PRAISE FOR *METABOLIC RIFTS*

"Ian Angus again demonstrates a wonderful ability to write clearly, informatively, and persuasively about science, history, economics, and social reality as he charts the multiple social and environmental catastrophes that capitalism brings. This remarkable book is essential for all who want to understand our world to help change it for the better." —PAUL LE BLANC, Professor of History, La Roche U., author, *Lenin: Responding to Catastrophe, Forging Revolution*

"One of the world's leading ecosocialists offers a sweeping journey through metabolic-rift theory, a powerful and highly readable account of Marxist ecological thought and the science of the Earth System. Urgent and uncompromising, *Metabolic Rifts* convincingly shows how capitalism is driving planetary crises, and why only a mass ecosocialist movement can secure the Earth's survival."—ADAM HANIEH, author, *Crude Capitalism: Oil, Corporate Power, and the Making of the World Market*

"A clear, accurate and highly readable synthesis of how Earth's life support systems, for our species as well as for countless others, have been imperilled by the headlong rush of Anthropocene change. Ian Angus explores the economic forces so central to all this and illuminates how both sociopolitical and scientific key ideas have developed. Highly recommended."—JAN ZALASIEWICZ, founding chair of the Anthropocene Working Group; co-author, *The Cosmic Oasis*

"Bringing the illumination of Marxism to bear, Ian Angus reveals a system riddled with contradictions, depending on the natural world while simultaneously destroying it, a scenario demanding a drastic shift of global priorities and structures. If eco-suicidal capitalism is the problem, eco-socialism is the solution." —HELENA SHEEHAN, author, *Marxism and the Philosophy of Science*

"In this superb book, Ian Angus shows that Karl Marx's critique of capitalism's environmental destruction was rooted in the most advanced science of his time and updates his analysis for our own time. With clear explanations of the latest science, *Metabolic Rifts* is an impassioned call for a revolutionary new society that rationally organises its relationship with nature."—MARTIN EMPSON, author, *Socialism or Extinction: The Meaning of Revolution in a Time of Ecological Crisis*

"Ian Angus combines deep knowledge of Earth System science, capitalist development, and Marxist scholarship to argue the case for an ecosocialist revolution. *Metabolic Rifts* is an invaluable resource for environmental activists, ecosocialists and all those who struggle daily to protect our biosphere and build a society that can start to heal humanity's rift with nature."—SUSAN PRICE, founding member of Socialist Alliance (Australia); co-editor, *Green Left*

"In *Metabolic Rifts*, Ian Angus explains how today's planetary ecological crisis emerged from capitalism's expropriation of the universal metabolism of nature and why only a revolutionary ecological response can sustain the earth as a safe home for humanity. He provides one of the strongest, most accessible cases yet made for the necessity of the creation of a new ecosocialist civilization."—JOHN BELLAMY FOSTER, author, *Breaking the Bonds of Fate: Epicurus and Marx*

"If we want to win the Earth, we had better understand how it works and what's needed to heal its many wounds. Ian Angus masterfully takes us from the discovery of the metabolic rift theory and the scientists who illuminated Earth's rhythmic system, to a sweeping and comprehensive history of capitalist ruination. This is the book to read to get up to speed on the ecological crisis."
—JESS SPEAR, People Before Profit councillor, South Dublin County Council; chief editor, *Rupture* magazine

"The brilliant Ian Angus clearly and succinctly shows why our earth is being destroyed by capitalism. Capital's unceasing drive to accumulate has created what Marx called a metabolic rift between humanity and nature. To save the planet, humanity and the species living on earth, what is needed is not reorganized capitalism, but an ecosocialist revolution."—MICHAEL ROBERTS, economist; co-author, *Capitalism in the Twenty-first Century*

"With exemplary clarity, *Metabolic Rifts* introduces readers to the 'natural science basis of Marxist ecosocialism' and analyzes key aspects of the ecological crisis. These ideas are more important than ever, and I don't know anyone who does a better job of explaining them in a straightforward way than Ian Angus."
—DAVID CAMFIELD, Professor of Labour Studies, U. of Manitoba; author, *Red Flags*

"Reminding us of the scientific roots of ecosocialism, Angus highlights the essentials of our human-nature metabolism that are still overlooked today in leftist political strategy, even as catastrophe approaches. By examining metabolic rifts, Angus urges us to raise the bar of our ambitions in the Anthropocene. We must fight capital to repair the Earth System and secure any future at all."—SABRINA FERNANDES, author, *Sintomas Mórbidos: A encruzilhada da esquerda brasileira* (Morbid Symptoms: The Crossroads of the Brazilian Left)

"A brilliant examination of how capital's anti-ecological logic is disrupting the Earth System's fundamental metabolic cycles. In our fight for survival, we need this cogent analysis to inform the revolutionary transformations that are necessary for sustainable human development."—BRETT CLARK, Professor of Sociology, U. of Utah; co-author, *The Robbery of Nature*

Metabolic Rifts
Capitalism's Assault on the Earth System

IAN ANGUS

MONTHLY REVIEW PRESS
New York

Copyright © 2026 by Ian Angus
All Rights Reserved

Library of Congress Cataloging-in-Publication Data
available from the publisher

ISBN: 978-1-685690-161-5 (paper)
ISBN: 978-1-658690-162-2 (cloth)

Typeset in Minion Pro and Brown

MONTHLY REVIEW PRESS, NEW YORK
monthlyreview.org

5 4 3 2 1

Contents

Abbreviations | 6
Measurements | 7
Acknowledgments | 10
Introduction | 13

Part 1: The Discovery and Rediscovery of Metabolic Rift | 19
    1. We Are Not the Owners of the Earth | 20
    2. Ecosocialist Tradition: Bebel, Kautsky, Bukharin | 28
    3. Continuity Lost and Restored | 45

Part 2: The Universal Metabolism of Nature | 57
    4. Six Revolutions that Made the Biosphere | 58
    5. Justus von Liebig and the Nutrient Cycle | 75
    6. Vladimir Vernadsky and the Biosphere | 82
    7. Barry Commoner and the Broken Circle | 93
    8. "We're Not in the Holocene Anymore" | 102

Part 3: Capital versus the Earth System | 113
    9. Capital's Anti-Ecological Logic | 114
    10. Breaking the Carbon Cycle | 127
    11. Rising Seas, Burning Trees, Tipping Points | 142
    12. Nitrogen: From Shortage to Glut | 151
    13. Agriculture: The Great Separation | 175
    14. Triple Crises in the Oceans | 192

Part 4: A Fight for Survival | 209
    15. Can We Avoid the Hothouse? | 210
    16. We Only Want the Earth | 217

Appendices | 228
    1. Metabolism: Lost in Translation? | 228
    2. Has the Anthropocene Been Cancelled? | 232
    3. Can CO_2 Removal Cool the Planet? | 238

Notes | 247
Index | 274

ABBREVIATIONS

AWG	Anthropocene Working Group
BECCS	Bioenergy with Carbon Capture and Storage
°C	Degrees Celsius
CAFO	Confined (or Concentrated) Animal Feeding Operation
CDR	Carbon Dioxide Removal
CNS	*Capitalism Nature Socialism* (journal)
CO_2	Carbon Dioxide
COP	Conference of the Parties (to the UNFCCC)
DAC	Direct Air Capture
ERW	Enhanced Rock Weathering
ESS	Earth System Science
FAO	United Nations Food and Agriculture Organization
G20	Group of 20
ICS	International Commission on Stratigraphy
ICSU	International Council of Scientific Unions
IGBP	International Geosphere-Biosphere Program
IPCC	Intergovernmental Panel on Climate Change
IUGS	International Union of Geological Sciences
MECW	*Marx-Engels Collected Works*
MHW	Marine Heat Wave
N_2	Inert Nitrogen
Nr	Reactive Nitrogen
NASA	National Aeronautics and Space Administration
NDC	National Defined Contribution
NET	Negative Emissions Technology
NGO	Non-Governmental Organization
OAE	Ocean Anoxic Event
OMZ	Ocean Minimum Zone
PETM	Paleocene-Eocene Thermal Maximum
PBF	Planetary Boundaries Framework
pH	acidity level
ppm	Parts per million
SPD	Social Democratic Party of Germany
UNFCCC	United Nations Framework Convention on Climate Change
VW	Volkswagen

MEASUREMENTS

Except in direct quotations, all measurements use the scientific SI (metric) system. Readers not familiar with metric may find these conversions helpful:

TEMPERATURE
Water freezes at 0°C, boils at 100°C
30°C is hot, 40°C is extremely hot

DISTANCE
2.54 centimeters = 1 inch
1 meter = 3.28 feet
1 kilometer = 0.6 miles

AREA
1 hectare = 2.471 acres
1 square kilometer = 0.3861 square miles

WEIGHT
1 kilogram = 2.20462 pounds
1 metric ton = 1000 kilograms = 2200 pounds

Two scholars who profoundly influenced me died while I was writing this book. Economist Paul Burkett played a decisive role in the recovery and development of Marxist ecology. Earth System scientist Will Steffen led the way in identifying the Anthropocene, defining planetary boundaries, and so much more. I dedicate this book to their memory.

Acknowledgments

Parts of *Metabolic Rifts* were previously published in *Climate & Capitalism*, *Monthly Review*, and other publications. All have been extensively rewritten and updated for this book.

Many thanks to Margaret Scott for permission to use her art on the front cover, and to Ann Sanderson for her artwork in chapters 12, 13, and 14.

My discussion of Barry Commoner's four laws of ecology, in chapter 7, is adapted from an article by Simon Butler, with his kind permission.

Lis Angus, my best friend and companion for more than fifty years, and John Bellamy Foster, prolific writer on Marxist ecology and editor of *Monthly Review*, supported this project from the beginning. They helped me think through complex problems and offered detailed suggestions that improved virtually every page.

Members of the pathbreaking Anthropocene Working Group—in particular Martin Head, Colin Summerhayes, Julia Adeney Thomas, Colin Waters, Marx Williams, and Jan Zalasiewicz—have been more than generous in sharing their work and ideas with me and responding to my requests for still more.

The debt I owe to other researchers and scholars—far more than I can list here—is evident in my endnotes. In its short life,

Acknowledgments

the discipline known as Earth System Science has spawned an impressive global community to which I am proud to make a small contribution.

Finally, I have once again been very fortunate to work with the wonderful team at Monthly Review Press: Martin Paddio, Rebecca Manski, Erin Clermont, George de Stefano, Elliot Linzer, and Michael Yates. MRP's editorial director, who brilliantly stewarded this book and my three previous titles. I wish him all the best in his retirement.

Some men, faint-hearted, ever seek
Our program to retouch,
And will insist, whene'er they speak
That we demand too much.
'Tis passing strange, yet I declare
Such statements give me mirth,
For our demands most moderate are,
We only want the earth.
—JAMES CONNOLLY (1907)

INTRODUCTION

"The Basis in Natural History for Our View"

The long-term evolution of the Earth System has been shaped by a multitude of cycles and feedbacks that control the movement of matter and energy in the oceans, soil, and atmosphere, with living matter playing critical roles at all stages. When any of those metabolic processes are disrupted, living organisms must adapt. Those that cannot adapt, perhaps because the changes are too large or too fast, do not survive. Two hundred and fifty million years ago, for example, years of massive volcanic eruptions pumped unprecedented amounts of CO_2 into the air, the average global temperature nearly doubled, and 96 percent of life on Earth died.

Beginning about 12,000 years ago, a species that previously lived in small groups of hunter-gatherers took advantage of climate change. After the Ice Age, in milder and more stable climate conditions, humans invented agriculture. They formed large, settled societies that amplified their impact on local, regional, and eventually global environments.

The arrival of capitalism, and especially its fossil fuel–powered expansion after the Second World War, put that impact into hyperdrive, undermining Earth's life-support systems more rapidly and thoroughly than ever before. The heat, fires, rising waters, and pollution we see today are only the beginning of a long-term planetary crisis. If radical changes are not made soon, today's climate emergencies will appear benign by comparison.

In 1861, Karl Marx wrote that Darwin's theory of evolution provided "the basis in natural history for our view" of human history.[1] A few years later, he wrote that for his economic research, the findings of German agricultural chemist Justus von Liebig on the decline of soil fertility in England were "more important . . . than all of the economists put together."[2]

We can say, with no exaggeration, that Liebig's work provided "the basis in natural history" for Marx's views on the separation of humanity from the rest of nature and laid the groundwork for Marxist ecology and ecosocialism.

Two decades earlier, Marx and his comrade Frederick Engels had developed a materialist philosophy that began with the undeniable fact that we cannot live unless we obtain food, air, water, and other essentials from the world around us. As Marx expressed it, nature is "man's inorganic body," an essential part of us that is not contained in our biological organs. "Man *lives* on nature—means nature is his *body*, with which he must remain in continuing dialogue if he is not to die."[3]

When Marx wrote that in 1844 he didn't know the word *metabolism*, but he had begun to think seriously about the constant flows of energy and matter that make life on earth possible. The concept would become central to his understanding of the relationship between society and the natural world and of the damage that capitalism inflicts on that relationship.

Like an autoimmune disease that attacks the body it dwells in, capitalism is simultaneously part of the natural world and at war with it. It both depends upon and undermines Earth's life-support systems. The theory of metabolic rift, which Marx developed by studying Liebig, describes what happens when the profit-and-growth–focused capitalist system disrupts Earth's life-sustaining natural cycles.

Until recently, it was common for environmentally conscious writers, including Marxists, to assert that Marx had little to say about nature, that his work is of no relevance to today's environmental concerns. That view has been decisively overturned by several scholars, most importantly by John Bellamy Foster in *Marx's Ecology: Materialism and Nature*. As historian Andreas Malm writes, since that book was published in 2000 "one Marxist line of inquiry into environmental problems has outshone all others in creativity and productivity: the theory of the metabolic rift."[4]

Apart from the first chapter, this book does not spend much time establishing the bona fides of Marx and Engels as ecological thinkers, nor does it engage in polemics with people who reject Marxism in general or metabolic rift theory in particular. Other writers have done those things well. My concern, rather, is to discuss the natural science basis of Marxist ecosocialism, with particular focus on the deadly rifts in two of the most important metabolic systems that make life on Earth possible, the carbon and nitrogen cycles.

In doing this, as I wrote in *A Redder Shade of Green*, I am motivated by

> the conviction that ecosocialism cannot succeed unless it is more than a pious wish for a better world. It must be based on a concrete scientific understanding of how our world has evolved, how it is changing today, and where those changes may take us. The way we build socialism, and the kind of socialism that can be built, will be profoundly shaped by the state of the planet we must build it on. If our programs and activity don't have a scientific basis, all our efforts to change the world will be in vain.[5]

This book is divided into four main parts.

The Discovery and Rediscovery of Metabolic Rift reviews the development of metabolic rift theory and Marxist ecology. Chapter 1 discusses how Marx and Engels developed and presented their views on metabolic rift. Chapter 2 presents the nearly forgotten work of three socialists who adopted and built on those views. Chapter 3 examines how, after decades of neglect by most socialists, these ideas have become central to a rebirth of Marxist ecology in the twenty-first century.

The Universal Metabolism of Nature discusses Earth's metabolism from a natural science perspective. Chapter 4 reviews what science now knows about the revolutionary changes that created the biosphere over four billion years. Chapters 5, 6, and 7 introduce the work and ideas of three scientists—Justus von Liebig, Vladimir Vernadsky, and Barry Commoner—who made important contributions to our understanding of the Earth System. Chapter 8 examines the multiple rifts that are now driving a new epoch in Earth System history, the Anthropocene.

Capital Versus the Earth System examines how conflicts between capitalism and two of Earth's most important metabolic cycles underlie major global crises. Chapter 9 outlines the characteristics of capitalism that lead to constant conflict with the natural world. Chapters 10 and 11 assess the carbon cycle and how breaking it is overheating the planet. Chapter 12 illustrates how industrial production has overwhelmed the nitrogen cycle; chapter 13 shows how the nitrogen glut has transformed agriculture and is destroying soil worldwide. Chapter 14 discusses the combined role of the carbon and nitrogen rifts in creating a triple crisis in the world's oceans.

A Fight for Survival considers the prospects of Earth's life-support systems. Chapter 15 examines the possibility that catastrophic changes may occur even if greenhouse emissions are halted, and chapter 16 discusses the kind of movement we need to prevent a global disaster.

The book concludes with three appendices: how translation problems have obscured Marx's views on ecology; how and why a major scientific organization failed to recognize the Anthropocene; and why much-hyped CO_2 removal technologies cannot save the climate.

My next book, *Social Murder*, will extend the arguments here by examining how capitalism's global attack on the Earth System's metabolism is driving a new wave of deadly diseases, while poisoning the air and water we all depend on.

PART 1

The Discovery and Rediscovery of Metabolic Rift

CHAPTER 1

We Are Not the Owners of the Earth

> We do not regard Marx's theory as something completed and inviolable; on the contrary, we are convinced that it has only laid the foundation stone of the science which socialists must develop in all directions if they wish to keep pace with life.
>
> —V. I. LENIN[1]

More than two thousand years ago, the Roman philosopher-poet Lucretius described recycling as a fundamental principle of the universe:

> Things, therefore, do not utterly perish, which seem to do so, since Nature recruits one thing from another, nor suffers any thing to be produced, unless its production be furthered by the death of another.... I have shown that things cannot be produced from nothing and also that when produced they cannot return to nothing.[2]

In 1260 CE, the Arab physician Ibn al-Nafis offered the earliest definition of metabolism: "The body and all its parts are in a continuous state of dissolution and nourishment, so they are inevitably undergoing permanent change."[3]

Despite such early intuitions, scientific understanding of life's metabolism was minimal until the nineteenth century. The difference between living and non-living matter was typically explained by *vitalism*, the view that all living things contain an invisible vital fluid or life force. Vitalists held that the complex carbon compounds found in plants and animals could only be created if the mysterious vital fluid was present. The term "organic chemistry" for the study of carbon compounds originated in that mistaken view.

The modern life sciences originated in a series of major discoveries in the late 1700s and early 1800s. In the 1770s, after Joseph Priestley showed that fire removes something essential for life from the air and green plants restore it, Antoine Lavoisier isolated the "something" and named it oxygen. In 1789, Jan Ingenhousz demonstrated that plants use energy from light to absorb carbon dioxide and emit oxygen. In 1828, Friedrich Wöhler achieved what previous scientists thought was impossible by synthesizing an organic compound (urea) in his laboratory. In the 1830s, Matthias Schleiden and Theodor Schwann showed that all plants and animals are composed of living cells, that "there is one universal principle of development for the elementary parts of organisms, however different, and that this principle is the formation of cells."[4]

In the 1840s, Julius Robert Mayer discovered the law of conservation of energy and showed, in *The Relation of Organic Motion to Metabolism*, that it applied to living things. Photosynthesis doesn't *create* new energy; it *converts* solar light energy into chemical energy.

These and many other discoveries contributed to a science of metabolism, a concept so new that English didn't even have a word for it until the 1870s. In about 1815 German scientists began using the word *Stoffwechsel*, which literally means "continuous material exchange." The definition given by a medical encyclopedia in 1844 shows that it was not used literally: "By *Stoffwechsel* is meant the conversion of body substance into other forms and the rapid production of new and precisely similar body structures by means of the constant supplying of nourishing materials."[5]

That understanding of life became the basis of metabolic rift theory, the central insight of Marxist ecology.

Destruction and Regeneration

Marx and Engels viewed humans as part of and dependent upon the rest of the natural world. As physical beings, we have always depended on and will continue to depend on exchanges of matter and energy with the rest of the natural world.

In his early works, Marx used various terms for the dynamic relationship between human society and the rest of nature. In 1851, however, he learned about *metabolism* from an unpublished manuscript by Roland Daniels, a doctor, scientist, and fellow member of the Communist League. Daniels defined "organic metabolism" as the "simultaneous destruction and regeneration" that characterizes all living bodies and distinguishes them from the non-living. He argued that the concept could usefully be applied to the analysis of society, a conclusion Marx accepted and integrated into his own work.[6] In *Capital*, his most important work, he used the concept of metabolism in three closely related ways:

- *Universal metabolism of nature* refers to Earth's fundamental life-support systems. These biological, chemical, and geological cycles constantly process the matter and energy on which all life depends.
- *Social metabolism* refers to the specific ways in which a given social order relates to the rest of nature. Humans have always obtained the necessities of life from nature, but the ways they have done so have changed significantly through history.
- *Metabolic rift* refers to capitalism's tendency to disrupt Earth's natural cycles and processes by subordinating the satisfaction of human needs to its inherent drive for profit and wealth accumulation. In the process, capitalism "disrupts the metabolic interaction between man and the earth," and causes "an irreparable rift in the interdependent process of social

metabolism, a metabolism prescribed by the natural laws of life itself."[7]

Marx could not have known how broad, deep, high, and complex the metabolism was. Scientists in his time were just beginning to study the metabolic processes that make life possible at every level, from cells to the entire planet, and even today vast parts are not well understood. But he grasped the essence of the matter, and his insights provide a basic framework for understanding what is happening to the Earth System at all levels today.

To understand the specific relationship between any particular social order and the natural world, we must examine the concrete social circumstances in which humans produce and reproduce. That's particularly important with capitalist society, which physically separates humans from the natural world their lives depend on:

> It is not the *unity* of living and active humanity with the natural, inorganic conditions of their metabolic exchange with nature, and hence their appropriation of nature, which requires explanation or is the result of a historic process, but rather the *separation* between these inorganic conditions of human existence and this active existence, a separation which is completely posited only in the relation of wage-labour and capital.[8]

Marx's research for *Capital* included careful study of Justus von Liebig's work on agricultural chemistry, which he described as "more important for this matter than all the economists put together."[9] Liebig showed that English agricultural and social practices were depleting the soil of essential nutrients, forcing farmers to use ever-increasing amounts of manufactured fertilizers.

Capitalist farming, Marx wrote, "disturbs the metabolic interaction between man and the soil, that is, it prevents the return to the soil of its constituent elements consumed by man in the form of food and clothing; hence it hinders the operation of the eternal natural conditions for the lasting fertility of the soil."[10] Nutrients that natural cycles had returned to the soil now polluted growing cities: "In London ... they find no better use for the excretion of four and a half million human beings than to contaminate the Thames with it."[11]

His closest friend and comrade, Frederick Engels, played an important role in disseminating their shared views to the growing socialist movement in Europe. Writing in the socialist newspaper *Der Volksstaat* in 1872–73, for example, he restated Marx and Liebig's view that rational agriculture required that "man shall give back to the land what he takes from it." He described the massive urban pollution that resulted from violating that law. In some of his most powerful environmental statements since his 1844 book on conditions in Manchester, he condemned the "pestilential air and the poisoned water" that made working-class neighborhoods in capitalist countries "the breeding places of all those epidemics which from time to time afflict our towns."[12]

But of all the works Engels wrote to educate German socialists, none was more influential than *Herr Eugen Dühring's Revolution in Science*, now better-known as *Anti-Dühring*, written in reply to a philosophy professor who condemned Marxism and class struggle. As the American socialist scholar Hal Draper observed, it was "the only more or less systematic presentation of Marxism" that Marx and Engels ever wrote.[13] Serialized in a socialist newspaper in 1877 and then published as a book in 1878, it included their most complete published account of nature's metabolic processes.

After retiring from his family's business in 1870, Engels immersed himself in studying the natural sciences. He brought that research to *Anti-Dühring*, frequently citing recent scientific findings to illuminate or expand on the materialist conception of nature. In his discussion of the relationship between living matter and the rest of nature, for example, Engels drew on findings in microbiology, a brand-new field at the time, to show that metabolic recycling is a law of life:

> *Life is the mode of existence of protein*, and this mode of existence essentially consists in the constant self-renewal of the chemical constituents of these bodies....
>
> But what are these universal phenomena of life which are equally present among all living organisms? Above all the fact that a protein absorbs other appropriate substances from its environment and assimilates them, while other, older parts of the body are decomposed and excreted.... From the moment when this uninterrupted metamorphosis of its constituents, this constant alternation of nutrition and excretion, comes to an end in protein, from that moment the protein itself comes to an end, it decomposes, that is, dies. Life, the mode of existence of protein, therefore consists primarily in the fact that every moment it is itself and at the same time something else. ... The metabolism, which takes place through nutrition and excretion, is a self-implementing process which is inherent in, native to, its bearer, protein, without which it cannot exist.[14]

In his notes for *Dialectics of Nature*, written at about the same time, Engels made the same points more concisely:

> Life is the mode of existence of protein bodies, the essential element of which consists in *continual, metabolic interchange with the natural environment outside them*, and which ceases with the cessation of this metabolism, bringing about the decomposition of the protein....
>
> Metabolism is the characteristic activity of protein bodies. ... Metabolism consists in the absorption of substances, the chemical composition of which is altered, which are assimilated by the organism, and the residua of which are excreted together with the decomposition products of the organism itself resulting from the life process.[15]

Few other authors of that time could have so clearly summed up the importance of metabolism to life.

It's important to understand that, for Marx and Engels, metabolism was not a metaphor. It was a material reality, comprising the social, biological, chemical, and geological processes that made life on Earth possible. When nature's metabolic processes are disrupted, humanity suffers.

> Let us not, however, flatter ourselves overmuch on account of our human victories over nature. For each such victory nature takes its revenge on us.... At every step we are reminded that we by no means rule over nature like a conqueror over a foreign people, like someone standing outside nature—but that we, with flesh, blood and brain, belong to nature, and exist in its midst, and that all our mastery of it consists in the fact that we have the advantage over all other creatures of being able to learn its laws and apply them correctly.[16]

They defined socialism in metabolic terms:

> Freedom, in this sphere can consist only in this, that socialized man, the associated producers, govern the human metabolism with nature in a rational way, bringing it under their own collective control rather than being dominated by it as a blind power; accomplishing it with the least expenditure of energy and in conditions most worthy and appropriate for their human nature.[17]

Freedom is not, as capitalists and ecomodernists would have it, about governing *nature*, but about governing our *metabolism* with nature.

All of their discussions of metabolism and metabolic rift should be read with Marx's statement in Volume 3 of *Capital* in mind, which has been justly called "the most radical conception of sustainability ever developed."[18]

From the standpoint of a higher economic form of society,

private ownership of the globe by single individuals will appear quite as absurd as private ownership of one man over another. Even a whole society, a nation, or even all simultaneously existing societies together, are not the owners of the earth. They are only its possessors, its usufructuaries, and, like boni patres familias [good heads of households], they must hand it down to succeeding generations in an improved condition.[19]

CHAPTER 2

Ecosocialist Tradition: Bebel, Kautsky, Bukharin

> Kautsky's book is the most important event in present-day economic literature since the third volume of *Capital*. Until now Marxism has lacked a systematic study of capitalism in agriculture. Kautsky has filled this gap.
>
> —V. I. LENIN, 1899[1]

The term "ecosocialist" is a recent invention, and there is no question that socialist movements have focused on environmental issues more in recent decades than they did in the mid-twentieth century. Some critics have concluded from this that Marxist ecology is a recent invention, based on a few scattered sentences in Marx's *Capital*.

And it's not uncommon to hear ecosocialists say, with a sigh, that our theoretical discussions would go more smoothly if only Marx or Engels had written a single work on the metabolism between capitalism, agriculture, and soil, rather than dealing with the subject piecemeal in their longer books. But, as the epigraph suggests, socialists at the beginning of the twentieth century not only believed that such a book already existed, but it also addressed concerns that they considered important. The word *ecosocialism* didn't yet exist, but important elements of its program did.

For Lenin to rank Karl Kautsky's book *The Agrarian Question* with the final volume of *Capital* was the highest possible praise. And yet, modern accounts of the development of Marxist ecology rarely mention it. Another widely read but now virtually forgotten book, August Bebel's *Women and Socialism*, also addressed agricultural and environmental issues. A third relevant book, Nikolai Bukharin's *Philosophical Arabesques*, was suppressed for seventy years and is still rarely read.

Bebel and Kautsky both knew Marx and Engels personally and had many face-to-face conversations with them about capitalism, socialism, and the Earth's future. Bukharin was a leader of the Russian Revolution, which implemented the most progressive environmental measures the world had ever seen. Their books built on and extended the ecological ideas and views of the founders of modern socialism; they embody the continuity of Marxist ecology into the twentieth century.

August Bebel: Woman and Socialism *(1879)*

Engels's book *Anti-Dühring* was widely read in the late 1800s, but its influence paled in comparison to *Women and Socialism*, first published in 1879. The author, August Bebel, was a founding member of the first German Marxist party and later the undisputed leader of the Social Democratic Party (SPD). He was a socialist member of the Reichstag (Parliament) from 1867 until he died in 1913, except for a three-year period when he was jailed for treason.

Lenin described him as "the German Social-Democratic leader who had the greatest influence among the working class and was most popular with the masses."[2]

Although not an original theorist, Bebel was a brilliant popularizer of socialist ideas. Apart from his many speeches—Eleanor Marx said he was "perhaps the finest orator of his country"[3]—his greatest achievement in promoting Marxism was *Die Frau und der*

Sozialismus (Women and Socialism), published in 1879 in defiance of Bismarck's Anti-Socialist Law.[4]

The book was widely circulated by the underground socialist movement in Germany in the 1880s, and its distribution increased even further after the ban was lifted in 1890. Hundreds of thousands of copies were printed—more than fifty editions in German and at least fifteen other languages before the First World War. In her Introduction to a Russian translation in 1918, Alexandra Kollontai called it the bible of the socialist women's movement.[5] For many years, it was one of the most widely read socialist books in the world.

The book primarily addressed the economic and social oppression of women. Bebel situated that discussion in the context of a general Marxist critique of capitalism and the socialist alternative, including environmental concerns.

In a socialist society, Bebel wrote, factories and mines would be redesigned to take "the utmost precautions against danger," and to ensure "the removal of disagreeable odors, gases and smoke . . . of all sources of injury or discomfort to health." At the same time, housing would be "separated from places of work and . . . freed from the disagreeable features of industrial and other manual work." Such changes "cannot be applied in capitalist society because they are expensive, and there is no obligation to do more than what is absolutely necessary for the workingman."[6]

Elsewhere, he condemned "the senseless ravaging of forests, for the sake of profit."[7]

However, the environmental problem that concerned him most was the loss of soil fertility, and here his views were clearly influenced by reading and speaking with Marx and Engels. "Manure," he wrote, echoing Liebig, "is to the soil what food is to man." To remain fertile, "the soil must receive back exactly the same chemical substances that it gave up through a crop." This was prevented by an agricultural system that wasted valuable manure.

Animal and human excrements are particularly rich in the

chemical elements that are fittest for the reproduction of human food. Hence the endeavor must be to secure the same in the fullest quantity and cause its proper distribution. On this head too modern society sins grievously. Cities and industrial centers that receive large masses of foodstuffs, return to the soil but a slight part of their valuable offal.

Marx called this a robbery system. Bebel called it "soil-vandalism . . . that cripples the land and decreases the crops."[8]

A rational system would return urban food waste and excrement to the farms, but that wasn't done because it was cheaper to import guano from Peru. Instead of fertilizing crops, "a large portion of the city excrement runs out into our rivers and streams and pollutes them."[9]

Bebel referred to and quoted Liebig several times as an authority. In this, and in the rest of his account of the soil crisis, he closely followed Marx. As a result, far from being forgotten in unpublished notebooks, the Marxist analysis of soil fertility and metabolic rift was familiar to millions of readers of one of the most influential books in the era of the Second International.

Karl Kautsky: The Agrarian Question *(1899)*

Karl Kautsky is mainly remembered today for his role in the great betrayal of 1914, when socialist leaders across Europe abandoned internationalist principles and supported their countries' war efforts, and for his hostility to the Russian Revolution.

But for decades before that, he was a highly respected Marxist theorist. He worked closely with Engels in London from 1885 to 1890. He edited the Marxist journal *Die Neue Zeit* (New Times) for more than thirty years. He was Engels's choice for editor of Marx's *Theories of Surplus Value.* In 1891, he was the principal author of the SPD program, which became a widely adopted model throughout the Second International. Lenin, for example, based his 1896 draft program for Russian socialists on it.

The Agrarian Question was the first major Marxist work to examine "whether and how capital is seizing hold of agriculture, revolutionizing it, making old forms of production and property untenable and creating the necessity for new ones."[10] For years, socialists accepted it as the authoritative study of the past, present, and probable future of agriculture. Kautsky's most radical conclusion, a break with the socialist orthodoxy of his time, was that the disappearance of small farms was not inevitable, and that in many cases "the small farm is superior to the large as far as rational cultivation is concerned."[11]

What farms of all sizes faced, however, was a crisis caused by the "two basic features" of modern agriculture: "private property in land, and the commodity-character of agricultural products."[12] That crisis was a decline in soil fertility that was not just a technical problem or a result of scientific ignorance: it was driven by the necessities of farming in capitalist society.

Kautsky had access to the latest scientific research and a wealth of new data on the state of agriculture in Europe and North America. The agrarian crisis was much further advanced in the 1890s, so his analysis went considerably beyond what Marx wrote.

Like Marx and Liebig, Kautsky argued that the primary cause of lost soil fertility was intensive agricultural production for "a market which does not return the vast bulk of the nutritional material which it takes from the land."[13]

> The outflow of so much value into the towns, uncompensated by any flow of counter-values, corresponds to a constantly mounting loss of nutrients in the form of corn, meat, milk and so forth which the farmer has to sell to pay taxes, debt-interest and rent.[14]
>
> As a result, the soil becomes depleted of the mineral elements on which plants are dependent for growth. Improved methods of cultivation, the growing of fodder crops with deep roots and deep-ploughing may all increase the yield of the fields, but at the cost or a more intense and rapid depredation and exhaustion of the soil.[15]

Liebig had insisted that nutrients should be returned to farms by using urban sewage for fertilizer. Although a few farms took small amounts of urban sewage from nearby sources, "no one has yet succeeded in devising a system for the removal of human excrement from large cities which meets the requirements of both agriculture and hygiene, without incurring a heavy financial penalty." The solution was not new technology, but social change:

> If the antithesis between town and country were to be overcome, and the population distributed more evenly over the land, this issue could be very simply resolved without great cost and even with a profit at the present level of technology using the sewage farm system. The prevailing mode of production rules such a solution out, however.[16]

While the natural fertilizer produced in cities was polluting lakes and rivers, farmers were forced to use artificial fertilizers:

> Without supplementary fertilisers, and given the current relationship between town and country, and current techniques of cultivation, this would soon lead to the complete collapse of agriculture. Such fertilisers allow the reduction in soil fertility to be avoided, but the necessity of using them in larger and larger amounts simply adds a further burden to agriculture—not one unavoidably imposed by nature, but a direct result of current social organisation.[17]

Clover and legumes had recently been shown to be a source of soil nitrogen. A crop rotation system that included them could help maintain fertility, but that meant reducing the area devoted to cash crops, which further reduced farmers' incomes. Farmers who produced for the market had "the greatest interest in extracting highest possible yield from the soil. . . . The quicker they suck the fertility out of the soil, the more profit they make."[18]

For tenant farmers, investments in soil fertility only benefited the landlord, so they tended to do as little as possible, letting fertility decline over time. Owner-farmers who maintained the quality of their soil by doing what science recommended had higher costs and had to compete with those who did not. By the end of the nineteenth century, this meant competing with farmers on the other side of the globe.

Three decades earlier, in *Capital*, Marx argued that "for a century and a half England has indirectly exported the soil of Ireland, without even allowing its cultivators the means for replacing the constituents of the exhausted soil."[19] In *The Agrarian Question*, Kautsky showed that many more countries had become victims of capitalist soil robbery. "Capital is engaged in an unceasing metabolism," he wrote.[20] It is constantly in motion, seeking new sources of profit. In the latter half of the nineteenth century, immense amounts of capital were invested in transportation systems—railroads and steamships—that could move food around the world cheaply and rapidly. European farmers, with high costs resulting from depleted soils, were now in direct competition with overseas farmers who had no such disadvantages:

> It was not the *volume* of imported food which threatened European agriculture, but rather the *conditions under which it was produced*. Such produce did not have to bear the burdens imposed on agriculture by the capitalist mode of production. Its appearance on the market made it impossible for European agriculture to continue shifting the rising burdens imposed by private property in land and capitalist commodity-production on to the mass of the consumers.[21]

For most of the century, Europe's major competitors were the United States and Australia, countries where "immeasurable tracts of unowned fertile land abound as the land's original rulers—the small number of indigenous peoples—have been exterminated or forced into small reserves."[22]

The soil is not yet exhausted—it is still completely virgin. It does not require fertilising and crop-rotation, and will continue to produce a rich yield for years ahead with the same crop. The farmer does not need to buy or make fertiliser: he can stick to a single crop—such as wheat—and will be more inclined to do so, the more developed the transport system, and the more the farmer is exclusively involved in commodity production and no longer needs to produce for his own consumption.[23]

In the United States, farming was virtually nomadic:

Agriculture there is based on robbing the soil which it sooner or later exhausts. This makes it necessary for the farmer to exchange fresh land for his exhausted land from time to time—either by having such a large farm in the first place that it can include both a cultivated and a non-cultivated part, or—if his entire holding is exhausted—by moving on to as yet uncultivated areas and making a new plot of land cultivable. . . . Abandoned land is left waste until it has recovered, or is taken over by a farmer who begins to farm using European methods, manuring and crop rotation. At any event, sooner or later this old land will become unusable for extensive depredatory cultivation. Soils on which wheat can be grown uninterruptedly for 40 years without fertiliser are extraordinarily rare.[24]

However, "all the fertile land in the United States is now private property. . . . The soil is exhausted, and new land cannot be had for nothing. Fertilizers, crop rotation, stock-keeping become necessary—but all this requires additional labour and money."[25] Farmers' debts were rising, and farms were shrinking.

All this implies that agriculture in the United States will become increasingly burdened, and its competitiveness on the world market correspondingly reduced.

The competition from European Russia and India will also lose its edge with the passage of time. Depredatory agriculture will lead to the bankruptcy of the prevailing agricultural methods even sooner than in the United States, since reserves of land are smaller, the older cultivated areas already more exhausted and the means of cultivation more exposed to deterioration with the increasing poverty of the peasants and the forced surrender of their livestock to the usurer and tax collector.[26]

This meant that competition in its existing form would end, "but it would be wrong to conclude from this that the agrarian crisis will soon be surmounted." Capital was already targeting new places for robbing the soil. "Siberia, with its 100 million hectares of grain land has been opened up by rail to the world market. Railways are encroaching on Central Africa from north, south, east and west and the opening up of China by rail is expected imminently." When soils are exhausted in those countries, "Central America, Northern Brazil, large parts of Africa, India, South Eastern Asia ... [will] also join the ranks of European grain farmers' competitors."[27]

Eventually, there would be no unexhausted soil left anywhere. Modern critics who claim that classical Marxism didn't recognize natural limits evidently haven't read Kautsky's argument that "in agriculture, the decisive means of production, the land, constitutes a fixed magnitude under given circumstances and cannot be increased at will."[28] Peaceful coexistence between capitalism and rational agriculture is impossible.

> The surface of the earth is finite and the capitalist mode of production is expanding at a dizzy pace. ... Constant expansion is the life principle of capitalism: technical revolution and the accumulation of capital are unceasing; production becomes increasingly mass production, whilst the share of the masses in their own product steadily diminishes. The agrarian crisis can therefore only end with a general crisis of capitalist society

as a whole. This point may arrive earlier or later; but as long as capitalist society continues, agrarian crisis will be its permanent accompaniment.[29]

As we've seen, Kautsky expanded on Marx's discussion of the metabolic rift in agriculture, showing that from its beginnings in England, the rupture in the soil-nutrient cycle had become a global phenomenon. That alone would warrant viewing *The Agrarian Question* as an important contribution to the development of Marxist ecology.

But Kautsky had more to say about what we now call environmental issues, including problems that were just emerging in his time but have become major crises in ours. For example, his discussion of deforestation has a very modern resonance. Kautsky argued for nationalization of forests, on the grounds that "rational husbandry of woodlands is incompatible with the exigencies of capitalist profit grubbing.... Where capitalist considerations alone decide, merciless felling can all too easily spell the total extinction of the forests."[30] His concern was not with the loss of wood as a resource, but with broad environmental protection:

> The forests are of such significance for the habitability and fertility of a country, its climate, the regularity of water levels, the mitigation of floods and the silting of rivers, [and] the protection of cultivable soil in mountainous and coastal areas that their uncontrolled devastation will cause the most serious damage to the cultivation of the land.[31]

He also wrote that deforestation reduced biodiversity by eliminating nesting opportunities for birds. With fewer birds eating harmful insects, "the costs of fertilisers are joined by those of pesticides," pushing European farmers' costs even further above those of their overseas competitors.[32]

Kautsky's criticism of sheep and cattle breeding in his time also sounds modern, especially if you are familiar with today's mass-produced chickens, which grow so large that their legs can't support them.

Natural selection leads to the selection and reproduction of those individuals most fitted to maintain the species. Artificial selection in capitalist society ignores this aspect and is simply concerned with breeding individuals which offer the greatest profit, incur the least cost, mature early and in which the exploitable parts are as large as possible, and the non-useful organs as atrophied as possible. Such "refined" strains yield a much higher profit than natural breeds, but their stamina and resistance is abnormally low.[33]

At the same time, "The modern mode of production generates increasingly serious hazards to the health of animals and crops, and opens the door to animal and plant epidemics."[34] Kautsky cited recent epidemics—"vine-pest and Colorado beetle, foot-and-mouth disease, red murrain and swine fever"—that "threaten to devastate the agriculture of entire countries."[35]

Today, raising animals in confined quarters is common, but in Kautsky's day, it was a recent development. Farmers who had switched to artificial fertilizers no longer needed manure in their fields, so increasingly they kept animals indoors year-round, in conditions that were ideal for infectious diseases. Kautsky's comment could be inserted without change in any twenty-first century account of influenza epidemics: "Modern breeding reduces the resistance of plants and animals to the tiny organisms which threaten them, [and] modern transport facilitates the rapid spread of these pests and allows them to devastate ever larger areas."[36]

Nikolai Bukharin: Philosophical Arabesques *(1937)*

As we've seen, the Russian revolutionary leader V. I. Lenin strongly praised Karl Kautsky's 1899 book *The Agrarian Question*, comparing it to Marx's *Capital*. He subsequently included concepts from Kautsky's book in his own articles and talks. In 1901, for example, he defended Marx and Liebig against populist writers who argued that the development of artificial fertilizers had overcome the nutrient rift:

> Liebig proved that it is necessary to restore to the soil as much as is taken from it. He was therefore of the opinion that throwing city refuse into the seas and rivers was a stupid and barbarous waste of materials essential for agriculture....
>
> Needless to say, the possibility of substituting artificial for natural manures and the fact that this is already being done (*partly*) do not in the least refute the irrationality of wasting natural fertilisers and thereby polluting the rivers and the air.[37]

In 1903, he incorporated Marx's ideas on the metabolic rift in agricultural soil, which he termed "abnormal metabolism," into a series of lectures on the agrarian question:

> Capitalism creates large-scale production and competition, which are attended by rapacious use of the productive forces of the soil. Concentration of the population in the cities creates depopulated territories and an abnormal metabolism. Cultivation of the land is not improved, or not improved as it should be....
>
> There is no doubt that capitalism has upset the equilibrium between the exploitation of the land and fertilization of the land.[38]

After the 1917 Russian Revolution, the new government placed support for pure and applied science high on its agenda. As historian Loren Graham writes, "No previous government in history was so openly and energetically in favor of science."[39] Andy Byford adds that the Bolsheviks "seized on science as an essential tool of revolutionary change—an instrument whose power and legitimacy was wielded as decisive to the stream of radical transformations into which the country was imminently thrown."[40]

Their commitments to ecological research and protecting biodiversity through conservation were particularly strong, as Douglas Weiner shows in *Models of Nature*:

> Through the early 1930s the Soviet Union was on the cutting edge of conservation theory and practice. Russians were the first to propose setting aside protected territories for the study of ecological communities, and the Soviet government was the first to implement that idea. Furthermore, Russians pioneered the suggestion that regional land use could be planned and degraded landscapes rehabilitated on the basis of those ecological studies.[41]

As ecologist Salvatore Engel-Di Mauro observes, "Under early Bolshevik government, environmentalism had a sort of roaring 20s, the likes of which no state-based society had ever witnessed."[42] In addition to implementing world-leading environmental policies, the government encouraged vigorous debates on the philosophy of science, including both communists and noncommunists in discussions of the relationship between society and the environment.

Among the Bolshevik leaders, Nikolai Bukharin was particularly active in studying and advancing Marxist views on the universal metabolism of nature. Described by Lenin as "the most valuable and biggest theoretician of the party,"[43] he closely followed the latest developments in contemporary science. This practice is very visible in his written work.

Students in Communist Party leadership schools in the 1920s, where Bukharin's textbook *Historical Materialism* was required reading, learned that the "material process of 'metabolism' between society and nature is the fundamental relation between environment and system, between 'external conditions' and human society."

In a prescient passage, he describes a concern that has come to the fore in the twenty-first century—the possibility that local deforestation could trigger a planet-wide cascade of environmental decline:

> The world being in constant motion, we must consider phenomena in their mutual relations, and not as isolated cases. All portions of the universe are actually related to each other and exert an influence on each other. The slightest motion, the slightest alteration in one place, simultaneously changes everything else. The change may be great or small—that is another matter—at any rate, there is a change. For example: let us say the Volga forests have been cut down by men. The result is that less water is retained by the soil, with a resulting partial change in climate; the Volga "runs dry" ... the animals formerly living in the forests disappear; new animals, formerly not dwelling in these regions, put in their appearance; the former animals have either died out or migrated to forest areas, etc.; and we may go even further: with a change in climate, it is clear that the condition of the entire planet has been changed, and therefore an alteration in the Volga climate to a certain extent changes the universal climate.[44]

In his famous address at the 1931 International Congress on the History of Science and Technology in London, Bukharin discussed the fundamental tenet of historical materialism, that to live, social man must produce. "Production is the real starting point of social development. In the process of production there takes place a 'metabolism' (Marx) between society and nature." As a result, humanity has "changed the face of the whole of the earth. Living and working in the biosphere, social man has radically remoulded the surface of the planet."[45]

Tragically, Bukharin fell victim to Stalin's purges, and his most important writings on the metabolism of society and nature were suppressed for more than seventy years. While in the Lubyanka prison in 1937, before his show trial and execution, he wrote a novel, a book of poetry, and two major political works. The manuscripts of all four were hidden in the Kremlin's archives and not published until this century.[46]

Of the four, *Philosophical Arabesques* was Bukharin's masterpiece. The title referred to Eugen Dühring's charge that Marx's *Capital* was a confusing mess of "dialectical frills and mazes and conceptual arabesques."[47] Indeed, we can describe it as an *Anti-Dühring* for the twentieth century, a defense of Marxism and historical materialism against the capitalist philosophies of our time, drawing on modern scientific understanding of the relationships between individuals, societies, and the natural world.

As Helena Sheehan writes, "*Philosophical Arabesques* was an ambitious and systematic work of philosophy . . . [that] set Marxism within the whole history of philosophy, within the whole battle of ideas of world culture of his times."[48]

For Bukharin, philosophy and ecology were not separate subjects, because he began with the concrete assertion that "living matter is a fact."

> There exists a huge, complex organic world; there exists what Academician Vladimir Vernadsky termed the earth's biosphere, full of infinitely varied life, from the smallest microorganisms in water, on land and in the air to human beings. . . .
>
> This life is linked inseparably to the "whole" and is part of the whole, one of its aspects, phenomena, facets, properties. It does not exist by chance, but is essential; it is inherent in the whole, as a stage in the historical development of its parts. On the earth, humanity is the most complex product of nature, its flower, so to speak.[49]

Vernadsky demonstrated that the biosphere constantly recycles matter and energy, and that living organisms, including humans, play an essential role in those vast operations. Bukharin agreed, viewing the metabolism between human beings and nature as a defining fact of human existence:

If human beings are both products of nature and part of it; if they have a biological basis when their social existence is excluded from account (it cannot be abolished!); if they are themselves natural magnitudes and products of nature, and if they live within nature (however much they might be divided off from it by particular social and historical conditions of life and by the so-called "artistic environment"), then what is surprising in the fact that human beings share in the rhythm of nature and in its cycles?[50]

Human labor, without which we cannot eat and drink, "conditions the metabolism between humanity and nature, . . . [establishing] the basis for the reproduction of the entire life of social humanity."[51] The character of the metabolism changes when society's historical form changes:

Capitalism with its principle of profit, with its competition and machines, immediately accelerated the process of mastering nature many times over, in both the material-practical and theoretical fields this acceleration of the process of mastering the objective world preceded both in breadth and in depth, and was truly unprecedented in human history.[52]

The "bourgeoisie has proven powerless" to control the forces it unleashed. "Its social science has degenerated into an apology for its practice, while this practice which expresses the anarchic functioning of capitalism, has never been able to exert control over the elemental social spontaneity of the system and overcome the irrationality of the social process that is innate to capitalism."[53]

The only way out is socialism, in which "society takes control of itself in practical fashion, just as it takes control of itself theoretically as well."[54]

Philosophical Arabesques isn't perfect. In particular, with an eye to the censors, Bukharin refrained from any criticism of conditions in the USSR, and even, knowing he faced possible execution, inserted a few hypocritical phrases praising Stalin. He also, however, subtly cited "Marx's position that real movement includes spirals, circles, regressions and halts," in support of his statement that "the idea that progress is uninterrupted . . . is false. So too is the idea of universal progress."[55]

The very existence of these books disproves the canard that socialists of the late 1800s and early 1900s did not know or care about the universal metabolism of nature or the environmental destruction caused by rifts in that metabolism.

They knew those concepts well and saw the fight to heal humanity's metabolism with nature as an integral part of the fight for socialism. They made major contributions to the development and extension of the environmental insights first enunciated by Marx and Engels.

And yet, if you ask an ecosocialist today to name a single book by Bebel, Kautsky, or Bukharin—let alone one that they have *read*—the most likely response is silence. After the great betrayal of 1914, socialists around the world stopped reading Bebel, Kautsky, and most other leaders of the Second International. Stalin's purges rendered Bukharin and many others unpeople whose books were wrong by definition.

But the books do exist, and the insights they offer into capitalism's anti-ecological essence remain valuable. They deserve pride of place on every ecosocialist's bookshelf.

CHAPTER 3

Continuity Lost and Restored

The Soviet Union was born in revolutionary struggle, but by the end of the 1920s, political power had been captured by privileged officials who had abandoned the egalitarian ideals of 1917. They used the words, but in practice they equated social progress with improvements in their own wealth and status. Nikolai Bukharin was only one of thousands of dedicated revolutionaries who were executed because Stalin and the bureaucrats whose interests he represented viewed them as a threat.

That degeneration underlay a sharp turn in environmental policy, away from Marx's insistence that every society has a responsibility to protect the planet. Official policy, misleadingly dubbed socialist construction, demanded increased industrial and agricultural production, regardless of the cost to people and nature.

That productivist perspective was adopted by socialists worldwide, not only by the dominant pro-Soviet current in the Marxist left, but also by socialists who were otherwise sharply critical of the Soviet Union and Stalinism. As Raymond Williams wrote in 1983, the common capitalist argument that poverty can only be eliminated by "production, and more production," became left-wing orthodoxy:

Socialists for three or four generations, with only occasional exceptions . . . made the case that production is an absolute human priority, and that those who object to its effects are simply sentimentalists or worse; moreover, that they are people who speak in bad faith from their own comfort and privilege, about the effects of reducing poverty in the lives of others. . . .

Under the spell of the notion of conquest and mastery, with its mystique of overcoming all obstacles, of there being nothing too big for men to tackle, socialism in fact lost its own most important emphasis. . . . The essential socialist case is that the wealth and poverty, the order and the disorder, the production and the damage, are all parts of the same process. . . .

That central socialist case was always put; there is not a generation in which somebody has not been seriously putting it. Yet under capitalist and imperialist influence, and especially since 1945 under North American influence, the majority position among socialists has been that the answer to poverty, the sufficient and only answer, is to increase production.[1]

The pollution and environmental destruction that such policies caused in the Soviet Union and Eastern Europe have been well documented, but for this discussion, the important point is that Soviet adoption of environmentally destructive policies, and the defense of those policies by many socialists, led many environmentalists to conclude that socialism and capitalism are anti-environmental twins. Ecologist Anna Bramwell's blunt assessment was typical: "Ecologists are not anthropocentric, Marx is. Marx does not *like* nature. . . . Marx's argument against nature on the grounds of the necessity of historical development is, indeed, overwhelmingly subsumed in his resentment of unaltered nature."[2]

Similarly, the author of *Small Is Beautiful,* E. F. Schumacher, wrote that socialists "treat as valueless everything that we have not made ourselves. Even the great Dr. Marx fell into this devastating error when he formulated the so-called 'labour theory of value.'"[3]

Depending on which green critic you consulted, you would

hear that Marx ignored the environment, or was hostile to it, or thought it was inexhaustible, or—at best—had some ecological insights but did not integrate them into his overall analysis of capitalism.[4] Perry Anderson, then editor of *New Left Review*, declared that "problems of the interaction of the human species with its terrestrial environment [were] essentially absent from classical Marxism."[5]

When new environmental movements emerged in rich countries in the 1970s, some socialists gave credence to the greens' anti-Marxist prejudices by condemning environmentalism as a diversion from the *real* class struggle.[6] Others used accounts of pollution to illustrate capitalism's failures, but didn't develop their environmental critique beyond declaring that capitalism fouls things up.[7] Environmental concerns weren't integrated into their programs and activities. With a few exceptions, such as the union-led "green ban" campaigns in Australia, socialist organizations abstained from (or just gave lip service to) the mass environmental campaigns and protests of the 1970s.

This is not to say that all socialists ignored environmental questions. On the contrary, as John Bellamy Foster shows in *The Return of Nature*, left-wing thinkers throughout the twentieth century made significant contributions to a materialist understanding of the society and nature relationship and challenged capitalism's accelerating environmental destruction. Barry Commoner is an important example: his best-selling 1971 book *The Closing Circle* employed a metabolic rift approach to explain the growing environmental crisis, without using those words.

Less well known to the general public is István Mészáros who, well before *The Limits to Growth* became a best-seller, identified the problem of uncontrolled material growth and traced it to capital's inexorable drive for profits and wealth accumulation. Responding to capitalist ideologues who claimed that everyone in the world could eventually enjoy U.S.-style mass consumption, he pointed out that "the ecological resources of our planet would be exhausted . . . several times over" before that could happen. In his January 1971 Deutscher Memorial Prize lecture, he described the "affluent society" as actually a "society of suffocating *effluence*" that has "failed to cope even with rat infestation in the slums and ghettos."

> The capitalist system of control . . . cannot separate "advance" from destruction, nor "progress" from waste—however catastrophic the results. The more it unlocks the powers of productivity, the more it must unleash the powers of destruction; and the more it extends the volume of production, the more it must bury everything under mountains of suffocating waste.[8]

In his later works, especially in *Beyond Capital*, Mészáros adopted and substantially expanded Marx's concept of social metabolism. On that subject as well, he was far ahead of the rest of the left.

Hybrid Ecosocialism

The word *ecosocialism* originated in Germany in the late 1970s as *ökosozialismus*. It made its first English-language appearance in the pamphlet *Eco-Socialism in a Nutshell*, published in England in 1980.[9] In both cases, the term referred to an eclectic mix of social-democratic and environmental reforms, but the very existence of the word reflected a growing interest in bringing the socialist and environmental movements together.

Over the next three decades, many attempts were made to combine Marxism and environmentalism—a difficult task, since, as Derek Wall writes, the radical green movement was marked by "intellectual confusion and a chaotic mismatch of contradictory assumptions."[10] Any catalog of the various green currents would include, at the very least, liberals, anti-corporatists, Malthusians, localists, primitivists, currency reformers, eco-feminists, anarchists, and autonomists. It is not surprising that no coherent red-green worldview emerged from attempts to combine the various forms of green with the diverse forms of red.

A more coherent approach, championed by the academic journal *Capitalism Nature Socialism*, attempted to revise Marxism to address environmental issues. In the 1990s and early 2000s, CNS hosted the most substantial discussions on that question. Most contributors accepted green criticisms of Marx's supposed failure to address environmental issues. They proposed, in various ways, to graft elements of green thought onto a Marxist base.

Joel Kovel, for example, argued that Soviet society's environmental crimes occurred because "an integral appreciation of nature's intrinsic value is not at the heart of socialism. . . . Marx may not have been Promethean, [but] there remains in his work a foreshortening of the intrinsic value of nature."[11] In his view, Marxists should incorporate "the spiritual dimension of existence," and learn from religious groups who "integrated spirituality into their conceptions about matter and nature."[12]

James O'Connor argued that Marx had failed to recognize that ecological destruction could ultimately lead to the end of capitalism. To be complete, crisis theory needed to incorporate what he called "the second contradiction of capitalism"—that by undermining its conditions of existence, capitalism tends to self-destruct.[13]

The 1990s and early 2000s were a time of vigorous and exciting debate among socialists who challenged the traditional approaches of both reds and greens, making important contributions to the development of ecological socialism. In 2001, Kovel and Michael Löwy co-wrote the first *Ecosocialist Manifesto*, which stimulated discussions among ecosocialists around the world.

Important as those contributions were, they were weakened by the unquestioned assumption that Marx had little to say about humanity's relationship with nature, and that what he did say was irredeemably productivist and anti-ecological. Re-reading the debates and discussions of that period, I am struck by the lack of direct engagement with what Marx and Engels and other socialists actually wrote about society and nature. The same few out-of-context quotations appeared again and again, as if each writer assumed the point had been proven elsewhere.

Of course, no one suggests that Marxism is complete and needs no additions or revisions. In Samir Amin's words, "To be a 'Marxist' is to continue the work that Marx merely began.... It is not to stop at Marx, but to start from him."[14] But to start from Marx, ecosocialism first had to learn what he actually said.

Marxist Ecosocialism

Late in the 1990s, two scholars, aware of each other's work but working independently, returned to basics and studied, in detail, what Marx actually wrote about the relationship between human society and nature. They showed, contrary to conventional green assumptions, that Marx's work included key elements of an ecological critique of capitalism.

In *Marx and Nature: A Red and Green Perspective,* published in 1999, Paul Burkett argued that Marx's "social-scientific approach to nature . . . enables us to see how the social forms of production lend historical specificity to ecological processes, of which humanity is an increasingly determinant element. This is an important first step toward understanding the ability (or lack thereof) of particular production systems to ecologically sustain any given qualitative development of human life."[15]

Focusing on "the unique synthesis of materialist and class-relational analysis in Marx's approach to nature," Burkett systematically demonstrated that common green criticisms of Marxism—for example, that Marx favored industrial growth at all costs, or that he thought nature had no limits and no value—were incorrect. Marx's work in political economy, he showed, "provides original and useful insights into the sources of environmental crisis under capitalism, the relations between ecological struggles and class struggles, and the requirements of a healthy and sustainable coevolution of humanity and nature."[16]

After disproving the common argument that "Marx's diagnosis

Continuity Lost and Restored

of the contradictions and crises of capitalism had nothing to do with the natural conditions of production," Burkett showed that Marx identified two different kinds of specifically environmental crises. On the one hand, there are crises caused by shortages of natural materials—for example, cotton in the 1860s, oil in the 1970s. On the other hand, there are crises caused by the deterioration of the conditions necessary for life:

> [It is] essential to distinguish environmental crises of *capital accumulation* from environmental crisis in the sense of *a general deterioration of the conditions for the development of people as a natural and social species*. The latter type of crisis by no means automatically implies the former, even though both are products of capitalism—which is to say that from the standpoint of human development, capitalism is an ecologically and socially irrational system.[17]

In 2000, in *Marx's Ecology: Materialism and Nature*, John Bellamy Foster undertook a systematic recovery of Marx's materialist understanding of history and nature. "Marx's work," he wrote, "cannot be fully comprehended without an understanding of his materialist conception of nature, and its relation to the materialist conception of history. Marx's social thought, in other words, is inextricably bound to an ecological worldview."[18]

A central achievement of Foster's research was the rediscovery of the importance of metabolism and metabolic rift in Marx's analysis of capitalism.

> An essential component of the concept of metabolism has always been the notion that it constitutes the basis on which the complex web of interactions necessary to life is sustained, and growth becomes possible. Marx employed the concept of a "rift" in the metabolic relation between human beings and the earth to capture the material estrangement of human beings within capitalist society from the natural conditions which

formed the basis for their existence—what he called "the everlasting nature-imposed condition[s] of human existence."[19]

In the second edition of *Marx and Nature*, Burkett reemphasized the importance of the two kinds of environmental crisis, relating them specifically to Marx's concept of metabolic rift. Together, those insights provided a framework for analyzing and understanding the ecological crises of the twenty-first century:

> In light of more recent work by Foster and others, it is now possible to affirm that Marx's metabolic rift approach—when properly reconstructed and updated to account for developments in technology, natural science, and the further globalization of capital accumulation—can help us understand the systemic roots of the contemporary problems of climate change, depletion and degradation of oceanic ecosystems by industrial fishing and aquaculture, and disruptions to the global nitrogen cycle brought on by overuse of inorganic fertilizers in industrial agriculture. The rift approach has also been proven useful for demonstrating how *ecological imperialism* (the guano trade, sugar plantations, etc.) and resultant ecological crises have been central to the entire history of capitalist development and underdevelopment on a global scale.[20]

Method, Not Scripture

Marx's Ecology and *Marx and Nature* were major works of de-revision. Foster and Burkett systematically examined what Marx and Engels actually wrote about nature and ecology, and in the process demolished myths and distortions that had inhibited the development of ecological Marxism. What they did *not* do is treat Marx and Engels as infallible or "consider the original Marxian canon as the true and sufficient guide to save nature from capitalism," as Kovel charged.[21] Foster called that suggestion "an absolute absurdity."

> No rational individual could believe that Marx's nineteenth-century analysis, notwithstanding all its brilliance, constitutes a "sufficient guide" to solving the global ecological crisis in an age of planetary climate change, ocean acidification, and fracking. Naturally, whatever methodological insights are to be derived from Marx's dialectic with respect to the ecological and social critique of capitalism . . . have to be synthesized with a vast body of historical and scientific knowledge that has arisen subsequently, and with the conditions of contemporary social praxis.[22]

Marx himself didn't believe in and certainly didn't offer eternal truths about the human-nature relationship:

> He aimed instead at comprehending material limits under respective concrete conditions of natural sciences and technology. Where exactly this contradiction manifests itself is not given a priori; it requires a concrete analysis of each situation. Natural sciences provide the basic knowledge for such an analysis. Otherwise, a critique would only be able to say that capitalism must destroy the environment. Marx was never satisfied with such an abstract thesis.[23]

What Burkett and Foster and other students of ecological Marxism have found in Marx is not inerrant scripture, but rather "a solid methodological foundation for the analysis of capital's historical process of antagonism between humanity and nature."[24] Andreas Malm summarizes its key elements:

> Nature consists of biophysical processes and cycles. So does society: human bodies must engage in metabolic exchanges with nonhuman nature. That need not be particularly harmful to any of the parties. Over the course of history, however, the relations through which humans have organized their *Stoffwechsel* [metabolism] might be fractured and forcibly

rearranged, so that they not only harm the people disadvantaged by this change, but also, at the very same time, disturb the processes and cycles of nature. A metabolic rift has opened up.[25]

The importance of metabolism to Karl Marx's thought has been thoroughly researched and documented, and metabolic rift theory is now accepted as an important part of left-wing ecological thought, even by its critics. Most articles and papers on capitalism's ecological crimes at least nod in the direction of metabolism/metabolic rift as a possible basis for analysis.

This, unfortunately, does not mean that everyone understands the fundamental concepts. A common misunderstanding in articles on metabolic rift, whether the authors support or reject the concept, is treating it as a metaphor rather than as a description of real global circumstances. One critic insists that Foster and Marx "misapprehend" the real meaning of metabolism, which is "simply the collection of all the chemical processes in your body that keeps you alive."[26] Metabolism, writes another, is "a seductive metaphor," and metabolic rift is "a metaphor of separation," whose "central diagnostic metaphor is 'planetary catastrophe.'"[27] A third describes it as "the foremost metaphor in contemporary Marxist framings of nature-society relations."[28]

On the contrary, Marx was not confused about the word's meaning and did not deploy metabolism as a metaphor. As Mackenzie Wark writes, "He means that there is an actual, planetary metabolism . . . [and] we can now say that earth science confirms this speculative insight."[29]

> The Anthropocene is a series of metabolic rifts, where one molecule after another is extracted by labour and technique to make things for humans, but the waste products don't return so that the cycle can renew itself. The soils deplete, the seas recede, the climate alters, the gyre widens: a world on fire. Earth, water, air: there is a metabolic rift where the molecules

are out of joint are potassium nitrate, as in Marx's farming example; or where they are dihydrogen-oxide as with the Aral Sea; or where they are carbon dioxide as in our current climate change scenario.

It used to seem as if exhausting the soil here or diverting water there were local problems. The Anthropocene is the recognition that some metabolic rifts are global in scope.[30]

Recovering Marx's ecological method is only a beginning. To be true to Marx's method, ecosocialists must, as he did, base our understanding of the relationship between society and nature on concrete analysis of socioeconomic trends and the best contemporary scientific work on the metabolism of the Earth System.

As Howard Waitzkin writes in his landmark book on capitalism's impact on medicine and human health, theory is not enough; a materialist approach requires historical specificity. "Marxist analysis tries to explain social problems with historical concreteness and with reference to specific material reality. Although general analytic principles may be appropriate to the study of different problems, each problem has its own context which demands concrete explanation."[31]

In that respect, it is significant, as historian and environmentalist Andreas Malm writes, that "one Marxist line of inquiry into environmental problems has outshone all others in creativity and productivity: the theory of the metabolic rift."[32] Over the past two decades, there has been a remarkable outpouring of articles and books that use the concept of "an irreparable rift in the interdependent process of social metabolism" to concretely analyze a wide range of environmental issues, including planetary boundaries, the carbon metabolism, soil depletion, fertilizer production, the ocean metabolism, the exploitation of fisheries, the clearing of forests, forest fire management, hydrological cycles, mountaintop removal, the management of livestock, biofuels, global land grabs, antibiotic resistance, and the contradiction between town and country.

This book extends that work by examining how capitalism's violation of fundamental planetary boundaries is dangerously disrupting Earth's life-support systems. A second book, now in production, will focus on how these disruptions have given birth to a new age of plagues.

PART 2

The Universal Metabolism of Nature

CHAPTER 4

Six Revolutions that Made the Biosphere

The real world itself is a historically changing quantity, eternally in flux. . . . Nature has a history just like human history and there is no fundamental difference here.
— NIKOLAI BUKHARIN[1]

The conditions on the young earth produced life; life then at once modified the conditions of the earth, so that this single extraordinary act of spontaneous generation could not be repeated. In one form or another, action and interaction between life and its surroundings have been going on ever since.
—RACHEL CARSON[2]

There's an old joke about a gardener who refused to buy a new rake: "The rake I'm using is the best I've ever had," he said. "I've replaced the handle three times and the head twice." All living things, like that rake, are continuous wholes composed of discontinuous parts. In Steven Rose's words, "Our bodies are in continuous flux. Nothing about us as organisms is permanent."

Living organisms must constantly maintain and rebuild themselves, and that requires constant exchanges of matter and energy with their surroundings. Within a single cell's lifetime, "each of five thousand or so different proteins will completely interchange with the surroundings thousands of times. . . . This energetic maintenance of unity while components are continuously or intermittently rearranged, destroyed and rebuilt, broken and repaired, is metabolism."[3]

Right now, there are trillions of biochemical reactions taking place simultaneously in your body. That's only possible because you, like all organisms from bacteria and fungi to blue whales and giant sequoia trees, constantly draw energy and matter from the world outside your body, and process them in tiny biological factories that no human-built system can emulate.

A report prepared for the U.S. National Research Council puts it this way: "The metabolism inside a cell has profound consequences for the environment in which that cell exists," because it always involves exchanges with the world outside the organism.[4] Living organisms cannot exist without ingesting matter and excreting waste. The earth is a sphere surrounded by a vacuum, so the amount of matter available for organisms to use is finite, and their wastes have nowhere else to go. For life to exist, the entire planet must constantly recycle and reuse the elements that make life possible.

Perhaps the best-known cycle links plants, which inhale carbon dioxide and exhale oxygen, with animals, which inhale oxygen and exhale carbon dioxide. Every breath you take contains billions of oxygen molecules that were previously the waste products of photosynthesis, many times over. That vital process is just one of the many cycles that comprise Earth's life support systems:

> Elements like carbon, necessary to life, are continually moved from one place to another, whether from cell to cell within an organism or around the globe, by transfers that may be nearly instant or take hundreds of millions of years. Living

organisms—above all bacteria, fungi, and plants—are the driving agents of these transfers, but atmosphere, waters, and geo-tectonic processes provide no less indispensable means of exchange among the various reservoirs in which the cycled elements come temporarily to rest. Without this cycling, there would have been no evolution of complex life, and the fortunes of modern civilization depend more on it than on the provision of particular resources, be they fuels or metals.[5]

If metabolisms were linear, if inputs were simply consumed, the nutrients needed by living organisms would soon be depleted. Plants could consume all the carbon dioxide in the atmosphere in about eight thousand years, and all the nitrogen in a million years. Life has lasted billions of years because vast recycling operations endlessly reprocess and reuse its essential elements and compounds:

> Almost all of the rocks composing the continents have been processed at least once through a chemical and physical cycle involving weathering, formation of sediments, and subduction, being subjected to great heat and pressure to produce new igneous rocks. The water in the oceans has been evaporated, rained out, and returned via rivers and groundwater flow many tens of thousands of times. The main gases in the atmosphere (nitrogen and oxygen) are cycled frequently through living organisms. The combined effect of these dynamic transports and transformations is a planet that is in a state of continual, chemical and biological evolution.[6]

This permanent recycling regime would be impossible if Earth were a totally closed system because, as the second law of thermodynamics says, totally closed systems eventually run down. Entropy (disorder) increases until everything comes to a stop. The Earth System is effectively closed to external matter—about five thousand tons of space dust and rock enter the atmosphere each year, but that's an insignificant amount for a planet with a mass of 6.585 billion trillion tons. Fortunately for us, the Earth System is open to external energy. Light from the sun, captured by plants and converted into chemical energy, is the principal source of energy for life on Earth.[7]

The metabolic cycles that support life on Earth have not always existed, nor have they always taken the same forms or worked in the same ways. They are products of our planet's long history, both cause and effect of its long-term evolution from a ball of molten rock through innumerable ice ages and continental reorganizations.

The history of life on Earth, and thus of humanity, is ultimately the history of the changing ways in which living things have obtained, processed, and exchanged matter and energy, and changed the planet as they did so. Four billion years of co-evolution have produced innumerable species and life-webs that are metabolically connected at every level, from the smallest cell to the entire planet.

Some historians use the term *longue durée* to refer to the period since Columbus invaded the Western Hemisphere. Compared to a human life, five hundred years is indeed a long time, but it barely begins to address the tightly integrated metabolic processes that developed long before humans evolved. Capitalism isn't just overusing resources; it is disrupting the entire Earth System. To understand what that means, our historical perspective must extend back billions of years.

The Earth formed 4.5 billion years ago. It took hundreds of millions of years to cool. When it did, there was no free oxygen—the atmosphere was mostly composed of nitrogen, carbon dioxide, and methane. The Sun was dimmer than it is now, but carbon dioxide, in concentrations 10 to 200 times greater than today, kept Earth's surface temperature above freezing, so liquid oceans existed, covering most of the surface. Because there was no oxygen, there was no protective ozone in the stratosphere, so the surface was constantly bathed in deadly ultraviolet radiation.

There was no biosphere, because there was no life.

The emergence of living matter was the first of many revolutionary transformations that created the biosphere and what we now call the Earth System. The first organisms immediately began changing the world and were themselves changed in the process. There was no plan and no designer: the modern biosphere is the result of billions of years of biological and geological experiments, filtered by natural selection so that the most successful carried on. The six revolutions discussed here were among the most important.

Revolution 1: Living Cells

In 1871, Charles Darwin speculated that life began in "some warm little pond with all sorts of ammonia and phosphoric salts, light, heat, electricity et cetera present."[8] In the 1920s, two socialists, working independently, extended Darwin's thought. The Russian chemist A. I. Oparin and the British geneticist J. B. S. Haldane argued that life must have originated spontaneously in the early ocean, when lightning and solar power triggered the formation of complex carbon-based molecules in that "prebiotic soup." Eventually, those organic molecules would combine to form living cells, and life itself then changed conditions on Earth that life could not form spontaneously again.

The Haldane-Oparin hypothesis has held up in broad outline, but subsequent research has revised most of the details. We now know that the composition of the atmosphere was very different from what they believed, and that ultraviolet radiation would have killed any living thing that was exposed to the sun. We still don't know for certain, but life may have originated in or near hydrothermal vents deep in the ocean, where seawater is drawn deep into the ocean floor, is heated and returns containing essential elements of life, including carbon, nitrogen, and sulfur—the "prebiotic soup" in a different form. Laboratory experiments have demonstrated that amino acids and other basic building blocks of life form spontaneously in such conditions.

Stephen Jay Gould thought it was significant that life emerged so early in Earth's history: "We can only infer from this rapidity that it is not 'difficult' for life of bacterial grade to evolve on planets with appropriate conditions. The origin of life may be a virtually automatic consequence of carbon chemistry and the physics of self-organizing systems—given favorable conditions and the requisite inorganic constituents."[9]

We don't know when living matter first arose. The oldest surviving traces are approximately 3.5 billion years old. By then, microscopic cells had already evolved, with semi-permeable skins that separated them from their environment, a coding system that stored genetic information so they could reproduce accurately, and metabolic systems that obtained and processed the energy and matter necessary for survival. There were two lineages with distinct biological characteristics, bacteria and archaea, but all were prokaryotes, single-celled organisms that lack a nucleus.

As biologist Tyler Volk emphasizes, those early cells were vastly more complex than even the most intricate assemblages of atoms and molecules that had previously existed on Earth. They were living factories that constantly ingested matter and energy from the surrounding ocean, and just as constantly discarded waste products:

> The cell . . . is a different creature because it is literally a creature. . . . Many of the creature's molecules exist only because they are inside it and functional. The cell uses its imports and exports for the molecular manufacturing of its thousands to tens of thousands of special types of molecules.[10]

Unlike anything that came before, the new living cells required constant "inputs of nutrients and energy as well as waste outputs. These inputs and outputs are revolutionary new relations." Just by living, they changed their environments by removing certain chemicals and excreting others. The "titanic consequence" was the emergence of biological evolution, as cells were forced to adapt or die in constantly changing conditions.[11] The existence of life led inexorably to new forms of life:

> Ancient cells related to each other in rich ways. They all took in nutrients. They all exuded waste. Thus, they affected their shared chemical environments and each other.
>
> Evolving, some species of cells discovered the means to utilize the wastes from others as nutrients for themselves. They established food webs based on these wastes, on other nutrients, and on parasitism, attack, and defense among various species.... Virtually from the start, modes of both competition and cooperation played off each other in ways that became ever more sophisticated and interwoven within the ancient microbial ecosystems.[12]

Although the sizes and shapes of bacteria changed little, their metabolic processes evolved in many directions. Biochemist Nick Lane describes the result as "a cauldron of bacteria, displaying an inventiveness of biochemistry we can only wonder at."[13]

Using the basic building blocks of life—carbon, hydrogen, oxygen, nitrogen, phosphorus, and sulfur—bacteria created complex new molecules that enabled them to survive and prosper in many different environments. By 3.2 billion years ago, "bacteria had invented most forms of metabolism, including multiple forms of respiration and photosynthesis."[14]

Revolution 2: Photosynthesis

The first living organisms obtained energy from chemical reactions occurring in the surrounding sea. That worked, but the supply was limited and unreliable. If a hot vent cooled or water currents shifted, microbes in that area could starve. Those that learned to use solar power were freed from energy scarcity: they multiplied and spread across the planet.

A major metabolic challenge faced by early organisms was

obtaining the elements they needed to assemble organic molecules, especially carbon, oxygen, and hydrogen. The first two were readily available as carbon dioxide, but even near hydrothermal vents, the supply of free hydrogen was limited. The first microbes to harness solar power used photons to split molecules such as hydrogen sulfide into their component elements—in this case, hydrogen and sulfur. The hydrogen was combined with carbon dioxide to make sugars, and the sulfur was discarded. That method, and others like it, may have been used by some bacteria as early as 3.5 billion years ago.

A more significant change occurred later, about 2.5 billion years ago, when cyanobacteria (often inaccurately called blue-green algae) evolved the ability to capture higher-energy photons from sunlight and used them to split water into hydrogen and oxygen. The new technology worked anywhere there was water and light, which was just about everywhere. More important, as we'll see, it led to another revolution. Donald Canfield estimates that "in the end, the use of water in photosynthesis resulted in an increase in rates of primary production [the formation of organic matter] on Earth by probably somewhere between a factor of ten to a thousand."[15]

On Earth's surface and in the upper layers of the ocean, most organisms today either use light and photosynthesis to power their metabolisms or obtain energy by eating organisms that do. The giant molecule that ancient bacteria created to perform the first steps of photosynthesis—ribulose-1,5-bisphosphate-carboxylase/oxygenase, conveniently abbreviated as Rubisco—is still playing that role today and remains the most abundant protein on Earth.

It was once thought that photosynthetic organisms supplanted their predecessors. However, recent research has found that organisms that use other sources of energy are not only still extant, but also abundant. One estimate is that 10^{30} non-photosynthetic organisms live deep in the oceans and in Earth's crust—that's 10 followed by 30 zeroes, an order of magnitude more than the number of Earth's inhabitants that capture and use light.

Revolution 3: Oxygen

Photosynthesis gave cyanobacteria the hydrogen and energy necessary for growth and spread. The leftover oxygen—a waste product—changed the world.

Oxygen is extremely volatile: given the slightest chance, it will combine with (oxidize) a large variety of other elements, to the extent that more than 99 percent of Earth's oxygen is embedded in mineral compounds, not in the atmosphere. The first oxygen produced by cyanobacteria was removed through various chemical reactions, so the atmosphere remained oxygen-free for many years, until a tipping point was reached. Scientists disagree on the cause of the transition. Some believe that the supply of oxygen-consuming chemicals declined because of reduced volcanic activity; however, there are other possibilities. What's certain is that it led, about 2.45 billion years ago, to what's called the *Great Oxygenation Event* or *Oxygen Revolution*. The waste product of innumerable microscopic organisms began to transform the atmosphere.

The amount of free oxygen in the atmosphere remained far below modern levels, but its volatility meant that small amounts had major effects. A layer of ozone (a form of oxygen) formed in the upper atmosphere, blocking deadly ultraviolet radiation. This allowed cyanobacteria to flourish on and near the surfaces of lakes, rivers, and oceans, where they produced still more oxygen. Oxygen reactions created two-thirds of the world's 4,500 known minerals—"all of them previously unknown in our Solar System"—and removed dissolved iron from the oceans, depositing bands of iron oxide that contain 90 percent of the world's iron ore.[16]

For two billion years, the greenhouse gases carbon dioxide and methane had kept the average temperature above freezing, at levels we would probably find comfortable. Methane's greenhouse effect is about 86 times greater than carbon dioxide's. However, it doesn't play a large role in today's climate because it breaks down in the presence of oxygen. Two and a half billion years ago, there was much more than there is today, and it lasted longer, so its role in climate was decisive.

In a geologically short time after the oxygen revolution began, chemical reactions with oxygen removed most of the methane from the air. At roughly the same time, the largest landmass in the Northern Hemisphere, the supercontinent Kenorland, began to break up, exposing large rock faces that absorbed CO_2 as they weathered. The greenhouse effect weakened, and Earth's average temperature fell below water's freezing point.

In three phases, between 2.4 and 2.1 billion years ago, kilometers-thick ice spread over land and sea. The combination of oxygen and ice undoubtedly killed many organisms, leading some researchers to call it the first mass extinction, although evidence is limited. For some time, the entire planet may have been totally covered in ice, "a climate disaster triggered by the evolution of oxygenic photosynthesis."[17]

Revolution 4: Symbiotic Life

Eventually, the glaciers retreated, and there wasn't another ice age for 1.5 billion years. The post-glacial world wasn't just much warmer; it was the setting for another metabolic revolution:

> There was a lot more energy to go around in the post-oxidation world, because respiration of organic matter with oxygen yields an order of magnitude more energy than breaking food down anaerobically. Amongst the first organisms to take advantage of this energy source were the first eukaryotes—complex cells with a nucleus and many other distinct components.[18]

Bacteria and archaea have survived for nearly four billion years, but their basic physical structure has limited their size. Growing would require more energy, and their structure imposes physical limits on how much they can acquire. The oxygen that cyanobacteria produced made more energy available, but they and their relatives could not use it efficiently.

We will never know how many failed biological experiments took place when the oxygen revolution and the first ice age changed the conditions of life permanently. But about two billion years ago, natural selection produced a major success, the eukaryotes.

Like bacteria, they were single-celled, but on average, they were 15,000 times larger by volume. Their DNA was enclosed in a nucleus, a structure that no bacteria ever developed, and they had so many new parts and features that Nick Lane describes them as "crammed with assorted jumble."

> Hundreds or even thousands of tiny, specialized organs, called organelles, such as mitochondria (in virtually all eukaryotes) and chloroplasts (in algae and plants), mixed up with small sacs of membrane, stacks of folded membranes and a protein skeleton. This riot of compartmentalization gives eukaryotic cells the look of evolution by conglomeration, which is indeed what happened.[19]

Margulis and Sagan call the new cells "bacterial confederacies ... [that] cooperated and centralized, and in doing so formed a new kind of cellular government."[20] Symbiosis, where different organisms live cooperatively, isn't unusual, but in this case, bacteria took up residence *inside* archaea, and the benefits to each were great enough that a permanent division of labor was established. The host provided nutrients for the guest, and the guest provided sugars and energy. If more energy were required, the guest could multiply, enabling increases in size and complexity that could never occur in bacteria. Over many millennia, the host's descendants acquired most of the guests' DNA, and the guests evolved into mitochondria.

Eukaryotes were not just new species, but an entirely new kind of life, a qualitative leap beyond bacteria and archaea. "The void between bacterial and eukaryotic cells is greater than any other in biology," Lane writes. The new life-forms "gave rise to the great fountain of life we see all around us."[21] That's true, but it took well over a billion years for Eukaryotes to evolve into animals, plants, and fungi. Indeed, as Stephen Jay Gould points out, "The time between the emergence of the first eukaryotic cell and the first multicellular animal is longer than the entire period of multicellular success."[22]

Revolution 5: The Cambrian Explosion

It has been called Darwin's Dilemma. In his day, the oldest-known fossils were of complex multi-cellular animals that lived during the Cambrian Period, now dated to about 540 million years ago. There was no evidence of earlier life anywhere. As Darwin wrote, this "sudden appearance" of complex creatures could "truly be urged as a valid argument" against his conclusion that all living organisms descended from earlier forms:

> If the theory be true, it is indisputable that before the lowest Cambrian stratum was deposited long periods elapsed, as long as, or probably far longer than, the whole interval from the Cambrian age to the present day; and that during these vast periods the world swarmed with living creatures. . . . To the question why we do not find rich fossiliferous deposits belonging to these assumed earliest periods prior to the Cambrian system, I can give no satisfactory answer.[23]

The Cambrian explosion remained a dilemma for a century. It wasn't until the 1950s and 1960s that scientists, using new methods and new technologies, produced incontrovertible evidence that "the world swarmed with living creatures" for billions of years before the Cambrian.[24] We now know for certain that living organisms have existed on Earth for at least 3.5 billion years.

But recent research has also produced incontrovertible

evidence that the Cambrian explosion wasn't an illusion caused by an incomplete fossil record. However, the explosion's fuse was lit earlier than formerly believed. After billions of years in which all living organisms were single cells, metazoans—multicellular animals—burst onto the scene and changed the world. The "explosion" lasted millions of years, which is a very long time in human terms, but a geological instant, a tiny fraction of the three billion years of unicellular life that preceded it.

The oldest undisputed fossils of multicellular animals are embedded in rock that formed in what is now Newfoundland, during the Ediacaran Period, thirty million years before the Cambrian. They were followed by "one of the major evolutionary transitions in the history of life."

> Some 120 million to 170 million years after the origin of sponges, the scrappy fossil record improved with a bang, geologically speaking. Following a prelude of a diverse suite of enigmatic, soft-bodied organisms beginning about 579 million years ago, a great variety and abundance of animal fossils appear in deposits dating from a geologically brief interval between about 530 to 520 million years ago, early in the Cambrian Period. During this time, nearly all the major living animal groups (phyla) that have skeletons first appeared as fossils.[25]

The causes of this revolution are still debated, but the "Snowball Earth" hypothesis, published in 1998 by geologist Paul Hoffman, has won wide support.[26] Hoffman showed that the period immediately before the Ediacaran was marked by long episodes in which most of the planet was covered kilometers deep in ice. Those episodes were separated and followed by periods of high CO_2 and unusually high temperatures. To survive those intense icehouse-hothouse cycles, organisms would have been under intense environmental pressure to adapt. That, together with a small increase in oxygen levels in shallow coastal waters, may have driven what paleontologist Rachel Wood calls an "astonishing burst of diversification" in which "a riot of novel forms burst into existence."[27]

Further research will probably modify our understanding of the explosion. There is no question, however, that the Ediacaran-Cambrian Period marks a revolutionary shift in the nature of the biosphere. A world with animals was fundamentally different from a world dominated by bacteria, archaea, and single-celled eukaryotes:

> Animals do not just occupy the modern biosphere; they permeate its structure and define how it works. Their unique combination of organ-grade multicellularity, motility and heterotrophic habit makes them powerful geobiological agents, imposing myriad feedbacks on nutrient cycling, productivity and environment. . . .
>
> The Ediacaran–Cambrian emergence of metazoans marks the tipping point between two alternative stable states of biospheric expression: on the one hand, an exclusively microbial world driven largely by physical circumstance and, on the other hand, a Phanerozoic world dominated by engineered biological environments. . . .
>
> The Ediacaran–Cambrian radiations undoubtedly established a new world order.[28]

Today, biologists recognize three biologically distinct "kingdoms" of multicelled life—plants, fungi, and animals. All three were fully formed by the early Cambrian, and all three have played decisive roles in creating the modern biosphere.

Revolution 6: Conquering the Land

For most of Earth's history, all organisms lived in the planetary ocean. Continents and islands existed, but they were barren, like the present surface of Mars.

Cartoons usually depict the arrival of complex life on land as air-breathing fish with short legs walking up a beach, but if that ever happened, the fish would have been 100 million years late. Long before any animals showed up, the land was colonized by plants. Ocean-based plants had changed Earth, but "even more radical changes transformed the planet when plants evolved the means to break free of their watery shackles and colonize dry land. In a period of less than 1 percent of the total age of life itself, this great invasion of land by plants changed all the rules—as well as the history of life on our planet."[29]

Life in the sea has significant advantages: the water counters gravity, delivers nutrients directly to the plants' permeable surfaces, and protects them from direct solar radiation. To live on land, plants evolved thicker skins that held them upright and kept them from drying out in the sunlight, and new ways of obtaining essential nutrients. The big payoffs for making those difficult changes were freedom from predators (because there were no land animals yet) and direct access to solar energy that could power rapid growth and diversification.

This revolution began with symbiosis. About 475 million years ago, freshwater algae formed an alliance with fungi. Algae obtained energy through photosynthesis, but on land they had no means of getting the nutrients they needed to grow. Fungi could obtain nutrients by dissolving rock, but they couldn't capture or use solar energy. Together, they formed the ancestor of lichens, in which the upper layer obtains energy from the sun while the lower layer obtains nutrients from minerals. To this day, more than 80 percent of land plants receive essential minerals from underground networks of fungi and provide sugars and fats in return.

That alliance, coupled with increased access to solar energy (because water wasn't in the way), triggered "an unparalleled burst of evolutionary innovation and diversification."[30] In about 65 million years (a geological blink of an eye), land plants evolved from lichens to flowering plants to trees, and changed the world. David Beerling describes trees and their symbiotic fungi as "the bioengineers of global change over millions of years." [31] They turned the terrestrial environment from gray to green.

Plants broke up rock and mixed it with organic matter, creating a surface layer that allowed even more life to flourish on land, and in the process reshaped the biosphere again:

> The formation of these soils dramatically changed life on Earth. Soils altered terrestrial landscapes, water courses, nutrient and mineral cycling and even the composition of the atmosphere. . . . Soils are the key interface between geology, the atmosphere and the water and nutrient cycles. The advent of deep soils transformed the interaction between these parts of the Earth.[32]

Above all, in 200 million years, land plants produced more free oxygen than ocean-based photosynthesizers had produced in two billion years. During the Cambrian explosion, oxygen probably comprised less than 2 percent of the atmosphere—far below the metabolic requirements of animals larger than worms and insects. Photosynthesis in early land plants drove oxygen concentrations up to and even above modern levels by about 350 million years ago, enabling the eventual emergence of amphibians, lizards, birds, and mammals, including (much later) humans.

Plants have changed the world and in turn have been changed, making the world ever more hospitable for ever more plants—and eventually, for animals, whose activity as ecosystem transformers cannot be overstated. In Nicholas Butterfield's words, "Animals figure disproportionately in the maintenance of the modern Earth System, not least because they invented it."[33]

This account barely skims the surface of a long and complex process. Still, it demonstrates four important facts about Earth's life-support systems.

1. The biosphere is a *historical* phenomenon. The metabolic

interaction between living matter and a formerly dead planet created the constantly changing global environment that scientists now call the Earth System. Life made more life possible.
2. Living matter and the rest of the planet have co-evolved, changing and being changed by each other. Every major change eliminated the conditions that made previous changes possible.
3. The rate of change has been anything but steady. Long periods of virtual stasis have been interrupted by intervals of rapid (in geological terms) change. The long-term pattern was summarized by Stephen Jay Gould and Niles Eldredge as *punctuated equilibrium.*
4. Tipping points are real. Relatively small changes—1 percent or 2 percent increases in oxygen levels, for example—have caused major changes in the global environment. As we'll see in subsequent chapters, we now face changes that are disrupting the entire biosphere.

This chapter began with a quotation from the great ecologist Rachel Carson emphasizing the constant interaction between organisms and environments that created our world. It seems appropriate to conclude with another quote, in which she urges careful attention to the dynamic systems that have been produced by so many years of co-evolution:

> The balance of nature is not the same today as in Pleistocene times, but it is still there: a complex, precise, and highly integrated system of relationships between living things which cannot safely be ignored any more than the law of gravity can be defied with impunity by a man perched on the edge of a cliff. The balance of nature is not a status quo; it is fluid, ever shifting, in a constant state of adjustment. Man, too, is part of this balance. Sometimes the balance is in his favor; sometimes—and all too often through his own activities—it is tilted to his disadvantage.[34]

CHAPTER 5

Justus von Liebig and the Nutrient Cycle

I have been going to the Museum in the daytime and writing at night. I had to plough through the new agricultural chemistry in Germany, in particular Liebig and Schönbein, which is more important for this matter than all the economists put together.

—KARL MARX, 1866[1]

Modern agricultural science began with the German chemist Justus von Liebig, who published three hundred papers on organic (carbon-based) chemistry between 1830 and 1840, and more than two thousand in his lifetime.[2] As his student Carl Voit later wrote:

Liebig was the first to establish the importance of chemical transformations in the body. He stated that the phenomena of motion and activity which we call life arise from the interaction of oxygen, food and the components of the body. He clearly saw the relation between metabolism and activity and that not only heat but all movement was derived from metabolism. He investigated the chemical processes of life and followed them step by step to their excretion products.³

In the 1830s, Liebig developed the first reliable methods for analyzing the chemical composition of soil, including simplified procedures that produced accurate results quickly. Through that work, his laboratory, the most advanced in the world, developed a new understanding of plant nutrition.

When Liebig began his studies, the accepted scientific opinion, based on the vitalist view that only living matter could create other living matter, was that plants grew by absorbing living material through their roots. In 1814, the most respected chemist of the day, Sir Humphrey Davy, wrote that "vegetable and animal substances deposited in the soil, as is shown by universal experience are *consumed* in the process of vegetation. . . . The great object in the application of manure should be to make it afford as much soluble matter as possible to the roots of the plant."⁴ He was correct that organic material in the soil contributed to plant growth, but wrong about the process.

Liebig showed that plants cannot use organic matter directly. It must first be broken down into its inorganic elements, which, in proportions that differ from one type of plant to another, combine with carbon and oxygen from the air to build plant matter. That discovery made the scientific formulation of artificial fertilizers possible for the first time. Modern fertilizers are still labeled to indicate how much of the three most important elements they contain. A fertilizer labeled 5-10-5, for example, is 5 percent nitrogen, 10 percent phosphorus, and 5 percent potassium.⁵

Liebig's work formed the basis of a new chemical approach to agriculture, and his 1840 book *Organic Chemistry in Its Application to Agriculture and Physiology* (usually referred to as *Liebig's Agricultural Chemistry*) became the new science's most-read textbook. He revised and updated it seven times—the eighth edition appeared in 1865—and published many other books and articles on soil chemistry.

Liebig's practical aim was to understand and help overcome declining soil fertility across Europe. This was particularly important in England, where farmers could only maintain production by applying ever-increasing amounts of fertilizers.

Traditionally, food grown on farms was consumed locally, so the elements it took from the soil were returned as food waste and excrement, which nourished future crops. The shift to market-oriented farming changed that: most crops were produced for sale and consumed in distant cities, where food waste and excrement were discarded. The essential nutrients in food were not returned to the soil, leading to a long-term decline in fertility. The problem intensified as the urban population increased—more people in towns and fewer in the country meant ever more nutrients left the land. Liebig saw artificial fertilizers as, at best, a temporary solution: Agriculture would continue to decline unless ways were found to return the nutrients that were being shipped away and discarded.

"Rational agriculture," he wrote, "is based upon the principle of restitution; by giving back to the fields the conditions of their fertility, the farmer insures the permanence of the latter."[6] In contrast, European (especially English) farming was a "robbery system," in which essential elements were stolen from the soil and never returned, impoverishing the land. The only long-term solution would be to re-create, in the new social conditions, the natural cycles that had made agriculture possible in the first place—to heal the rift between human society and a critically important life-support system:

> If it were practicable to collect, without the least loss, all the solid and fluid excrements of the inhabitants of towns; and to return to each farmer the portion arising from produce originally supplied by him to the town, the productiveness of his land might be maintained almost unimpaired for ages to come, and the existing store of mineral elements in every fertile field would be amply sufficient for the wants of the increasing populations.[7]

Liebig's Blind Spot

Liebig's work and ideas were a major step toward understanding the cyclical processes that comprise Earth's life-support systems and the role of several key elements in plant nutrition. However, that understanding couldn't develop fully until other scientists got past a major misconception that had prevented Liebig from understanding how the cycles work.

Chemical analysis showed that all plants contain nitrogen, leading Liebig to conclude, correctly, that nitrogen is one of a handful of essential elements for plant growth. Plants simply cannot live without it. But where did it come from? Liebig found no source of nitrogen in soil, and only small amounts in animal manure, so he concluded, reasonably enough, that it must come from the air, which is less than 1 percent carbon dioxide and more than 78 percent nitrogen. If plants can get all the carbon dioxide they need from the air, why not nitrogen as well?

Atmospheric nitrogen is inert—under normal conditions, it won't combine with any other chemical—but it was known that lightning forced it to combine with oxygen, producing nitrogen oxides, which are soluble in water. Liebig argued that plants obtain nitrogen that was created by lightning and dissolved in rain. As a result, he believed, there was no need to include nitrogen in fertilizers, because plants could get all they needed from the air.

In the mid-1840s, that assumption led him to develop and market a commercial fertilizer that contained no nitrogen compounds. Practical tests by working farmers showed that it produced no appreciable improvement in crop growth, and the business failed. It took years for Liebig's reputation to recover.

John Lawes and Joseph Gilbert at the Rothamsted Experimental Station in England showed that fertilizers containing nitrogen promoted far more plant growth than those without it. Liebig was correct that plants need nitrogen, but wrong about where they found it. (Lawes and Gilbert, we should note, had no better idea than he about where unfertilized plants obtained nitrogen.)

The answer was not found until after Liebig's death. He might have found it earlier, or at least contributed to the solution, if he had not been committed to a purely chemical explanation of metabolism. He attributed both the decomposition of dead things and human diseases to "fermentation," which he insisted was a purely chemical process. He ridiculed the suggestion that yeast is alive. He rejected Louis Pasteur's proof that microorganisms were responsible for spoiling wine and beer. One of his last major projects, in 1868, was a series of lectures criticizing Pasteur's work and denying that bacteria played any role in fermentation, decay, or disease.

As Frederick Engels noted, these and other arguments showed "how much of a dilettante Liebig was in biology, although the latter is a science bordering on chemistry."[8]

The science Pasteur founded—microbiology—solved the nitrogen puzzle. In the mid-1880s, Hermann Hellriegel and Hermann Willfarth showed that certain species of bacteria, most of which live in the roots of beans, clover, and other legumes, capture and "fix" nitrogen into compounds that plants can use.[9] The amount of nitrogen available is limited because only a few types of bacteria can do this, and over time, other bacteria convert the nitrogen back to its inert form and return it to the atmosphere.[10]

The discovery of this nitrogen cycle, together with the realization that bacteria and fungi are responsible for the eventual decomposition of all organisms, showed that living matter itself is a major factor—indeed, the *essential driver*—in the vast recycling operations that make life possible.

Although Liebig missed the role of living organisms in driving the nutrient cycle, he was one of the first scientists to insist that all living organisms are linked to each other and the rest of the earth through complex metabolic cycles:

> All the innumerable products of vitality resume, after death, the original form from which they sprung. And thus death—the complete dissolution of an existing generation—becomes the sources of life for a new one.[11]

His controversial Introduction to the 1862 edition of *Agricultural Chemistry* made a powerful statement about nature's metabolic unity:

> Our present research in natural history rests on the conviction that laws of interaction not only exist between two or three, but between all the phenomena of the animal, vegetable and mineral spheres which determine life on the surface of the earth. Thus, none of them are separate but are always linked to one, or to several others, and these in turn to yet more, all ultimately linked together, without beginning or end. The sequence of these phenomena, their origins and their departures, can be compared to a wave motion within a cycle. We consider Nature as a whole; all its manifestations are connected like the knots in a net.[12]

That passage was written four years before Ernst Haeckel coined the word *ecology*, and six decades before Vladimir Vernadsky discovered that "there is a continual migration of atoms from inert matter to living matter and back again ... *Biogeochemical phenomena* are the basis of the biosphere."[13]

Postscript: Did Liebig solve the metabolic rift?

A recent article accused Marxist ecosocialists of misrepresenting Liebig's work: "He did not just alight upon the unidirectional nature of the flow of nutrients within agricultural production, but used this discovery to figure out *how it could be corrected*."[14]

According to the authors, Matt Huber and Leigh Phillips, "His [Liebig's] development of nitrogen-based fertilizer" overcame any "assumed limits" on agricultural production. If this were true, it would mean that Marx's concern that capitalism produces an "irreparable rift" was disproven before it was published. Indeed, Phillips has written elsewhere that "there is no metabolic rift."[15]

Anyone familiar with Liebig's work will recognize that the

Justus von Liebig and the Nutrient Cycle

real misrepresentation lies in calling him the "father of fertilizer" as Huber and Phillips do. Despite his pioneering analysis of soil chemistry, Liebig never understood how plants obtained nitrogen. As a result, the commercial fertilizer he developed did not significantly improve plant growth. In any event, he viewed manufactured fertilizers as only temporary expedients—the long-term solution would be restoration of the nutrient cycle. As he wrote in 1865:

> During the last twenty-five years I have strenuously endeavoured to draw attention to the source of our existence, to show that the art of Agriculture does not consist only in making the earth produce, but also in rendering its productiveness permanent, and that of the various means for doing so there is only a single one which can be safely relied on to secure the perpetual fertility of our fields, viz. The Utilization of the Sewage of Towns.

Only that solution, he concluded, was "founded on the immutable Laws of Nature."[16]

Despite the widespread and constantly increasing use of fertilizers, the fertility of the world's soils continues to decline. Clearly, chemical fertilizers have not solved the nutrient rift in agriculture.

CHAPTER 6

Vladimir Vernadsky and the Biosphere

> Humankind, as living matter, is constantly connected with the matter-energy processes of the defined geological envelope of the Earth—its biosphere. Not for a single moment can humankind be physically independent of its environment.
>
> —V. I. VERNADSKY[1]

The first scientist to undertake a serious study of the dynamic relationship between life and the earth was the Russian geochemist Vladimir Ivanovich Vernadsky. Born in 1863 and educated in St. Petersburg, Munich, and Paris, he was well known by 1900 both as a geologist and as a liberal opponent of tsarist autocracy. A founder of the Constitutional Democratic (Kadet) Party and member of its central committee for many years, he represented the universities' constituency in the Duma (Parliament) from 1906 to 1911, when he resigned to protest government attacks on academic freedom. In 1915, he founded the Commission for the Study of the Natural Productive Forces of Russia to identify sources of strategic raw materials. The commission's work continued under the Soviet government until 1930. Although Vernadsky opposed the Bolshevik Revolution, he resigned from the Kadet

Party when it supported military action against the new government. After the civil war, Lenin supported Vernadsky's return to Petrograd and reappointment as head of the Academy of Sciences.

In the early 1930s, Vernadsky criticized the Soviet government's takeover of scientific institutions and objected to attempts to impose dialectical materialism as an official and mandatory philosophy. He frequently intervened privately to aid scholars who faced official censorship or persecution. But for the most part, he refrained from publicly opposing Stalin's policies to avoid endangering his scientific work. He wasn't a Marxist, but he was a patriot, eager to contribute to the country's development, and that probably saved him from the fate of many other scientists in the purges. As his biographer notes, "It was not uncommon for Stalinists to worry more about Marxists with whom they disagreed and whom they distrusted, than they did about non-Marxists who worked loyally for the regime, did not intrigue, and were no real threat to Stalin's position."[2]

In 1922, while studying and teaching in Paris, Vernadsky sent "a plea for the establishment of a biogeochemical laboratory" to scientific bodies in Europe and the United States, hoping to get international funding. He was turned down by, among others, the British Association for the Advancement of Science, the U.S. National Research Council, and the Carnegie Institution. Only the young Soviet government responded positively. He established his laboratory—really a small research institute—in Leningrad in 1926.

Vernadsky's focus on biogeochemistry—he created both the word and the science—reflected his conviction that the composition and principal characteristics of our planet could not be explained by geology and chemistry alone. "I realized," he later wrote, "that the basis of geology lies in the chemical element—in the atom—and that living organisms play a prominent role, perhaps the leading one, in our natural environment—the biosphere."[3]

He summarized his views in 1926 in the pathbreaking book *Biosfera* (*The Biosphere*). Geologists recognized the existence of three "envelopes" surrounding the planet: atmosphere (air), hydrosphere (water), and lithosphere (soil and rock). The biosphere was a fourth, "a specific, life-saturated envelope of the Earth's crust," comprising all living matter on Earth and all parts of Earth where life exists, from the crust to the upper atmosphere.[4] His argument was revolutionary in two major respects: it treated the entire planet as an object of study, and it identified *life itself* as a major factor in shaping the planet.

> No chemical force on Earth is more constant than living organisms taken in aggregate, none is more powerful in the long run. The more we learn, the more convinced we become that biospheric chemical phenomena never occur independent of life. . . .
>
> Life is, thus, potently and continuously disturbing the chemical inertia on the surface of our planet. It creates the colors and forms of nature, the associations of animals and plants, and the creative labor of civilized humanity. And also becomes a part of the diverse chemical processes of the Earth's crust. There is no substantial chemical equilibrium on the crust in which the influence of life is not evident, and in which chemistry does not display life's work.[5]

Vernadsky described living organisms as "transformers" that use solar energy to power their metabolic relationships with the rest of the planet. "This transformation of energy can be considered as a property of living matter, its function in the biosphere."

> The radiations that pour upon the Earth cause the biosphere to take on properties unknown to lifeless planetary surfaces and thus transform the face of the Earth. Activated by radiation, the matter of the biosphere collects and redistributes solar energy and converts it ultimately into free energy capable of doing work on Earth.
>
> The outer layer of the Earth must, therefore, not be consid-

Vladimir Vernadsky and the Biosphere

ered as a region of matter alone but also as a region of energy and a source of transformation of the planet. To a great extent, exogenous cosmic forces shape the face of the Earth, and as a result, the biosphere differs historically from other parts of the planet. This biosphere plays an extraordinary planetary role.

The biosphere is at least as much a creation of the sun as a result of terrestrial processes.[6]

He identified recycling as the primary characteristic of global metabolism.

The biosphere's 10^{20} to 10^{21} grams of living matter is incessantly moving, decomposing, and reforming. The chief factor in this process is not growth, but multiplication. New generations, born at intervals ranging from tens of minutes to hundreds of years, renew the substances that have been incorporated into life.

Because enormous amounts of living matter are created and decomposed every 24 hours, the quantity which exists at any moment is but an insignificant fraction of the total in a year.

It is hard for the mind to grasp the colossal amounts of living matter that are created, and that decompose, each day, in a vast dynamic equilibrium of death, birth, metabolism, and growth.[7]

In 1938, he described the intimate connection of living organisms with their environments through metabolic processes.

Living organisms are connected with the biosphere through their nutrition, breathing, reproduction, metabolism. This connection may be precisely and fully expressed quantitatively by the migration of atoms from the biosphere to the living organism and back again—the biogenic migration of atoms. . . . There is no natural phenomenon in the biosphere more geologically powerful than life. . . .

> Between the living and inert matter of the biosphere, there is a single, continuous material and energetic connection, which is continuously maintained during the processes of respiration, feeding, and reproduction of living matter, and is necessary for its survival: *the biogenic migration of atoms* of the chemical elements, from the inert bodies of the biosphere into the living natural bodies and back again.[8]

Until his death in 1945, Vernadsky and his colleagues conducted cutting-edge research on the composition and dynamics of the biosphere. A recently translated selection of papers he wrote in that period includes studies of the oxygen and carbon cycles, the organic origins of coal and petroleum, the sources of atmospheric carbon dioxide, and more.[9] On these subjects and others, Vernadsky's work was well ahead of science in other countries.

Vernadsky insisted that biogeochemistry was not concerned with the origin of life as such. Science could not yet explain life, so discussions of it tended to be "permeated with philosophical and religious concepts alien to science."[10] Nor did biogeochemistry study individual organisms: that was the domain of biology. Biogeochemistry addressed planetary questions, so its concern was with the planetary impact of "living matter as a whole—the totality of living organisms."[11]

Vernadsky did not, however, adopt the artificial holism that is sometimes invoked as an alternative to dualism. As the research topics listed above show, he was fully aware of the need to investigate specific parts of the biosphere to build a picture of the whole. He knew that the planetary cycles cannot be understood without knowledge of the differing metabolisms of the species involved. For example, his work in the 1930s included consideration of the different planetary impacts of autotrophs (organisms that live by photosynthesis) and heterotrophs (organisms that live by directly or indirectly consuming autotrophs).

Above all, he was very aware of the unique biospheric impact of one particular species: *homo sapiens*.

Long before he developed his views on the biosphere, Vernadsky's practical work as a geologist made him aware of the destructive effects of extractive industries on the environment. In 1913, for example, after visiting the nickel and cobalt mines in Sudbury, Ontario, he wrote home to his wife:

> This new technology—American technology—which has given so much to mankind, has its dark side. Here we see it in everything: a beautiful land has been made ugly, the forest burned out; for tens of miles the land turned into a wasteland, all plant life poisoned and burned out, and all of this in order to achieve a single goal: the quick mining of nickel.[12]

After the Revolution, he and two of his former students convinced the Bolshevik government to ban mining and other commercial activity in a geologically significant region of the southern Urals. On May 4, 1920, Lenin signed a decree establishing that area as the first territory in the world to be protected for scientific study.[13]

In the 1920s, Vernadsky began to consider whether intelligent matter (humans) might be having an overwhelming impact on the rest of living matter. In his 1926 book *The Biosphere*, he noted that human intelligence had enabled our species to "reach places that are inaccessible to any other living organisms," which made it difficult to determine what the limits of the biosphere might be.[14] What's more, humanity was making unprecedented changes in the "film of life" that covers the land:

> Civilized humanity has introduced changes into the structure of the film on land which have no parallel in the hydrosphere. These changes are a new phenomenon in geological history and have chemical effects yet to be determined. One of the principal changes is the systematic destruction during human history of forests, the most powerful parts of the film.[15]

Research on biogeochemical cycles convinced him that industrialization was significantly changing the biosphere. He wrote this passage in the 1930s, long before anyone else identified the world-changing effects of CO_2 emissions:

> The release of carbonic acid [carbon dioxide] by Man in the process of his technical work is considered biogenic, such as the release occurring in factory furnaces, calcinating lime, fermentation, and in many other processes is a very interesting and characteristic fact in the history of carbon that the quantity of carbonic acid released by mankind in this way increases with the progress of civilization. It has already reached such an order that it must be taken into account in the geochemical history of the biosphere. . . .
>
> Such an increase acquires the status of an important geochemical phenomenon. In this way, civilized Man breaks the established terrestrial balance. With the civilization of *Homo sapiens*, a new geological power has appeared.[16]

In the 1930s, Vernadsky concluded that human activity was creating a new planetary envelope, which he dubbed the noösphere (pronounced NO-osphere), from "nous," ancient Greek for "mind" or "intelligence." He borrowed the word from Pierre Teilhard de Chardin, a Jesuit priest and geologist, whom he met in Paris in the 1920s..

That borrowing has been a source of confusion, since the two men defined the word in radically different ways. Teilhard, a Catholic mystic, defined the noösphere as the spiritual realm that humanity would achieve when it evolved beyond the material world, beyond the biosphere—the "omega point" where humans would meet Christ. Vernadsky, an atheist and materialist (he called himself a "cosmic realist"), viewed the noösphere as the part of the biosphere that was being physically transformed by human activity. So it's important, when the word appears, to determine which version the writer means, or if the writer is even aware of the difference.

In his unfinished book *Scientific Thought as a Planetary Phenomenon*, Vernadsky wrote that the new planetary envelope began to take form with the invention of agriculture, which "radically transforms nature . . . clearing the land from other living organisms."

> You might say that within the last five to seven thousand years the continuous creation of the Noösphere has proceeded apace, ever increasing in tempo, and that the increase of the cultural biogeochemical energy of mankind is advancing steadily without fundamental regression, albeit with interruptions continually diminishing in duration. There is a growing understanding that this increase has no insurmountable limits, that it is an elemental geological process.[17]

Vernadsky viewed evolution as an inevitable progressive advance to a better future, and believed that any negative side effects caused by the expansion of the noösphere would be overcome by human intelligence. It was already having positive social effects:

> Profound social changes, giving support to the broad masses, advanced their interests into the first rank, and the question of eliminating malnutrition and famine became a realistic option that can no longer be ignored.
>
> The question of a planned unified activity for the mastery of nature and a just distribution of wealth associated with a consciousness of the unity and equality of all peoples, the unity of the noösphere, became the order of the day.[18]

In one of his last articles, one of the few published in English during his lifetime, Vernadsky wrote that in modern times, human economic activity was literally changing the chemical composition of the biosphere:

> That mineralogical rarity, native iron, is now being produced

by the billions of tons. Native aluminum, which never before existed on our planet, is now produced in any quantity. The same is true with regard to the countless number of artificial chemical combinations (biogenic "cultural" minerals) newly created on our planet. The number of such artificial minerals is constantly increasing. All of the strategic raw materials belong here. Chemically, the face of our planet, the biosphere, is being sharply changed by man.[19]

He described the noösphere in terms that sound very like twenty-first-century discussions of the Anthropocene:

> Proceeding from the notion of the geological role of man, the geologist A. P. Pavlov [1854–1929] in the last years of his life used to speak of the *anthropogenic era* in which we now live. . . . He rightly emphasized that man, under our very eyes, is becoming a mighty and ever-growing geological force. . . . In the twentieth century, man, for the first time in the history of the earth, knew and embraced the whole biosphere, completed the geographic map of the planet Earth, and colonized its whole surface.[20]

The noösphere would be "the last of many stages in the evolution of the biosphere in geological history." For him, progressive geological evolution and the fight against Nazi barbarism were related.

> Now we live in the period of a new geological evolutionary change in the biosphere. We are entering the noösphere. This new elemental geological process is taking place at a stormy time, in the epoch of a destructive world war. But the important fact is that our democratic ideals are in tune with the elemental geological processes, with the laws of nature, and with the noösphere. Therefore we may face the future with confidence. It is in our hands. We will not let it go.[21]

There are obvious parallels between Vernadsky's view that human activity was transforming the biosphere into the noösphere and the twenty-first-century view that human activity has so changed the Earth System that a new epoch, the Anthropocene, has begun. His description of humanity's impact on the biosphere could easily fit into any modern account of the profound disruption of biogeochemical cycles—that is, of metabolic rifts:

> Man always increases the number of atoms leaving the ancient cycles—the geochemical "eternal" cycles. He intensifies the breach of these processes, introduces new ones, and interferes with old ones. With Man, an enormous geological power has appeared on the surface of our planet. The balance of the migrations of elements that had been established in the course of geological time is being broken by the reason and activities of Man. At present we are changing the thermodynamic equilibrium inside the biosphere in this way.[22]

Vernadsky's influence on the development of Earth System science was limited because his work was virtually unknown outside of the Soviet Union until recently. When he died, fewer than half a dozen of his papers had been translated into English, and only a handful more into French or German. A full English translation of *The Biosphere* wasn't published until 1997. Even in the Soviet Union, most of his work was unavailable until the publication of his *Selected Works* in 1967.

In 1970, the influential magazine *Scientific American* published a special issue on the biosphere, edited by George Evelyn Hutchinson, a Yale professor often called the father of modern ecology. His introductory article provided an overview of biospheric science, incorporating recent advances and fully crediting Vernadsky as the originator of the field. He concluded by arguing that Vernadsky's optimistic view of the noösphere is difficult to maintain now that growing environmental crises are threatening the very survival of the biosphere.

The *Scientific American* articles generated new interest in Vernadsky's work, but its impact was limited, particularly because so little of his work was available in languages other than Russian. Perhaps publishers and translators don't think his thoroughly interdisciplinary works will sell in Western academia, where geologists study geology and biologists study biology, and the twain never meet. As Jacques Grineveld writes, "The revolutionary character of the Vernadskian science of the Biosphere was long hidden by the reductionist, overspecialized and compartmentalized scientific knowledge of our time."[23]

Fortunately, his groundbreaking work is now attracting wider attention. Vernadsky's insights into the nature and development of the biosphere illuminate our efforts to understand global metabolism—and global metabolic rifts.

CHAPTER 7

Barry Commoner and the Broken Circle

We have come to a turning point in the human habitation of the earth. . . . Continued pollution of the earth, if unchecked, will eventually destroy the fitness of this planet as a place for human life.

—BARRY COMMONER[1]

The Second World War saw "the explosive birth of big science," as historian of science Cliff Connor documents. Isolated individuals making big discoveries on their own in small labs were replaced by "large teams of professional researchers working on a grand scale with substantial governmental and corporate funding."[2] The paradigmatic case was the Manhattan Project, which employed 130,000 people and cost $2 billion (the equivalent of $27 billion today) to plan, design, and build the bombs that killed over 200,000 people in Hiroshima and Nagasaki.

Following the war, the U.S. military continued to invest heavily in big, expensive science, especially in geophysical studies of direct value to military operations—mapping the ocean floor, and launching weather satellites, for example. It financed large-scale projects that it directly controlled and paid for research grants at a handful of elite universities. Much of the research that ultimately led to the emergence of what's now called Earth System Science was financed by military money. For the scientists involved, this had the advantage of allowing them to undertake large projects that they couldn't otherwise afford—but it also skewed research priorities toward military needs, and limited participation to people who could obtain the necessary security clearances.

There is, therefore, some irony in the fact that one of the first American scientists to publicly describe the earth as a system and identify the causes of planet-wide environmental destruction had received no military funding and could not get security clearance—a socialist and ecologist who taught at Washington University in St. Louis, Missouri.

Barry Commoner rose to prominence in the 1950s as a leader of the campaign against nuclear bomb tests. His scientific research into the extent and impact of radioactive fallout—a deadly threat whose very existence the U.S. military and government denied—made him very aware that humanity now could poison our world on a scale never before possible. In the 1960s, as founder of the Center for the Biology of Natural Systems, he brought that understanding to his study of other types of pollution.

Time magazine wrote in 1970 that Commoner had "probably done more than any other U.S. scientist to speak out and awaken a sense of urgency about the declining quality of life." His *Washington Post* obituary in 2012 said, "He was among the first scientists to step out of the laboratory and declare that scientists had a moral obligation to keep the public informed about the dangers posed by advances in science and technology." Ralph Nader called him "the greatest environmentalist of the 20th century."[3]

In 1966, Commoner warned that humanity's relationship with what scientists now call the Earth System was in crisis:

> As a biologist, I have reached this conclusion: we have come

to a turning point in the human habitation of the earth. The environment is a complex, subtly balanced system, and it is this integrated whole which receives the impact of all the separate insults inflicted by pollutants. Never before in the history of this planet has its thin life-supporting surface been subjected to such diverse, novel, and potent agents. I believe that the cumulative effects of these pollutants, their interactions and amplification, can be fatal to the complex fabric of the biosphere. And, because man is, after all, a dependent part of this system, I believe that continued pollution of the earth, if unchecked, will eventually destroy the fitness of this planet as a place for human life.[4]

In the same book, he was one of the first to warn that burning wood, coal, petroleum, and natural gas was changing the composition of the atmosphere. "Carbon dioxide makes a huge greenhouse of the earth, allowing sunlight to reach the earth's surface but limiting reradiation of the resulting heat into space. The temperature of the earth—which profoundly affects the suitability of the environment for life—is therefore certain to rise as the amount of carbon dioxide in the air increases."[5]

Commoner's 1971 book, *The Closing Circle*, was his most ambitious account of the nature and causes of the environmental crisis. Its title referred to what he called "the great fault in the life of man in the ecosphere." He didn't use the term "metabolic rift," but he described it dramatically:

We have broken out of the circle of life, converting its endless cycles into man-made, linear events: oil is taken from the ground, distilled into fuel, burned in an engine, converted thereby into noxious fumes, which are emitted into the air. At the end of the line is smog. Other man-made breaks in the ecosphere's cycles spew out toxic chemicals, sewage, heaps of rubbish—testimony to our power to tear the ecological fabric that has, for millions of years, sustained the planet's life.

> Suddenly we have discovered what we should have known long before: that the ecosphere sustains people and everything that they do; that anything that fails to fit into the ecosphere is a threat to its finely balanced cycles; that wastes are not only unpleasant, not only toxic, but, more meaningfully, evidence that the ecosphere is being driven towards collapse.[6]

For Commoner, the "circle of life" was not a mystical or religious concept, but the material reality that Marx described as the universal metabolism of nature, the processes in which energy and matter constantly cycle through the biosphere:

> In every natural system, what is excreted by one organism as waste is taken up by another as food. Animals release carbon dioxide as a respiratory waste; this is an essential nutrient for green plants. Plants excrete oxygen, which is used by animals. Animal organic wastes nourish the bacteria of decay. Their wastes, inorganic materials such as nitrate, phosphate, and carbon dioxide, become algal nutrients. . . .
>
> Nothing "goes away": it is simply transferred from place to place, converted from one molecular form to another, acting on the life processes of any organism in which it becomes, for a time, lodged.[7]

Declaring that "most of this book is an effort to discover which human acts have broken out of the circle of life, and why,"[8] Commoner began by setting out an "informal set of 'laws of ecology.'"

1. Everything is connected to everything else.
2. Everything must go somewhere.
3. Nature knows best.
4. There is no such thing as a free lunch.[9]

The first law states a simple fact about ecosystems. All healthy ecosystems are interconnected and self-stabilizing: If any part of a natural ecosystem is damaged or overstressed, it can trigger far wider problems. For example, the burning of fossil fuels is overloading the global carbon cycle, which in turn is triggering dramatic changes to climate, global ice cover, weather patterns, ocean acidification, farming yields, sea levels, government budgets, and worldwide refugee numbers. Any society that ignores Commoner's first law invites ecological and social turmoil.

Of the second law, Commoner wrote:

> One of the chief reasons for the present environment crisis is that great amounts of materials have been extracted from the Earth, converted into new forms, and discharged into the environment without taking into account that "everything must go somewhere." The result, too often, is the accumulation of harmful amounts of material in places where, in nature, they do not belong.[10]

He was particularly concerned about the production and accumulation of materials that nature cannot absorb or degrade:

> One of the striking facts about the chemistry of living systems is that for every organic substance produced by a living organism, there exists, somewhere in nature, an enzyme capable of breaking that substance down. In effect, no organic substance is synthesized unless there is provision for its degradation; recycling is thus enforced. Thus, when a new man-made organic substance is synthesized with a molecular structure that departs significantly from the types which occur in nature, it is probable that no degradative enzyme exists, and the material tends to accumulate.[11]

Scientists have recently concluded that the very production of untested "novel entities" is a planetary boundary violation that threatens the stability of the Earth System. That brings them into line with Commoner's conclusion, half a century ago, that we ought to "regard every man-made organic chemical not found in nature which has a strong action on any one organism as potentially dangerous to other forms of life."[12]

His third law, nature knows best, is not naive green romanticism, but a rejection of what he called "one of the most pervasive features of modern technology . . . the notion that it is intended to 'improve on nature.' . . . Stated baldly, the third law of ecology holds that any major man-made change in a natural system is likely to be *detrimental* to that system."[13]

He borrowed the fourth law from economics:

> In ecology, as in economics, the law is intended to warn that every gain is won at some cost. In a way, this ecological law embodies the previous three laws. Because the global ecosystem is a connected whole, in which nothing can be gained or lost and which is not subject to overall improvement, anything extracted from it by human effort must be replaced. Payment of this price cannot be avoided; it can only be delayed. The present environmental crisis is a warning that we have delayed nearly too long.[14]

The four laws are superficially simple, but books could be written elaborating on each of them. They formed the basis of Commoner's pathbreaking analysis of the global environmental crisis, and they are just as valid today.

Like today's Anthropocene scientists, he identified the years following 1945 as a turning point: "We know that *something* went wrong in the country after World War II, for most of our serious pollution problems either began in the postwar years or have greatly worsened since then."[15]

Contrary to ecologists who blamed overpopulation, Commoner argued that production had not only increased since 1945; *its fundamental character had changed*. As a result, the environmental crisis wasn't just bigger than in the past; it was qualitatively different and worse:

> The chief reason for the environmental crisis that has engulfed the United States in recent years is the sweeping transformation of productive technology since World War II. . . . Productive technologies with intense impacts on the environment have displaced less destructive ones. The environmental crisis is the inevitable result of this counter-ecological pattern of growth.[16]

In particular, Commoner pointed to the spectacular expansion of the petroleum, petrochemical, and related industries, which produced products and wastes that nature could not recycle, and which at the same time stimulated a huge expansion in the amount of energy used in production and transportation. Low-energy manufacturing gave way to high-energy processes, and natural products were replaced by synthetic ones that required petroleum as a raw material and for energy.

Once our attention focuses on changes in production technology, it's easy to see why the change occurred when it did. As Commoner pointed out, the decades before the Second World War saw revolutionary advances in basic science, especially physics and chemistry. Much of the new science was adopted for military purposes during the war, and then rapidly moved into industrial and agricultural production after it. "The period of World War II is, therefore, a great divide between the scientific revolution that preceded it and the technological revolution that followed it."[17]

The root problem, Commoner argued, was an economic system that puts profit ahead of the health of people and planet. "Private business has chosen to invest its capital preferentially in a series of new productive enterprises that are closely related to the intensification of environmental pollution." Corporations do this not because they have a perverse affection for pollution, but because "production based on the new technology has been more profitable than production based on the old technology it has replaced."[18]

The crucial link between pollution and profits appears to be modern technology, which is both the main source of recent increases in productivity—and therefore of profits—and of recent assaults on the environment. Driven by an inherent tendency to maximize profits, modern private enterprise has seized upon those massive technological innovations that promise to gratify this need.[19]

In *The Social Costs of Private Enterprise*, economist K.W. Kapp showed that after environmental costs were included, the total social cost of many industries exceeded their supposed benefits. Commoner summarized Kapp's work and incorporated it in his own analysis, concluding: "An economic system which is fundamentally based on private transactions rather than social ones is no longer appropriate and increasingly ineffective in managing this vital social good [the ecosphere]."[20]

In addition to spending hundreds of billions of dollars to restore already damaged ecosystems, nothing less than a total restructuring of the economy was required:

> If we are to survive economically as well as biologically, industry, agriculture, and transportation will have to meet the inescapable demands of the ecosystem. This will require the development of major new technologies, including systems to return sewage and garbage directly to the soil; the replacement of many synthetic materials by natural ones; the reversal of the present trend to retire land from cultivation and to elevate the yield per acre by heavy fertilization; replacement of synthetic pesticides, as rapidly as possible, by biological ones; the discouragement of power-consuming industries; the development of land transport that operates with maximal fuel efficiency at low combustion temperatures and with minimal land use; essentially complete containment and reclamation of wastes from combustion processes, smelting, and chemical operations (smokestacks must become rarities); essentially complete recycling of all reusable metal, glass, and

paper products; ecologically sound planning to govern land use including urban areas.[21]

He estimated that "most of the nation's resources for capital investment would need to be engaged in the task of ecological reconstruction for at least a generation."[22] Over half a century later, none of the necessary changes he identified have even begun, and new crises have been added to those he addressed. The time and resources required to ensure that we can "survive economically as well as biologically" are now vastly greater than Commoner expected.

The Closing Circle was and remains a masterpiece that everyone concerned about the environment should read. Inevitably, parts of it are out of date, but Barry Commoner's conclusions are more relevant than ever:

> We are in an environmental crisis because the means by which we use the ecosphere to produce wealth are destructive of the ecosphere itself. The present system of production is self-destructive; the present course of human civilization is suicidal.[23]
>
> There's something wrong, and I think the answer is that we have to now begin to think about replacing the capitalist organization of the economic system by a system which is governed by human need, by social need, and of course, with a small *s*, that's socialism.[24]

CHAPTER 8

"We're Not in the Holocene Anymore"

> Over this first 98% of the Holocene, we have still been in what has been, relatively speaking, very great stability of atmospheric composition and of climate. The last 2 percent of it has been extraordinary—unique, probably in Earth history—as regards what has happened to the atmosphere and to the Earth's surface.
>
> —JAN ZALASIEWICZ AND MARK WILLIAMS[1]

When dinosaurs roamed the world, and for millions of years after an asteroid wiped them out, the earth was hot—on average, 4°C warmer than today, and much warmer than that in the tropics. There was no permanent ice anywhere. It was hotter than any climate humans have ever experienced.

The hothouse age ended when plate tectonics ripped continents apart, driving what is now India northward into Asia, and shifting Antarctica to the South Pole—actions that started a long-term cooling trend. Polar ice caps first formed about 34 million years ago, and about 2.4 million years ago they expanded, until covering much of what we call North America, Europe, and Russia in ice several kilometers thick. The Ice Age had begun.

"We're Not in the Holocene Anymore"   103

Since then, long-term changes in Earth's orbit, rotation, and tilt, known as the Milankovitch cycles, have produced global temperature swings—initially every 40,000 years and then every 100,000 years. In the glacial (cold) phases, ice sheets covered much of the planet; in much shorter interglacial (warm) periods, the ice retreated toward the poles.[2] For the past 11,700 years, Earth has been in an interglacial period, which geologists refer to as the Holocene.

If that cycle had not been disrupted, the world's glaciers and polar ice caps would now be growing. Instead of global heating, Earth's future, in the next 11,000 years or so, would once again be global freezing.

However, as anyone even slightly aware of environmental issues knows, the world's glaciers and ice caps aren't expanding; they are shrinking fast. Between 1994 and 2017, Earth lost 28 trillion tons of ice, and the rate of decline has increased by 57 percent since the 1990s.[3] Even if greenhouse gas emissions are rapidly reduced, continental ice sheets won't return for at least 50,000 years. If emissions don't stop, the ice won't be back for at least half a million years.[4]

In short, as a direct result of greenhouse gas emissions caused by human activity, the Ice Age has been cancelled.

This is concrete proof of one of the most radical conclusions of twenty-first-century science:

> The earth has now left its natural geological epoch, the present interglacial state called the Holocene. Human activities have become so pervasive and profound that they rival the great forces of nature and are pushing the earth into planetary *terra incognita*.[5]

During the 1970s and 1980s, increasing numbers of scientists came to the conclusion that traditional environmental studies, focused on local or regional issues, were insufficient for understanding a new situation in which Earth had entered a period of extreme crisis, caused by human activity.

In 1972, for example, Barbara Ward and René Dubos wrote that "the two worlds of man—the biosphere of his inheritance, the technosphere of his creation—are out of balance, indeed potentially in deep conflict." Earth faced "a crisis more sudden, more global, more inescapable, and more bewildering than any ever encountered by the human species and one which will take decisive shape within the life span of children who are already born."[6]

Several bestselling books by James Lovelock promoted what he called the Gaia hypothesis—that living matter actively regulates the planetary environment to ensure optimal conditions that sustain life. His views were rejected by most scientists, but their popularity encouraged the study of the planet as a whole. Some scientists still use the word Gaia as a synonym for the Earth System.[7]

NASA formed an Earth System Sciences Committee in 1983, declaring that its goal was "to obtain a scientific understanding of the entire Earth System on a global scale by describing how its component parts and their interactions have evolved, how they function, and how they may be expected to continue to evolve on all time scales."[8] Millions of high-resolution photos of Earth obtained by the Landsat satellites, first launched in 1972, contributed to that effort.

In 1986, the International Council of Scientific Unions approved the formation of the International Geosphere-Biosphere Program (IGBP) "to describe and understand the interactive physical, chemical and biological processes that regulate the total Earth System, the unique environment that it provides for life, the changes that are occurring in this system and the manner in which they are influenced by human activities."[9]

The IGBP began operations in 1990, with a secretariat in Stockholm and a variety of international working groups that involved thousands of scientists. By any measure, it was "the largest, most complex, and most ambitious program of international scientific cooperation ever to be organized."[10] For the next twenty-five years, the most important work in Earth System Science was performed under the IGBP's umbrella.

An IGBP founding statement began: "Mankind today is in an unprecedented position. In the span of a single human generation, the Earth's life-sustaining environment is expected to change more rapidly than it has over any comparable period of human history."[11] That statement proved more insightful than anyone imagined in 1990. In 2000, at a meeting where the various working groups reported on a decade of research, Nobel Prize–winning atmospheric chemist Paul Crutzen declared that the accumulated changes had broken through the limits of the present geological epoch. "We're not in the Holocene anymore. We're in the Anthropocene!"[12]

The importance of that insight cannot be overstated. Anthropocene wasn't just a new word; it was a new reality and a new way of thinking about the crisis of the Earth System. Several leading participants in the development of Earth System Science (ESS) wrote recently:

> ESS, facilitated by its various tools and approaches, has introduced new concepts and theories that have altered our understanding of the Earth System, particularly the disproportionate role of humanity as a driver of change. The most influential concept is that of the Anthropocene, introduced by P. J. Crutzen to describe the new geological epoch in which humans are the primary determinants of biospheric and climatic change. The Anthropocene has become an exceptionally powerful unifying concept that places climate change, biodiversity loss, pollution and other environmental issues, as well as social issues such as high consumption, growing inequalities and urbanization, within the same framework. Importantly, the Anthropocene is building the foundation for a deeper integration of the natural sciences, social sciences and humanities, and contributing to the development of sustainability science through research on the origins of the Anthropocene and its potential future trajectories.[13]

Crutzen initially suggested that the Anthropocene may have begun with the Industrial Revolution in the eighteenth century, but subsequent research focused attention on the mid-twentieth century:

> Key to this understanding was the discovery of a sharp upturn in a multitude of global socio-economic indicators and Earth System trends at that time; a phenomenon termed the "Great Acceleration." It coincides with massive increases in global human-consumed energy and shows the Earth System now on a trajectory far exceeding the earlier variability of the Holocene Epoch, and in some respects the entire Quaternary Period.[14]

In 2004, the IGBP published *Global Change and the Earth System: A Planet Under Pressure*, synthesizing the results of their research on global change and arguing that "the Earth System is now in a no-analogue situation, best referred to as a new era in the geological history of earth, the Anthropocene."[15]

After outlining what IGBP researchers had learned about the complex dynamics of the Earth System, the authors described how human activities are now changing it in fundamental ways. Their account included the famous "Great Acceleration" graphs, which show the unprecedented increases in economic activity and environmental destruction that began about 1950. The great metabolic cycles that support life on Earth—carbon, nitrogen, water, and more—were disrupted, and "the most rapid and pervasive shift in the human-environment relationship began.... Over the past 50 years, humans have changed the world's ecosystems more rapidly and extensively than in any other comparable period in human history."[16]

A New Reign of Climate Chaos?

Karl Marx famously wrote that we humans make our own history but not under conditions of our own choosing. He was referring to the limits that the recent past imposes on our thinking and ability to act. His insight also describes the restrictions that the

Earth System placed on our ancestors for hundreds of thousands of years.

The first modern humans evolved from earlier primates about 300,000 years ago. These *homo sapiens* were every bit as intellectually and physically capable as we are: Place them in the twenty-first century, and they could quickly learn to use smartphones and automobiles. But for 300,000 years, all of our ancestors lived in small groups of hunter-gatherers until, beginning about 11,000 years ago, agriculture was invented in Mesopotamia and then independently invented in parts of China, Central America, India, Africa, North America, and South America. The world's first great cities—Çatalhöyük in Turkey; Eridu, Uruk, and Ur in Mesopotamia; Ain Ghazal in Jordan; Mehrgarh in Pakistan; Memphis in Egypt, and more—were built during the same period of rapid economic and social change.

Global climate played a critical role in this worldwide shift from small nomadic groups to farming and the emergence of the first great civilizations. Figure 8.1 (see page 108), adapted from a study of ice-core data by scientists at the Potsdam Institute for Climate Impact Research, shows the average annual temperature in Greenland over the past 100,000 years.[17] The first 90 percent of this time was the end of the Pleistocene, a 2.6 million-year-long epoch characterized by repeated glacial advances and retreats. The global climate was not only cold, it was, in general, extremely variable.

Modern humans walked the earth for all the time shown in this graph. Climate historian William J. Burroughs, who calls the time before the Holocene the "reign of chaos," argues compellingly that so long as rapid and chaotic climate change continued, agriculture and settled life were impossible. To succeed, agriculture needs not just warm seasons, but a stable and predictable climate—and indeed, not long after the Holocene began, humans on five continents independently took up farming as their permanent way of life. "Once the climate had settled down into a form that is in many ways recognizable today, all the trappings of

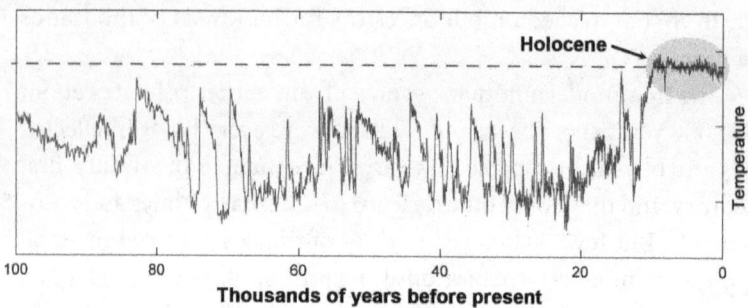

Figure 8.1: Millennia of climate chaos, followed by the Holocene epoch.

our subsequent development (agriculture, cities, trade etc.) were able to flourish."[18]

The Holocene has been one of the longest stable warm periods in the last half-million years.[19] From 11,700 years ago to the twentieth century, the average global temperature did not vary by more than one degree Celsius, up or down half a degree. That is not to say that Holocene weather was without extremes: the one-degree average variation included droughts, famines, heat waves, cold snaps, and intense storms. But overall, it was marked by a not-too-hot, not-too-cold Goldilocks climate.

Rarely has a new scientific concept won wide support as quickly as the Anthropocene. The decade following Crutzen's spontaneous declaration produced a large body of research that explored aspects of the Earth System's rapidly changing state. In 2012, when the IGBP and other Earth System science organizations held a conference on global change in London, more than three thousand people attended in person and three thousand more attended online. The meeting's final declaration was unequivocal:

> Research now demonstrates that the continued functioning of the Earth System as it has supported the well-being of human civilization in recent centuries is at risk. Without urgent action, we could face threats to water, food, biodiversity and other critical resources: these threats risk intensifying

economic, ecological and social crises, creating the potential for a humanitarian emergency on a global scale.[20]

Breaking Planetary Boundaries

When it comes to human well-being, everything we can see in the Anthropocene points to a serious deterioration of the conditions that have supported large and complex human societies for 10,000 years. That insight led a commission of leading Earth scientists to research and define the specific limits within which Holocene-like conditions would continue. They developed the *Planetary Boundaries Framework*, which identifies nine systems and processes that determine the environmental limits within which humanity can operate safely, without risking catastrophe.

The boundaries are not themselves tipping points—they can better be compared to guardrails on a mountain road that keep cars from getting dangerously close to the cliff edge:

> By combining improved scientific understanding of Earth System functioning with the precautionary principle, the Planetary Boundaries Framework identifies levels of anthropogenic perturbations below which the risk of destabilization of the Earth System is likely to remain low—a "safe operating space" for global societal development. A zone of uncertainty for each Planetary Boundary highlights the area of increasing risk.[21]

The initial framework, published in 2009, identified nine critical Earth System processes, three of which had already been crossed. Subsequent updates have refined most of the definitions and proposed hard numbers for all of them.

For information on the current status of the planetary boundaries, I recommend the annual *Planetary Health Check*, edited by Planetary Boundaries Science, an international scientific partnership established in 2023 "to elevate global awareness and drive action towards maintaining planetary stability."[22] The following summary is adapted from their 2024 report and from the more technical report published in the journal *Science Advances* in September 2023.[23]

Of the nine boundaries, only two are within the safe level. The ozone layer in the upper atmosphere has stopped shrinking. It is becoming thicker, providing improved protection from harmful ultraviolet radiation. This is a result of the 1987 Montreal Protocol, which outlawed the chemicals that were destroying ozone.[24]

Atmospheric aerosol loading, the amount of small particle pollution in the air, varies from place to place, but is generally within the safe level globally. However, the researchers report "high uncertainty" about where the zone of increasing risk starts.

Ocean acidification: The 2024 Planetary Boundaries update found that ocean acidity was just inside safe operating space, but subsequent research has concluded that "by 2020, the average global ocean conditions had already crossed into the uncertainty range of the ocean acidification boundary."[25]

Climate Change: Atmospheric CO_2 levels are at a fifteen million year-high, and greenhouse gas emissions continue to drive the warming trend that has accelerated since the late twentieth century. The planetary boundary is 350 parts per million, and the zone of increasing risk is from 350 ppm to 450 ppm. It briefly exceeded 429 in May 2025, and global average temperatures are now higher than at any point since human civilizations emerged on Earth.

Change in Biosphere Integrity: Of the world's estimated eight million plant and animal species, around one million are currently threatened with extinction. The current rate of actual extinctions is one hundred times greater than the historic background rate. At the same time, the proportion of food energy (net primary production) consumed by humans is increasing, squeezing out other species. The decline in the diversity, extent, and health of living organisms and ecosystems threatens the biosphere's ability to regulate the state of our planet by affecting the energy balance and chemical cycles on Earth.

Land System Change: The transformation of natural landscapes, such as through deforestation and urbanization, diminishes ecological functions like carbon sequestration, moisture recycling, and habitats for wildlife. Global and regional forests have been steadily declining over the last few decades across all major forest biomes. Most regions are already in the High-Risk Zone, well beyond their safe boundaries.

Freshwater Change: Alteration of the global hydrological cycle affects all natural functions on land, including carbon sequestration and biodiversity, and it can lead to large ecological shifts. Local streamflow and soil moisture loss have been in the increasing-risk zone since the early twentieth century.

Biogeochemical Flows: The massive overuse of mined phosphorus and synthetic nitrogen in agriculture has exceeded safe boundary levels, driving significant ecological changes, including air and water pollution, eutrophication, poisonous algal blooms, and dead zones in lakes and oceans—as well as contributing to global heating. Current annual use is about 23 million metric tons of phosphorus and 190 million metric tons of nitrogen. The safe levels would be under 11 million tons of phosphorus and 62 million tons of nitrogen.

Novel Entities: In the 1980s, scientists discovered that a chemical used in most refrigerators was destroying the layer of ozone that protects us from harmful solar radiation. The threat was blocked by a treaty that banned that specific chemical, but hundreds of thousands of other artificial substances that have never been tested singly or in combination have been released into the environment, including microplastics, endocrine disruptors, nuclear waste and genetically modified organisms. The risks are unknown, but potentially so high that the planetary boundary for untested novel substances has been set at zero.

In *The Ecological Rift*, Foster, Clark, and York argue convincingly that scientific research on planetary boundaries proves that "we are at red alert status. If business as usual continues, the world is headed within the next few decades for major tipping points along with irreversible environmental degradation, threatening much of humanity."

Although the ecological crisis is often described only in terms of climate change, "the analysis of planetary boundaries and rifts, as they present themselves today, helps us understand the full scale of the ecological crisis now confronting humanity. The simple point is that the planet is being assaulted on many fronts as the result of human-generated changes in the global environment." What we face is not an assemblage of separate problems, but "a potential terminal event in geological evolution that could destroy the world as we know it."

> Planetary boundaries and tipping points, leading to the irreversible degradation of the conditions of life on Earth, may soon be reached, science tells us, with a continuation of today's business as usual. The Anthropocene may be the shortest flicker in geological time, soon snuffed out.[26]

Since Foster, Clark, and York wrote that, the number of broken boundaries has more than doubled, but those in power have made no serious effort to prevent or even mitigate a terminal event.

In the 1930s, the German socialist Walter Benjamin wrote: "Marx says that revolutions are the locomotives of world history. But the situation may be quite different. Perhaps revolutions are not the train ride, but the human race grabbing for the emergency brake."[27] We face not just metabolic rifts, but metabolic chasms. Capitalism's inability to operate within reasonable planetary boundaries means that our exit from the Holocene is speeding up and may be irreversible. It is time to grab the emergency brake.

PART 3

Capital versus the Earth System

CHAPTER 9

Capitalism's Anti-Ecological Logic

> A system that has only one goal, the maximization of profits in an endless quest for the accumulation of capital on an ever-expanding scale, and which thus seeks to transform every single thing on earth into a commodity *with a price*, is a system that is soulless; it can never have a soul, never be green.
>
> — FRED MAGDOFF AND JOHN BELLAMY FOSTER[1]

The soulless system we face is *capitalism*, a world-spanning social order whose fundamental characteristics are in permanent conflict with the natural metabolic systems that make life on Earth possible.

In the briefest possible terms, capitalism is an economic and social system in which the owners of capital (capitalists) appropriate the surplus product generated by the direct producers (or workers), leading to the accumulation of capital—investment and amassing of wealth—by the owners. Production takes the material form of the production of commodities for a market with the aim of generating profit and promoting accumulation. Individuals in this system pursue their self-interest, checked only by their mutual competition and by the impersonal forces of the market.[2]

To understand why a system that once promised progress and liberation now threatens disaster, we must understand the perverse logic that drives it. Five tightly interconnected characteristics distinguish capitalism from all previous human societies and pit it against the natural world: generalized production of commodities; profit maximization; competition among multiple capitalists; short-termism, and unending capital accumulation.

1. *Everything is for sale.*

Volume 1 of *Capital* begins: "The wealth of societies in which the capitalist mode of production prevails appears as an immense collection of commodities."[3] Markets have existed for thousands of years, but only in capitalist societies is the entire economy organized to produce and sell commodities.

Marxist economist Ernest Mandel elaborates:

> The development of the capitalist mode of production implies the generalization of commodity production for the first time in mankind's history. This production no longer embraces merely luxury products, the surplus of foodstuffs or other goods of current consumption, metals, salt and other products indispensable for maintaining and extending the social surplus product. Everything that is the object of economic life, everything that is produced is henceforth a commodity: all foodstuffs, all consumer goods, all raw materials, all means of production, including labor-power itself.[4]

It is hard to grasp the size and complexity of modern capitalism's "immense collection of commodities." In July 2024, Amazon's U.S. website had more than 600 million products for sale, and that represents a tiny fraction of the global market for goods and services.⁵ If a commodity isn't actually illegal, some organization will offer it for sale. "When laws allowed slavery, the United States had an active market in human beings. In countries that permit child labor, children make toys for other children. And when laws allow damage to human health and the natural environment, the result is dirty air and foul water."⁶

In fact, even illegality can't stop the commoditization of everything. Despite the so-called war on drugs, the global trade in illegal narcotics generates well over $300 billion in sales a year.

As philosopher Michael J. Sandel says, "There are some things that money can't buy, but these days, not many." In 2012, he compiled a short list of things that could be purchased in an economy where "almost everything is up for sale." It included an upgrade to a private cell in a Californian prison ($90 a night); the right to shoot an endangered black rhino in South Africa ($250,000); and the right to emit a metric ton of carbon dioxide into the atmosphere in Europe ($10.50). "A market society is a way of life in which market values seep into every aspect of human endeavor. It's a place where social relations are made over in the image of the market."⁷

"A commodity," Marx wrote, "seems at first glance to be a self-evident, trivial thing," scarcely worth any consideration. However, on further analysis, it proves to be "a very vexatious thing, full of metaphysical subtlety and theological perversities." Behind the curtain, behind every item sold in your local store, lie vast and complex socio-economic systems. Millions of workplaces all over the world, staffed by millions of workers whose labor-power itself is a commodity, produce untold numbers of products and components of products. Distribution systems, so complex that "managing logistics" is itself a major business activity, move products to the point of sale and use, which may be (likely is) on the other side of the Earth. There are markets not only for consumer goods, but for the raw materials and machines that go into making products, and for the capital required to acquire the means of production.

Capitalism's Anti-Ecological Logic

The entire natural world has been drawn into the immense collection of commodities. In socialist geographer David Harvey's words:

> Nature is necessarily viewed by capital... as nothing more than a vast store of potential use values—of processes and things—that can be used directly or indirectly (through technologies) in the production and realisation of commodity values.... Natural use values are monetised, capitalised, commercialised and exchanged as commodities. Only then can capital's economic rationality be imposed upon the world.[8]

For capitalism, only things that can be sold have value. Things that can't be turned into commodities can be destroyed or discarded because they have no value to the system. Many of the world's greatest environmental disasters can be traced directly to that illogical logic.

2. Maximizing Profit

To succeed, capitalist corporations not only need to sell commodities, but to sell them for more than they cost to produce. Big banks, money funds, and billionaires only invest in production if there is a prospect of getting more money back. They really don't care if their money finances the production of cars, or clothes, or candy bars, so long as they get the largest possible return on their investment. The economist John Maynard Keynes was no Marxist, but he summed up capitalism's driving force in terms that Marx would certainly have agreed with:

> An entrepreneur is interested, not in the amount of product, but in the amount of *money* which will fall to his share. He will increase his output if by doing so he expects to increase his money profit.... The firm is dealing throughout in terms of sums of money. It has no object in the world except to end

up with more money than it started with. That is the essential characteristic of the entrepreneur economy.⁹

When deciding which products to produce, corporations select the most profitable, even if others are more socially desirable. The hyper-profitable pharmaceutical industry invests hundreds of millions of dollars to develop "lifestyle drugs" for toenail fungus, obesity, baldness, impotence, and the like, while spending pennies (if that) on research into the tropical diseases that kill millions of poor people in the Global South every year. In the words of investigative reporter Ken Silverstein, "One old, fat, bald, fungus-ridden rich man who can't get it up counts for more than half a billion people who are vulnerable to malaria but too poor to buy the remedies they need."¹⁰

The profit system creates and deepens inequality by ensuring that wealth flows inexorably to the already wealthy. In 2024, 1.6 percent of all adults owned 48.1 percent of the world's personal wealth, while the poorest 41 percent owned just 0.6 percent.¹¹ The combined holdings of America's twelve richest men were more than $2 trillion, up 193 percent since 2020.¹²

3. Competing Capitals

Although we often refer to the role of capital in general, in practice, capital only exists as multiple capitalist groups (firms, corporations, stores) that compete for market share and investment. Each group seeks to ensure that the commodities it offers generate an attractive profit on invested capital. A corporation with lower costs, or better-advertised products, or faster delivery can gain market share and even drive competitors out of business. There is constant pressure to expand physically, financially, and geographically.

This is not what mainstream economics texts call "perfect competition," where the presence of many competitors is said to ensure that no company can overcharge, cheat, or otherwise manipulate the market, and where Adam Smith's invisible hand somehow produces the best possible results for society as a whole.

In the few cases where such "perfect" competition does occur, it "always ends in the ruin of many small capitalists, whose capitals partly pass into the hands of their conquerors, and partly vanish entirely."[13] A noteworthy example is agriculture in North America, where owner-operated family farms once reigned. In the 1930s, there were nearly seven million farms in the United States; in 2015, there were only two million, and most of those produced so little income that the owners had to have off-farm jobs. Today, just 3 percent of farms take in more than half of all farm income.[14]

It is sometimes suggested that the existing economic system isn't "real capitalism"—it is "corporatism" or some similar label, and all the problems we describe would vanish if only we returned to a free market economy. Such arguments view capitalism as an abstract ideal, rather than as a product of history in which competition has consistently resulted in a few firms growing larger while most are squeezed out. As Istvan Mészáros wrote: "The necessary outcome is the increasing concentration and centralization of capital and the constitution of more and more powerful enterprises—the giant transnational corporations—which dominate the stage, without the slightest decrease in their appetite for gobbling up their competitors."[15]

Corporate concentration has reached new heights in the twenty-first century. In banking in 1995, the assets of six banks equaled 17 percent of U.S. GDP; by 2010, that had risen to 64 percent. Between 2004 and 2008, the world's 500 largest corporations had total annual revenue equal to 40 percent of world income. Most segments of the global economy are dominated by a handful of companies:

> More and more industries in the manufacturing sector of the economy are tight oligopolistic or quasi-monopolistic markets characterized by a substantial degree of monopoly. And—if anything—the trend is accelerating. . . .

There can be no doubt that such giant corporate enterprises increasingly represent a controlling interest in the world economy, with enormous consequences for the future of capitalism, the population of the world, and the planet.[16]

4. Short-Termism

Capital's need for profit has a corollary: the drive to grow faster. The circuit from investment to profit to reinvestment requires time to complete, and the longer it takes, the less total return investors receive. Competition for investment produces constant pressure to speed up the cycle, to go from investment to production to sale ever more quickly.

That's why it took sixteen weeks to raise a two-and-a-half-pound chicken in 1925, while today chickens twice that size are raised in six weeks. Selective breeding, hormones, and chemical feed enable factory farms to produce not just more meat, but more meat faster and thus more profit faster. The suffering of animals and the quality of the food are secondary concerns, if considered at all.

The need for quick returns on investment pits capitalism directly against the long-term requirements of environmental sustainability.

Fertile land is destroyed, forests are clear-cut, and fish populations collapse, all because of what Istvan Mészáros calls the "incurably short-term horizon of the capital system."[17] There is an insuperable conflict between nature's time and capital's time—between metabolic processes that have developed over hundreds of millions of years, and capital's need for ever-faster production, sale, and profit.

5. Capital Accumulation

If all the world's wealth were converted to hundred-dollar bills, and everyone were to sit on the stack of their own wealth, most of humanity would be sitting on the floor. Middle-class people in rich countries would be sitting at the height of a chair, and the world's two richest men would be sitting in outer space.[18]

That's a powerful image, but it conceals a fundamental distinction, a qualitative divide in the nature of wealth. The riches of the people on the floor and at chair height consist almost entirely of personal possessions. Most have no savings, investments, or income-generating property of any kind. Indeed, most owe more than they own. The wealth of the world's richest people, on the other hand, is mostly *capital*: wealth that is invested to produce more wealth. From 2015 through 2024, the total wealth of the world's billionaires rose to $14 trillion—a mind-boggling 121 percent increase.

Magdoff and Foster suggest a paraphrase of the Old Testament's First Commandment that captures the essence of capitalism: "Thou shalt have no gods before the accumulation of capital." In pre-capitalist societies, the ruling classes appropriated and consumed the surplus product produced by workers and farmers. Capitalists also consume part of their firms' profits, living extravagant lives that 99.9 percent of the population can never afford—but most profits go into expanding the ruling class's total productive wealth.

Capitalism aims not at material growth for its own sake, but at the endless expansion of capital itself:

> Capital ... recognizes no limits to its own self-expansion: there is no amount of profit, no amount of wealth, and no amount of consumption that is either "enough" or "too much." This means that the environment exists not as a place with inherent boundaries within which human beings must live together with Earth's other species, but as a realm to be exploited in a process of growing economic expansion. Businesses, according to the inner logic of capital, which is enforced by competition, must either grow or die, as must the system itself.[19]

In Marx's words: "Accumulation for the sake of accumulation, production for production's sake . . . [was] the historical mission of the bourgeoisie in the period of its domination."[20] All the world is measured against that narrow objective, and a zero-growth capitalist economy simply cannot exist.:

> The only utility whatsoever which an object can have for capital can be to preserve or increase it. . . . Growing wealthy is an end in itself. The goal-determining activity of capital can only be that of growing wealthier, i.e. of magnification, of increasing itself.[21]

The drive to extract, produce, and grow ever more stuff fills the air, soil, and water with poisons. Oceans are dying, species are disappearing at unprecedented rates, freshwater is running short, and soil is eroding faster than it can be replaced—but the growth machines push on. At the same time, corporate executives, economists, bureaucrats, and politicians continue to insist that growth is good and non-growth is bad. Unending material expansion is promoted by ideologues of every political stripe, from social democrats to conservatives. When the G20 met in Toronto in 2010, the word *growth* appeared twenty-nine times in their final declaration.

The growth imperative is not, as liberal environmentalists often argue, just a mistaken policy or a false ideology. It is a fundamental structural feature of capitalism. Uncontrolled growth is an inevitable result of the profit system, of capitalism's inherent drive to accumulate ever more capital:

> The uniqueness of the capital system is manifest in the structural imperative to "grow inexorably or perish." No other system of social metabolic reproduction in the whole of human history had even remotely resembled this inner determination of capital. . . .
> Growth, as the self-expansion of capital, becomes the overpowering end in itself, excluding all consideration of the inherent worth of the adopted targets in relation to genuine human objectives.[22]

Capitalism's Anti-Ecological Logic

As the Bolshevik economist Evgeni Preobrazhensky, explained, capitalism's crises and ongoing destructive nature flowed not from individuals' ignorance, but from the system's anarchic nature:

> If all the capitalists and merchants of contemporary economy possessed a perfect knowledge of Marx's *Capital*, they would probably calculate better within the limits of their sphere of activity and would possibly commit fewer stupidities; but they would not be able to overcome the consequences in the economy which ensue from its unorganized, elemental character.[23]

It doesn't matter if corporate profits involve spreading disease, destroying forests, demolishing ecosystems, and treating our water, air, and soil as sewers. So long as they contribute to the accumulation of capital, all is well in corporate boardrooms.

"The obsessive, obstinate, tyrannical, message of capital"

Marx filled the three large volumes of *Capital* with his unfinished analysis of how capitalism works, so this brief account barely skims the surface. Still, these five characteristics provide a framework for understanding why we live in a world in which it is not just acceptable but praiseworthy to pave paradise and put up parking lots.

We often refer to things that capitalism does, but of course capitalism is not alive, so it cannot actually do anything—these destructive actions are actually carried out by influential humans operating in a social order that rewards behavior that strengthens capital and punishes behavior that might weaken it. The major shareholders and executives, top managers of corporations, and pro-capitalist politicians act, in Marx's evocative phrase, as "personifications of capital."

The radical political ecologist Andre Gorz put it this way:

> A capitalist is not primarily someone who has a fortune and who lives off the work of others. That also describes the slave

owner, the usurer or moneylender, the feudal lord. The essence of a capitalist is that for him money is not primarily something that you spend (spent money by definition is not capital) but something that you invest in order to make a profit which in turn will be invested in order to make an even larger profit and so on forever. The growth of profit, of production, of the company, is the only criterion of success for its managers. And it matters little whether they are owners or salaried executives, bosses by divine right or managerial technocrats. In any case they must act like capitalists—that is, deliver the obsessive, obstinate, tyrannical, message of capital that can't say anything other than "more, bigger, faster."[24]

As individuals, the people who control the giant polluters may want their children and grandchildren to live in a clean, environmentally sustainable world. But no matter how they behave at home or with their children, at work they are capital in human form, and the imperatives of capital take precedence over all other needs and values. When it comes to a choice between protecting humanity's future and maximizing profit today, they choose the latter. Capitalists and their agents "have to submit to the objective imperatives emanating from the unalterable logic of capital expansion. If they do not do so, they will quickly cease to be capitalists, unceremoniously ejected from the overall reproduction process."[25]

As a case in point, consider Volkswagen, the world's second-largest automobile company. In 2009, regulators in Europe and North America introduced strict limits on automobile emissions of nitrogen oxide. This gas causes a wide range of illnesses. That was a big problem for Volkswagen, because much of their profit came from vehicles with diesel engines that did not meet the new standards.

But, as we are often told, capitalism encourages innovation. Just in time, VW announced that its engineers had solved the problem. Cars equipped with their new technology passed the tests—they fully met or exceeded the new standards. They advertised it

Capitalism's Anti-Ecological Logic

heavily as "Clean Diesel," and it was hugely successful. Between 2009 and 2016, Volkswagen sold over eleven million Clean Diesel cars worldwide.

That's pretty impressive—a giant corporation was doing well by doing good, making huge profits while protecting the environment and human health.

Or so it seemed.

In 2016, thanks to investigations by some dedicated engineers, the world learned that Clean Diesel was a hoax. Volkswagen had not invented new emissions technology; it had invented software that cheated on the tests. When the software detected that a test was being conducted, it reduced the engine's power and performance. Under laboratory conditions, VW's Clean Diesel cars met the emission regulations. On the road, they emitted up to forty times more nitrogen oxide than the legal limit.

Senior executives were fired and the company was fined, but that was after the fact, after seven years of big sales and profits, seven years of illegal pollution. The scandal illustrates two fundamental characteristics of capitalism: short-term gains are more important than long-term losses, and profit is more important than protecting human health and the environment.

Usually, big corporations don't have to break laws, because politicians and regulators ensure that laws are corporate-friendly, that regulations don't unduly interfere with profit-making. Boeing, for example, doesn't seem to have broken any laws when it concealed the dangerous changes it made to the 737-Max passenger jet, leading to crashes that killed 346 passengers and crew in 2024. But, as the Volkswagen scandal showed, when the stakes are high enough, the personifications of capital will not be restricted by legality, no matter who gets hurt.

Corporations are social machines for turning capital into more capital. That's what shareholders expect and want, and that's what managers and executives must deliver. A person who is unwilling to put the needs of capital first is not likely to become a corporate executive. If the screening process fails or if a CEO has an inconvenient attack of conscience, he or she will not last long in that position. It has been referred to as the "ecological tyranny of the bottom line."[26] When protecting humanity and the planet might reduce profits, corporations will always put profits first.

The result is a socioeconomic system that grows and prospers only by destroying human lives and natural systems. In Marx's words, "The profound hypocrisy and inherent barbarism of bourgeois civilization . . . resemble[s] that hideous, pagan idol, who would not drink the nectar but from the skulls of the slain."[27]

Unlike the pagan idol, capitalism has real power—and it is really endangering human survival.

CHAPTER 10

Breaking the Carbon Cycle

> The key to understanding the inextricable connections among Earth, carbon, and us is cycles. Carbon cycling lies at the heart of the rapid changes that humans are imposing on Earth, both planned and unintentional.
> —ROBERT HAZEN, *SYMPHONY IN C*[1]

If you've ever wondered what a scientific representation of a metabolic rift might look like, check out Figure 10.1 (see page 129).

The Keeling Curve is such a stunning example of important and clearly presented science that it has been designated a National Historic Chemical Landmark. Its creator received the highest U.S. award for lifetime achievement in science, the National Medal of Science, "for his pioneering and fundamental research on atmospheric and oceanic carbon dioxide, the basis for understanding global carbon cycle and global warming."[2]

(As I write this, we are waiting to learn if Trump will cut funding for the project, which would be an act of gross, anti-scientific vandalism.)

In July 1958, Dr. Charles Keeling of the Scripps Institution of Oceanography began measuring the amount of carbon dioxide in Earth's atmosphere. Using measuring equipment and techniques he developed, he collected air samples daily from an observatory 3,000 meters above sea level, on the remote north side of the Mauna Loa volcano on Hawaii's Big Island.

He continued connecting daily samples until his death in 2005, and his son, Ralph, also a climate scientist, has continued the work since. The result is the world's longest continuous record of atmospheric carbon dioxide.

In his first annual report, Keeling noted that the level at the end of the first year was higher than it had been twelve months earlier. That proved to be a permanent trend. From Keeling's first measurement in 1960 to 2025, the amount of CO_2 in the air we breathe has risen by 37 percent. The level has not been this high since the Pliocene Epoch, three million years ago.

But there is something else of note in the Keeling Curve. Before the steady upward trend became clear, Keeling noticed that atmospheric CO_2 levels rose from October to May and fell from May to October, creating a saw-tooth pattern. He was the first person to see Earth breathing.

The saw-tooth pattern reflects Earth's vegetation cycles. During the April-September growing season in the Northern Hemisphere, CO_2 is taken out of the atmosphere by living plants, and in the rest of the year, it is released by dead plants. The pattern is slightly offset by the opposite seasons in the Southern Hemisphere, but since most of the world's land and vegetation is in the north, the cycle is not overridden. This pattern has likely remained unchanged for as long as the continents have been in their present locations.

This illustrates the complex interworking of biological, chemical, and geological cycles that define the global metabolism. The tilt of Earth's axis causes seasons, which triggers cycles of plant growth and decay, causing atmospheric CO_2 to rise and fall. Although each of those cycles can be studied independently, they can only be fully understood as interacting elements of the whole Earth System.

Since 1958, the amplitude of the saw-tooth—the distance from high to low each year—has increased by as much as 50 percent.

Breaking the Carbon Cycle

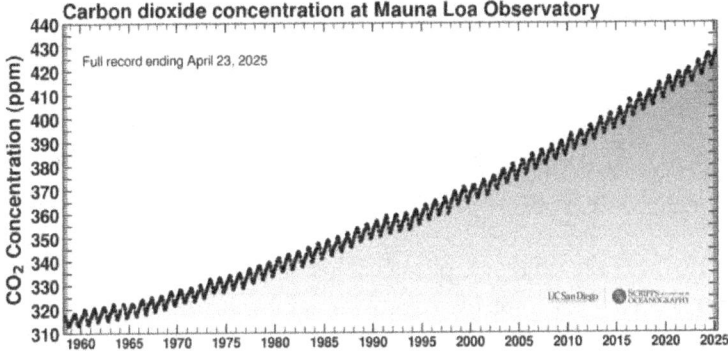

Figure 10.1. Keeling Curve 1959–2025: The concentration of CO_2 in earth's atmosphere approached 430 parts per million in 2025.

More CO_2 is being absorbed by forests and plants in spring and summer, and more is being released in fall and winter, but the change isn't balanced—the highs are increasing faster than the lows. Plants seem to be struggling to take in as much as possible, but they can't keep up. Other studies indicate that increased CO_2 intake helps plants such as corn to grow faster, but reduces the crop's nutritional content.

The Keeling Curve shows two separate but connected rifts in Earth's metabolism. First, the increase in total atmospheric CO_2 shows that carbon sinks are no longer offsetting carbon sources. Second, the increased level of atmospheric CO_2 is changing how plants absorb and emit it, altering a seasonal cycle that has remained unchanged for hundreds of millions of years.

In short, the Keeling Curve shows that Earth isn't just breathing, it is hyperventilating.

CO_2 and Climate

Carbon is the fourth most abundant element in the universe and the second most abundant in your body. No other element has carbon's ability to form so many different stable combinations with so many different elements. This characteristic has ensured its place as the stuff of life, at every scale. Every living thing, from microbes to whales and from algae to redwood trees, is composed of carbon molecules.

And the planetary climate is regulated by carbon dioxide.

Yes. Two centuries of scientific research confirm—despite the claims of science deniers—that the greenhouse effect is a proven fact.

In the 1820s, French physicist Joseph Fourier calculated the energy that Earth receives from the sun and the energy that is reflected back into space, and made a surprising discovery: If the only source of heat is direct solar energy, Earth should be much colder. He concluded that the atmosphere absorbs some of the energy that the planet reflects and returns some of it to the surface. This was later dubbed the *greenhouse effect*, a misleading expression since the atmospheric effect works quite differently from the glass walls of greenhouses, but the phrase caught on, and we're stuck with it.

The first scientist to identify carbon dioxide's role in the greenhouse effect was the American suffragist Eunice Foote, a participant in the famous 1848 women's rights convention in Seneca Falls, a signatory to its Declaration of Sentiments, and one of five women chosen to prepare the convention's proceedings for publication. At a time when women were not allowed to hold academic posts, she was a self-educated chemist who had a sophisticated laboratory in her home.

In experiments she designed and conducted in the 1850s, Foote demonstrated that carbon dioxide traps much more solar heat than hydrogen, ordinary air, or oxygen. She concluded that if there were more CO_2 in the atmosphere, Earth would be warmer. Her short paper, "Circumstances Affecting the Heat of the Sun's Rays," was presented at the 1856 meeting of the American Association for the Advancement of Science and published in the *American Journal of Science and Arts*. There was, however, no follow-up, and Foote's work was forgotten until an independent researcher found it in 2010.[3]

Breaking the Carbon Cycle

In 1859, Anglo-Irish physicist John Tyndall, unaware of Foote's research, showed that atmospheric heating is caused by the infrared part of light's spectrum, not by visible sunlight, and that nitrogen and oxygen, which together comprise almost 99 percent of the atmosphere, have no insulating effect at all. All atmospheric capture of solar heat, he reported, is caused by a few trace gases, particularly carbon dioxide, water vapor, and ozone. His findings laid the groundwork for modern climate science.[4]

In 1896, the Nobel Prize–winning Swedish chemist Svante Arrhenius was the first to measure the climate impact of industrial emissions from burning coal. Noting that "if now the quantity of carbonic acid in the air is increased, the temperature of the earth's surface increases," he calculated that if the amount of CO_2 in the air doubled, the earth would be 5.7°C warmer.[5] He was remarkably close. Climate scientists now estimate that doubling CO_2 levels will raise Earth's temperature by "between 2°C and 5°C."[6]

If there were no CO_2 in the atmosphere, Earth's average temperature would be *minus* 18°C instead of *plus* 15°C. The oceans would be frozen, and life as we know it would never have evolved. On the other hand, if, as on Venus, the atmosphere were entirely CO_2, Earth's surface would be hot enough to melt lead.

Carbon dioxide's warming effect is simple physics, as Stephanie Pappas explains:

> Sunlight enters the atmosphere as ultraviolet and visible light; some of this solar energy is then radiated back toward space as infrared energy, or heat. The atmosphere is 78 percent nitrogen and 21 percent oxygen, which are both gases made up of molecules containing two atoms. These tightly bound pairs don't absorb much heat.
>
> But the greenhouse gases, including carbon dioxide, water vapor and methane, each have at least three atoms in their molecules. These loosely bound structures are efficient absorbers of the long-wave radiation (also known as heat) bouncing back from the planet's surface. When the molecules in carbon

dioxide and other greenhouse gases re-emit this long-wave radiation back toward Earth's surface, the result is warming.[7]

Some science deniers claim that carbon dioxide emissions can't be a problem because they are such a small fraction of the atmosphere, less than 1 percent. That argument is precisely backwards: It is *because* a very small amount of CO_2 has warmed Earth for billions of years that *any* change is a concern. A small absolute increase is a large percentage increase. Anyone who says that increasing the amount of carbon dioxide in the atmosphere doesn't make Earth warmer has to explain why the laws of physics don't apply.

Recycling Carbon, Fast and Slow

Like the other elements required by living matter, the supply of carbon would have long ago been exhausted if it were not constantly recycled. Plants alone could consume all the carbon dioxide in the atmosphere in just 8,000 years. Life continues because carbon molecules are constantly recycled and reused in two separate but related metabolic cycles, a fast cycle controlled by biology, and a slow cycle driven by geology.

The fast carbon cycle takes from seconds to centuries to recycle carbon through living matter, soil, oceans, and the atmosphere. Its driving engine is photosynthesis, the complex process by which plants combine carbon dioxide, water, and solar energy to produce carbohydrates and release oxygen as a waste product. Since all animals either eat plants or eat animals that eat plants, photosynthesis is the basis of all food webs, and thus of all complex life.

Almost all of the CO_2 that plants use is eventually returned to the atmosphere, water, or soil. Some is respired almost immediately. Some CO_2 returns when plants die and decompose—for some trees, that can take decades or even centuries—or when they burn. Some is eaten by animals and moves elsewhere when they excrete and when they die. These processes ensure that plant life everywhere has ready access to the tens of billions of tons of carbon it needs every year. All the air you breathe and all the food you eat include carbon atoms that have passed through the fast carbon cycle many times over.

The slow carbon cycle takes from hundreds of thousands to millions of years to move carbon between the solid Earth, the atmosphere, and the oceans. Volcanoes leak or expel about 200 million tons of carbon dioxide into the atmosphere every year. Rain absorbs CO_2 from the atmosphere, creating a weak acid that slowly dissolves rocks, creating calcium carbonate that is washed into the sea. In the ocean, plankton, corals, and other animals use the carbon to build their shells and skeletons. Over time, those animals die and their hard parts sink, forming carbon-based rock that is carried by plate tectonics and eventually returned to the atmosphere by volcanoes.[8]

As geophysicist Roy Livermore explains, under normal conditions, feedback cycles ensure that the amounts of carbon added to the atmosphere by volcanoes and removed by weathering roughly balance over the long term:

> In a nutshell, an increase in supply of CO_2 through volcanism leads to an increase in surface temperature by means of the greenhouse effect, which leads to faster weathering, which leads to faster removal of CO_2 from the atmosphere, followed by transport of carbonates in rivers and deposition in the oceans, which leads to a reduction in atmospheric CO_2, which leads to a decrease in surface temperature.[9]

Breaking the Cycle

For at least 2.6 million years—starting long before our ancestor *homo erectus* walked the earth—the concentration of atmospheric CO_2 was never lower than 183 parts per million during glacial (cold) periods and never higher than 292 parts per million during interglacial (warm) periods. The average was about 230.

The fact that levels varied so little shows that there has long been a rough balance between additions and removals of CO_2. Now that balance has been shattered, thanks to the rapid extraction and burning of long-buried carbon.

Between 500 and 600 million years ago, untold numbers of tiny plants and animals were buried beneath the ocean floor. About 300 million years later, before fungi developed the ability to dissolve wood, huge numbers of newly evolved plants and trees were buried in swampy land. Over time, heat and pressure transformed the oceanic plankton into petroleum and natural gas, and the terrestrial plants and trees into peat and coal.

While they remained underground, the transformed remains of those long-dead organisms had no effect on climate. But now the extraction and burning of coal, petroleum, and natural gas is transferring billions of tons of carbon a year out of long-term storage into the atmosphere, far more rapidly than natural processes can remove it:

> Fossil hydrocarbons are so full of energy thanks to the strong carbon bonds inherited from living things and compressed by rocks and soils. This material memory of life on earth is formed over hundreds of millions of years. . . . Yet today we are expending several of those millennia each year to exploit the energy of carbon bonds and to fuel industry, releasing CO_2 into the atmosphere. In this way, we are consuming and burning the memory of past life; we are burning "buried sunshine," in the words of ecologist Jeffrey Dukes.[10]

As we have seen, the International Geosphere-Biosphere Program's (IGBP) research into global change led inexorably to the conclusion that "the last 50 years have without doubt seen the most rapid transformation of the human relationship with the natural world in the history of mankind."[11] In *Crude Capitalism*, Adam Hanieh quotes that sentence and goes on:

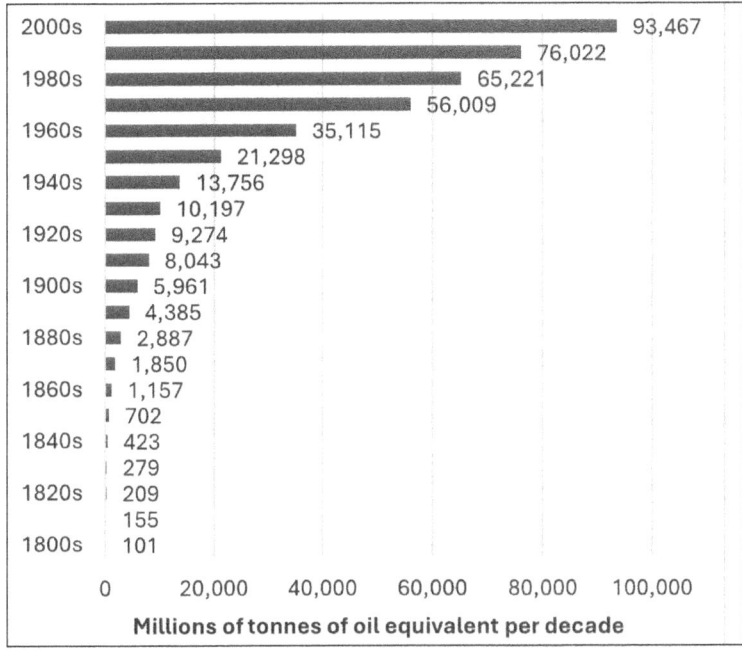

Figure 10.2. Fossil Fuel Production, 1800–2009: Data from Simon Pirani, *Burning Up: A Global History of Fossil Fuel Consumption* (Pluto Press, 2018), 10.

Why was the mid-20th century *the* turning point in humanity's impact on the earth's systems? The simple—but incomplete—answer is *oil*. Oil first began to emerge as a significant energy source in the U.S. during the early 1900s, although, at the time, coal remained the dominant fossil fuel. A major leap towards an oil-centered world occurred around the Second World War, when the shift from coal to oil was extended across Western Europe, and then later through newly industrializing countries in other parts of the world. The oil transition massively accelerated the world's consumption of fossil fuels and thus carbon emissions: nearly three-quarters of the human-driven increase in the atmospheric concentration of CO_2 has happened since 1950, and about half since the 1980s.[12]

Hanieh's account is correct, but his use of the word *transition* may be misleading. Although oil replaced coal in some applications—such as railroads and steamships, for example—the use of both has increased substantially since the 1950s. Coal remains, by a small margin, a greater source of greenhouse gas emissions. Globally, oil has been an addition to, rather than a replacement for previous fossil fuels.

Burning past sunshine, an essential feature of capitalism for centuries, has overwhelmed nature's ability to remove CO_2 from the atmosphere. In 2025, atmospheric CO_2 was 55 percent higher than the Holocene average, higher than at any time in at least the past three million years.[13] Greenhouse gas levels have never been this high while humans existed, and they have never before risen so quickly.

How Hot Will it Get?

The year 2024 was the warmest since records began being kept, 175 years ago. According to the World Meteorological Organization's latest *State of the Global Climate* report:

- Each of the years from 2015 to 2024 set a new global temperature record.
- Each of the years from 2017 to 2024 set a new record for ocean heat content.
- The eighteen lowest Arctic sea-ice extents on record were all in the eighteen years after 2007.
- The three lowest Antarctic ice extents occurred between 2022 and 2024.
- The largest three-year loss of glacier mass on record occurred between 2022 and 2024.
- The rate of sea level rise has doubled since satellite measurements began.[14]

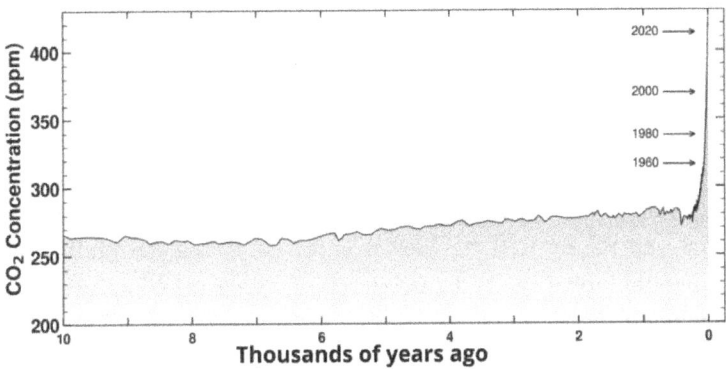

Figure 10.3. Carbon dioxide in the atmosphere: Burning coal, oil, and gas has produced far more carbon dioxide than natural processes can remove, ending the Holocene and causing climate chaos. (Source: Scripps Institution of Oceanography.)

There is no room for doubt: Earth is getting hotter. The question now is, *how hot will it get?*

In the Paris Agreement, adopted at the United Nations climate conference in 2015, 196 countries promised to "significantly reduce the risks and impacts of climate change" by "holding the increase in the global average temperature to well below 2°C above pre-industrial levels and pursuing efforts to limit the temperature increase to above pre-industrial levels."[15]

A May 2024 survey asked 380 leading climate scientists whether the 1.5°C goal would be achieved. Only 6 percent said yes. Seventy-seven percent believed that global temperatures will rise more than 2.5°C by 2100, and 42 percent thought the increase will be more than 3.0°C.[16]

Future Earth, the international agency that coordinates global change research, warns that "overshooting 1.5°C is fast becoming inevitable."

> Decades of insufficient action for mitigating GHG [greenhouse gas] emissions have set the world on the current trajectory to

overshoot the internationally agreed target of limiting global warming to 1.5°C, enshrined in the Paris Agreement. National mitigation commitments are inadequate to even stay well below 2°C of global warming, creating unacceptable risks for human societies and ecosystems, with vast yet unequally distributed costs. This is a dangerous gamble that could lead to irreversible impacts for life on Earth, including devastating loss of biodiversity and a rising risk of triggering climate tipping points.[17]

Under the Paris Agreement, each country determines its own targets, called National Determined Contributions (NDC). According to the UN, there is a "massive gap" between the treaty's objectives and the policies actually adopted by the largest polluters:

> Collectively the NDC targets of the G20 are far from the average global percentage reductions required to align with 2°C and 1.5°C scenarios. . . .
> A continuation of the mitigation effort implied by current policies is estimated to limit global warming to a maximum of 3.1°C (range: 1.9–3.8) over the course of the century.[18]

This isn't just a matter for future concern. 2024 was the hottest since pre-industrial times, the first full year in which the average temperature surpassed the 1.5 °C target. Actually exceeding the Paris goal requires at least a decade over 1.5°, but 2024 is almost certainly an indicator of what is to come, especially if, as noted climate scientist James Hansen argues, global warming is speeding up:

> Therefore, we expect that global temperature will not fall much below +1.5°C level, instead oscillating near or above that level for the next few years, which will help confirm our interpretation of the sudden global warming. High sea surface temperatures and increasing ocean hotspots will continue, with

harmful effects on coral reefs and other ocean life. The largest practical effect on humans today is increase of the frequency and severity of climate extremes. More powerful tropical storms, tornadoes, and thunderstorms, and thus more extreme floods, are driven by high sea surface temperature and a warmer atmosphere that holds more water vapor. Higher global temperature also increases the intensity of heat waves and—at the times and places of dry weather—high temperature increases drought intensity, including "flash droughts" that develop rapidly, even in regions with adequate average rainfall.[19]

It has become common in scientific reports to assert that it's still "technically possible" to meet the Paris objectives. That's just barely true, but unlikely. The United Nations Environment Program tells us just what needs to be done:

> Specifically, if action in line with 2°C or 1.5°C pathways were to start in 2024, then global emissions would need to be reduced by an average of 4 and 7.5 per cent every year until 2035, respectively. If enhanced action . . . is delayed until 2030, then the required annual emission reductions rise to an average of 8 per cent and 15 per cent to limit warming to 2°C or 1.5°C, respectively.[20]

None of that is going to happen if radical political and economic changes aren't made soon. Greenhouse gas emissions are going up, not down, and not one G20 government has shown willingness to slow the increase, let alone reverse it. The United States has withdrawn from the international climate process, and Trump has cancelled climate change programs. If other major emitters don't take up the slack or just fail to carry through on their Paris Agreement commitments, even 3°C will be passed, probably sooner than the climate modelers project.

Andreas Malm and Wim Carton sum up where things stand today:

Promises were, after all, just that, and most were not backed up by measures that could take them out of the realm of "blah blah blah," to use Greta Thunberg's phrase. When in 2023, eight years after Paris, one scratched away at the net zero façade and summated all the *actual* efforts—not promises—in place across the globe, the sobering result was that the world was on track for 2.7°C; or, rounding the number, 3°C, meaning a warming twice as large as that which the Global South had insisted on to stay alive. And we know that the warming does not produce a linear rise in damages: 3°C would be something far worse than just a doubling of the impacts at 1.5°C. But deep into the Paris era, this is where the world was heading.[21]

If three degrees doesn't sound like much, bear in mind that the average global temperature during the last ice age was just six degrees cooler than today. Even a small change in the average temperature can lead to a disproportionate increase in deadly extremes.

"There Is No Natural Savior"

The Anthropocene has been described as the epoch when human activity is "overwhelming the great forces of nature."[22] There is no doubt that industry and agriculture are overwhelming the global carbon cycle. In 2024, CO_2 emissions from fossil fuel combustion and land-use change reached an all-time record of 41.6 billion tons.[23] That's nearly 70 times the annual emissions produced by volcanoes. Even though the oceans have absorbed about 31 percent of the new emissions, the level of CO_2 in the atmosphere is growing fast.

The closest parallel in Earth's deep history is the Paleocene-Eocene Thermal Maximum (PETM) 56 million years ago, when global temperatures rose by 5° to 8°C and half of all ocean life died. The PETM was caused by a massive release of buried greenhouse gases, possibly from super-volcano eruptions in the North Atlantic. In two thousand years, a blink of an eye in geological time, over two trillion tons of long-buried carbon dioxide entered the atmosphere. After the eruptions stopped, it took more than 100,000 years for temperatures to return to pre-PETM levels.

Today, greenhouse gases are being added to the atmosphere ten times as rapidly as during PETM at its peak. Since 1750, emissions have totaled nearly 1.5 trillion tons, and more than half of that was emitted after 1988. If business as usual continues, total emissions will reach total PETM levels in this century. Rapid action to slash emissions could prevent that, but even then, future generations will face a much warmer global climate regime than humans have ever experienced.

At the IGBP meeting in 2000, where the Anthropocene epoch was first discussed, the Carbon Working Group reported research showing that "although natural sinks can potentially slow the rate of increase in atmospheric CO_2, no natural savior is waiting to assimilate all the anthropogenic CO_2 in the coming century. . . . It will affect Earth's biogeochemical cycles for hundreds of years to come."[24]

CHAPTER 11

Rising Seas, Burning Trees, Tipping Points

The current concentration of carbon dioxide in the world's atmosphere is not just the highest level ever directly measured, it's the highest in more than three million years, higher than humans have ever experienced.[1]

This is a direct result of carbon dioxide emissions from fossil fuels, industry, and other human sources that reached a record 41.6 billion metric tons in 2024.[2] The world's oceans, plants, and soils absorbed more than half of that, but the CO_2 that stayed in the air increased the total there by about 15 billion metric tons, further fracturing the global carbon cycle and intensifying what the UN Secretary-General says should now be called the "era of global boiling."[3]

If all anthropogenic emissions were to stop tomorrow, natural processes would gradually reduce the amount of CO_2 in the atmosphere; however, the key word is "gradually." As a leading climate scientist writes, "The lifetime of fossil fuel CO_2 in the atmosphere is a few centuries, plus 25 percent that lasts essentially forever."

The climatic impacts of releasing fossil fuel CO_2 to the atmosphere will last longer than Stonehenge. Longer than time capsules, longer than nuclear waste, far longer than the age of human civilization so far. Each ton of coal that we burn leaves CO_2 gas in the atmosphere. The CO_2 coming from a quarter of that ton will still be affecting the climate one thousand years from now, at the start of the next millennium.[4]

Other scientists put the very long-lasting fraction at 20 percent, but that is a trivial difference given that the amount of CO_2 in the atmosphere is now a trillion tons greater than when direct measurements started in 1958. Many centuries from now, the CO_2 emitted today will still be keeping Earth's temperatures well above Holocene levels.

Rising Waters

Sea level is inextricably connected to global warming. First, because warmer weather is melting glaciers and ice sheets, releasing ever more water into the seas. And second, because water expands as it warms and has nowhere to go except onto the land. So far, the two processes have roughly equal impacts.

Before the Holocene, ice sheets held so much water that the oceans were as much as 130 meters lower than they are today—it took ten thousand years of melting to bring the ocean surface close to what we see today. For most of the Holocene, the level remained stable or rose less than a millimeter per year. Records from thousands of tidal gauges introduced since the 1800s, and specialized satellites launched since 1993, show that the sea level rise rate increased slowly in the twentieth century, then speeded up. The growth rate has increased every year since 2010, and in 2024 it rose 5.9 millimeters, three times as fast as in any year in the 1900s.

Even if the global temperature increase is kept below 1.5 degrees (very unlikely), glaciers will continue to melt, sea water will continue to expand, and the oceans will continue to rise, probably for centuries. There seems to be a general scientific consensus that the waters will be about thirty centimeters higher in 2050, and up to a meter higher in 2100, depending on the level of greenhouse gas emissions. The wild card, as Figure 11.1 shows, is how much the Greenland and Antarctic ice sheets melt during this century. Ice sheet science is not well developed, and scientists do not have a clear understanding of how huge masses of ice resting on rock might move, break up, and melt. There is enough ice in Greenland to raise sea level 7 meters; enough in Antarctica to raise it 58 meters more. Neither is likely to melt completely in this century. Still, even a small fraction will radically change living conditions on much of our planet.

The Intergovernmental Panel on Climate Change (IPCC) has "high confidence" that by 2100, sea level rise will cause extreme sea level events that now occur only once in 100 years to happen at least annually in most coastal areas.

More than a billion people live on land that is less than 10 meters above sea level, and 230 million of them live within one meter. For them, a few more centimeters of ocean could be catastrophic. That's particularly true in coastal cities, where sea level rise may be magnified by long-term subsidence. Parts of New Orleans, for example, are now sinking as much as 20 millimeters a year—combined with higher seas, that pretty much guarantees massive flooding, sooner or later.[5] A recent study estimates that a 20-centimeter rise "would lead to average global flood losses of US$1 trillion or more per year for the world's 136 largest coastal cities." The study's authors argue that such a rise is possible by 2050. Based on present experience, it is certain that most of the pain will be felt by the poor.

Sea level rise poses a particularly difficult challenge because it combines short-term and long-term crises. Seawalls to protect against storm damage and frequent flooding may work in the short term, but they can actually increase climate risks by trapping water surges. Effective long-term responses, such as moving people, houses, and infrastructure inland, require international planning and coordination over centuries—activities that are not characteristic of capital's short-term profit focus.

Rising Seas, Burning Trees, Tipping Points

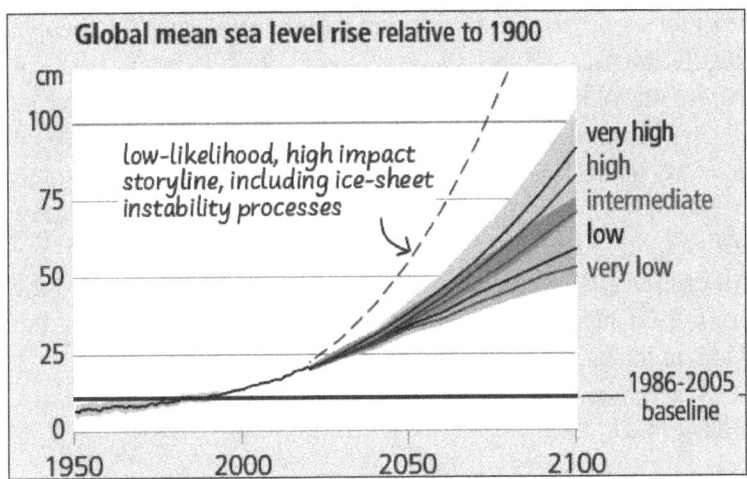

Figure 11.1: Global mean sea level rise to 2100 depends primarily on greenhouse gas emissions, but all bets are off if ice sheets collapse. (Source: IPCC, *Climate Change 2023*.)

Fire Weather

Fire has been an essential part of nature's metabolic systems since the first plants grew on land. Fires recycle carbon, open space for new growth, spread seeds, and more generally shape the world's landscapes.

Now, however, global warming is increasing the frequency and extent of the hot and dry conditions known to meteorologists as fire weather—conditions in which fires, regardless of how they are started, can grow rapidly into massive conflagrations. This metabolic shift is driving a radical increase in the number and intensity of extreme wildfires. There are now more than twice as many extreme wildfires every year as there were at the beginning of the century.[6]

In the last week of June 2021, the village of Lytton in central British Columbia experienced temperatures over 40°C for five consecutive days, reaching a Canadian record of 49.5 °C on June 29. On June 30, a grassfire was spotted outside the town. In less than ninety minutes, houses on the edge of town were burning, and a few hours later, the entire community was destroyed. Two people died in the fire; only the rapid evacuation of Lytton and adjacent First Nations communities prevented a much higher death toll.[7]

The Lytton fire was dramatic and destructive, but the burned area, 84,000 hectares, reaches barely halfway up a list of the largest twenty-first-century fires. The fire that destroyed Fort McMurray, Alberta, in 2016, burned 580,000 hectares. Wildfires in the Amazon in 2019 burned more than 85.9 million hectares, and the 2023–2024 bushfire season in Australia burned an astonishing 144.5 million hectares.

A Canadian government website describes Canada's worst wildfire year.

> Canada's 2023 wildfire season was the most destructive ever recorded. By the end of the year, more than 6,000 fires had torched a staggering 15 million hectares of land. To put that in perspective, that's an area larger than England and more than double the 1989 record. Normally, an average of 2.5 million hectares of land is consumed in Canada every year. And unlike previous years, the fires this year were widespread, from the West Coast to the Atlantic provinces, and the North. By mid-July, there were 29 mega-fires, each exceeding 100,000 hectares.[8]

The same year, Greece experienced Europe's largest wildfire ever, and fires killed more than 200 people in Hawaii and Chile. In the following year, 2024, extreme drought led to immense wildfires in Bolivia (10.7 million hectares), Venezuela (5.2 million hectares), Peru (0.30 million hectares), Guyana (0.26 million hectares), and Ecuador (0.09 million hectares). In Brazil, 30 million hectares burned—62 percent over the annual average, an area the size of Italy.[9]

These experiences highlight an important and dangerous feedback loop in climate change, shown in Figure 11.2.

Forests are natural carbon sinks. They absorb carbon dioxide

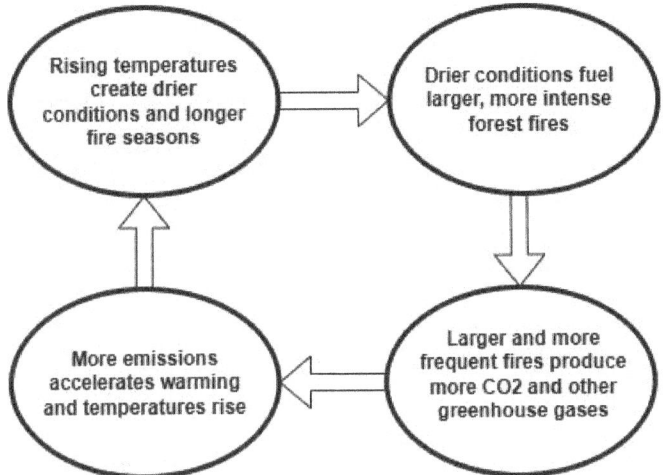

Figure 11.2: Forest Fire/Carbon Loop

from the atmosphere and store it in their roots, trunks, and leaves. When a forest burns, many years of stored carbon combine with oxygen and return to the atmosphere as carbon dioxide. Between 2001 and 2023, annual global carbon dioxide emissions from forest fires increased by 60 percent.[10]

Between May and September 2023, forest fires in Canada released about 647 million metric tons of carbon into the atmosphere. As a study published in *Nature* shows, that is "comparable to the annual fossil fuel emissions of large nations, with only India, China and the USA releasing more carbon per year."[11]

If wildfire emissions were included in calculations under the Paris Agreement, Canada would jump from twelfth place to fourth among the worst contributors to global warming. As it is, they are excluded, under the specious grounds that such emissions are "natural," despite the obvious role of human activity in making big burns inevitable. Besides, we're told that CO_2 will be reabsorbed when the forests grow back. In fact, it's unlikely that burned boreal forests will ever fully recover, particularly since climate change—including the fires themselves—is changing the environments they originally grew in.[12]

Tipping Points and Fat Tails

Even more alarming, recent studies suggest that the Amazon basin, so essential to the global carbon cycle, is nearing a tipping point at which it would switch from being a net absorber of CO_2 to being a net source. Amazon Frontlines, an NGO that works with Indigenous communities in the area, warns that massive fires and deforestation threaten to "transform the world's largest rainforest into billions of tons of carbon dioxide lodged in the atmosphere."[13] The 2023 *Global Tipping Points Report* argued that the shift has already begun:

> Analysis based on early warning signals indicates that over 75 per cent of the Amazon has lost resilience since the early 2000s. This decline is focused mostly closer to human disturbance, as well as in the drier south and east previously identified as "bistable" (i.e. with two possible alternative states) due to the forest-rainfall feedback and thus is more vulnerable to tipping. While the Amazon has acted as a carbon sink due to CO_2 fertilisation, in mature forest this sink peaked and started declining in the 1990s and when including degraded forest (also predominantly in the drier south and east) the Amazon as a whole is now a carbon source.[14]

There is a tendency to view the future as a straightforward extension of the present, and to assume that change will happen gradually. In IPCC reports, graphs of future heating forecasts display straight lines or smooth curves—we rarely see any disconcerting discontinuities.

That view gives some credence to the argument, made by many mainstream economists, that there is no urgency because serious climate change is almost entirely in the distant future. By the time a three-degree increase arrives in 2100, we'll probably have much better climate control technology available, so let's spend our limited public funds on today's problems and deal with the future when it arrives. The work of William Nordhaus has been particularly influential in this respect. He doesn't deny that climate change is real, but he has played a central role in justifying climate inaction for over three decades.

If we were certain that temperatures would increase gradually, with no tipping points or extreme events, there might be a (weak) case for Nordhaus's wait-and-see approach. But, as noted climate scientist Michael Mann writes, a deliberate delay policy downplays or ignores the very real possibility of extremely damaging climate events:[15]

> One of the most under-appreciated aspects of the climate change problem is the so-called "fat tail" of risk. In short, the likelihood of very large impacts is greater than we would expect under typical statistical assumptions....
>
> We are used to thinking about likelihoods and probabilities in terms of the familiar "normal" distribution, otherwise known as the "bell curve."...
>
> Global warming instead displays what we call a "heavy-tailed" or "fat-tailed" distribution. There is more area under the far right extreme of the curve than we would expect for a normal distribution, a greater likelihood of warming that is well in excess of the *average* amount of warming predicted by climate models....
>
> With additional warming comes the increased likelihood that we exceed certain "tipping points," such as the melting of large parts of the Greenland and Antarctic ice sheet and the associated massive rise in sea level that would produce.[16]

Even if temperatures on the right side of the curve are less likely than those in the middle, they are definitely possible, which makes decisive action more urgent than a "normal" distribution might imply.

If we are lucky, climate change might occur as Nordhaus hopes, giving us lots of time to prepare and adapt. However, there is increasing evidence that exceeding certain thresholds can quickly push components of the Earth System into qualitatively different modes of operation:

> The Earth System comprises a number of large-scale subsystems, the so-called tipping elements, that can undergo large and possibly irreversible changes in response to environmental or anthropogenic perturbations once a certain critical threshold in forcing is exceeded.... With continuing global warming, it becomes more likely that critical thresholds of some tipping elements might be exceeded, possibly within this century, triggering severe consequences for ecosystems, infrastructure and human societies.[17]

Scientists have identified more than twenty-five potential tipping points in the Earth System, including five that "are already at risk of crossing tipping points at the present level of global warming: the Greenland and West Antarctic ice sheets, warm-water coral reefs, North Atlantic Subpolar Gyre circulation, and permafrost regions." Those systems "pose threats of a magnitude never before faced by humanity." The danger is increased by the possibility of cascades, in which triggering one tipping point triggers another, "causing a domino effect of accelerating and unmanageable damage."[18]

Two decades ago, climate scientists believed that tipping points were unlikely to be reached until the global average temperature increased by 5°C or more. Now, the IPCC says that there is a high risk of "abrupt and irreversible change" when the 1.5°C threshold is passed.[19]

One or more tipping points could trigger a qualitative change, sending Earth toward an extreme hothouse state that stopping emissions will not cure.

CHAPTER 12

Nitrogen: From Shortage to Glut

> Nitrogen pollution is causing an environmental catastrophe with devastating consequences for planet Earth, yet the scale of the problem remains largely unknown outside of scientific circles.
>
> —UNITED NATIONS ENVIRONMENT PROGRAM[1]

If you ask environmental activists to identify their major concerns, climate change and species extinctions will likely be named first, followed by air pollution, deforestation, and maybe population growth. Most likely, they won't mention nitrogen at all. Although many scientific and technical studies have been conducted on the nitrogen crisis, few popular books on environmental issues have anything substantial to say about it. There are no anti-nitrogen demonstrations, no international nitrogen reduction treaties, no politicians defending or denying the science.

And yet, as the 2013 report *Our Nutrient World* tells us:

> While recent scientific and social debate about the environment has focused especially on CO_2 in relation to climate change, we see that this is just one aspect of a much wider and

even more complex set of changes occurring to the world's biogeochemical cycles. In particular, it becomes increasingly clear that alteration of the world's nitrogen and phosphorus cycles represents a major emerging challenge that has received too little attention.[2]

More than fifty years ago, in *Scientific American*, ecologist C. C. Delwiche warned: "Of all man's recent interventions in the cycles of nature the industrial fixation of nitrogen far exceeds all the others in magnitude."[3] The journal *Science* describes "massive disruption of the global nitrogen regime" as a "major component" of the Anthropocene.[4] The European Science Foundation says that industrial production of reactive nitrogen is "perhaps the greatest single experiment in global geo-engineering that humans have ever made."[5]

Planetary boundaries studies show that nitrogen flows are now well outside safe limits, posing a major threat to the stability of the Earth System:

> Human processes—primarily the manufacture of fertilizer for food production and the cultivation of leguminous crops—convert around 120 million tonnes of N_2 from the atmosphere per year into reactive forms—which is more than the combined effects from all Earth's terrestrial processes. Much of this new reactive nitrogen ends up in the environment, polluting waterways and the coastal zone, accumulating in land systems and adding a number of gases to the atmosphere. It slowly erodes the resilience of important Earth subsystems. Nitrous oxide, for example, is one of the most important non-CO_2 greenhouse gases and thus directly increases radiative forcing.
>
> Anthropogenic distortion of the nitrogen cycle and phosphorus flows has shifted the state of lake systems from clear to turbid water. Marine ecosystems have been subject to similar shifts, for example, during periods of anoxia in the Baltic Sea caused by excessive nutrients.[6]

Nitrogen: From Shortage to Glut

Essential for Life

Vaclav Smil summarizes the importance of nitrogen:

> Nitrogen is present in every living cell; in chlorophyll whose excitation by light energizes photosynthesis (the biosphere's most important conversion of energy); in the nucleotides of nucleic acids (DNA and RNA), which store and process all genetic information; in amino acids, which make up all proteins; and in enzymes which control the chemistry of the living world....
>
> It is the nutrient responsible for the vigorous vegetative growth, for the deep green of the leaves, for their large size and delayed senescence, as well as for the size and protein content of cereal grains, the staples of mankind. Nitrogen deficiency cannot be missed either: pale green or yellowing leaves, slow and stunted plant growth, low yields and depressed protein content of seeds.
>
> Nitrogen's importance for human beings is no less critical. We have to ingest ten complete, preformed essential amino acids in order to synthesize our body proteins needed for tissue growth and maintenance. Stunted mental and physical development are the starkest consequences of protein malnutrition.[7]

Of the elements that are essential for life, nitrogen is simultaneously the most abundant and the least available. Seventy-eight percent of the air we breathe is nitrogen, but more than 99 percent of it is in a form that most organisms cannot use.

Nitrogen atoms have an unusually strong ability to form stable compounds with various elements in multiple ways. In particular, they readily combine with various numbers of oxygen and hydrogen atoms to create ammonia, ammonium, nitric oxide, nitrite, nitrate, nitric acid, nitrous oxide, and a multitude of organic molecules. In these forms, it is called reactive nitrogen (Nr) because it can take part in biological and chemical processes, and because the various nitrogen compounds can and do turn into one another easily.

Mostly, however, nitrogen atoms combine with each other. Pairs of nitrogen atoms bind tightly to create dinitrogen (N_2). These chemically and biologically inert molecules comprise 78 percent of the air. The high energy and heat of lightning bolts can split dinitrogen molecules and combine them with oxygen to create nitrogen oxides, but that doesn't happen often enough or in enough volume to provide the reactive nitrogen that life on Earth needs.

Life as we know it is only possible because some bacteria long ago evolved the ability to fix nitrogen—they can split atmospheric N_2 molecules and create reactive nitrogen compounds. Their microscopic descendants are still the only organisms that can fix nitrogen. No other form of life has evolved the ability, but every other form of life depends on it.

Microbes are key players in a circular process that moves nitrogen from the atmosphere to living organisms and back again. In terrestrial ecosystems, there are three major stages, each involving metabolic transformations that only microscopic organisms can perform:

Fixation. Dinitrogen from the air enters soil and surface waters, where microbes convert it to ammonia. This reactive nitrogen gas dissolves in water to form ammonium.[8] In the soil, almost all ammonium is produced by a few species of bacteria that live in the roots of legumes such as alfalfa, clover, and beans, and in the roots of some trees. Farmers discovered thousands of years ago that growing legumes along with other crops or in rotations helped maintain soil fertility.

Nitrification. Other microbes convert ammonium into compounds that plants can absorb through their roots and use to make amino acids and proteins. When plants die and decompose, their nitrogen is eventually returned to the soil as organic compounds that decay into ammonium, which can then be used by other plants. Of course, some plants are eaten by birds or animals that use some of the nitrogen to build their bodies and excrete the rest—ultimately it too returns to the soil. In natural ecosystems, organic matter that has decomposed in soil is a primary source of the reactive nitrogen needed for new plant growth.

Denitrification. Some reactive nitrogen is buried in ocean sediments or deep soils, but most is consumed by other microbes that transform it into inert nitrogen, which then returns to the atmosphere. On average, the cycle from initial fixation back to the atmosphere takes about five hundred years in soils and five thousand years in the oceans.

This is a simplified account of a very complex process. Many books have been written to explain the nitrogen cycle, and most acknowledge that it remains not fully understood.[9] A nitrogen atom may undergo parts of the cycle many times over, in different ways and time scales, combining with other elements in multiple ways, passing through the air, water, soils, plants, animals, and humans on the way from the atmosphere and back.

What's more, the various biogeochemical cycles cannot be fully understood in isolation from each other. Each one strongly affects, and is strongly influenced by, the others, as the synthesis report of the International Geosphere-Biosphere Program pointed out:

> The atmospheric concentration of CO_2 can influence the amount of nitrogen taken up by plants that have nitrogen-fixing symbionts in their root structure by altering the biological nitrogen fixation rate. These particular types of plants can utilise increased availability of nitrogen to increase leaf nitrogen, which leads in turn to increased photosynthetic capacity. The biological nitrogen fixation rate, however, is also limited by another element, phosphorus. The CO_2 level can also alter the amount of phosphorus available to plants.[10]

If the soil contains insufficient water, plants can't grow and take up nitrogen. If temperatures are too warm, nitrogen fixing slows down. Many more examples could be cited.

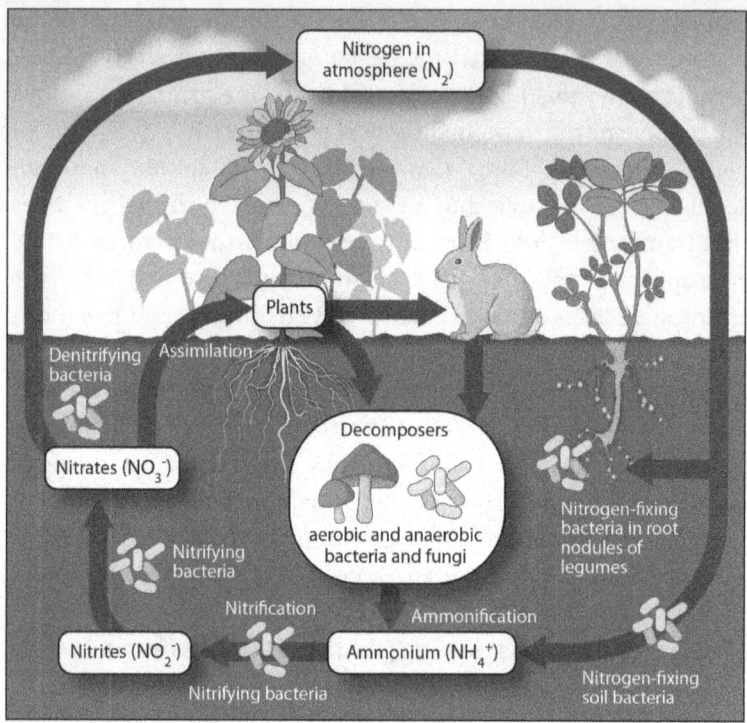

Figure 12.1. Nitrogen Cycle in Natural Ecosystems: Until the twentieth century, the amount of reactive nitrogen in the environment was limited by the ability of bacteria to fix it from the atmosphere, balanced by the amount that other bacteria could convert back into N_2. Very little escaped into the wider environment.

If nitrogen fixation were a one-way process and not part of a cycle, plants would have removed all the nitrogen in the atmosphere long ago. But, as has often happened in the history of living matter, evolution produced organisms that reversed the process. Over hundreds of millions of years, natural selection produced a rough balance between the conversion of N_2 to Nr by some bacteria and the conversion of Nr to N_2 by others. As a result, the volume of reactive nitrogen in the biosphere remained roughly constant over time—until now.

Nitrogen: From Shortage to Glut

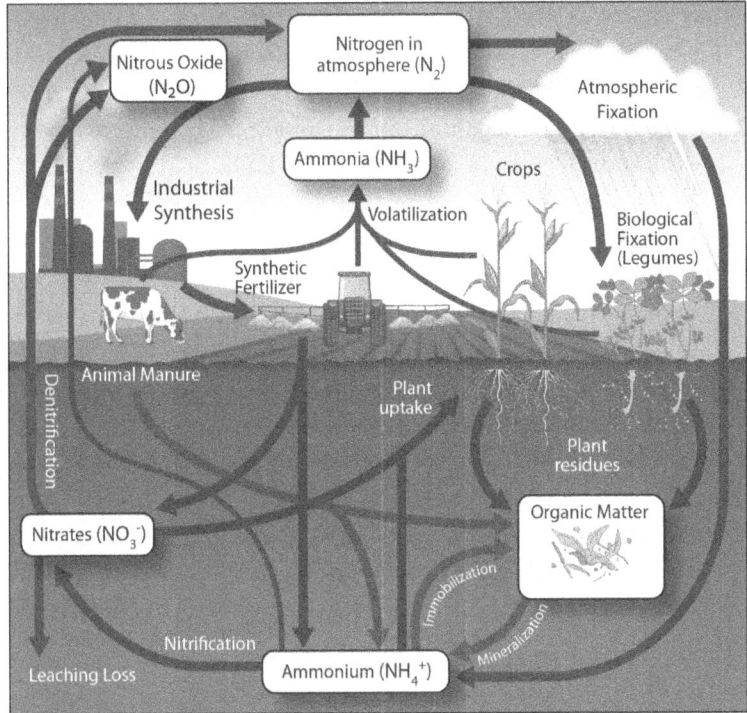

Figure 12.2. Metabolic Rifts in the Nitrogen Cycle: In the twentieth and twenty-first centuries, synthetic fertilizers, industrial agriculture, and fossil fuels have overwhelmed natural nitrogen cycles. Bacterial fixation is no longer the largest source of reactive nitrogen, and the small amounts that once escaped have become a flood that affects the entire biosphere. (Graphic by Ann Sanderson)

In the 1800s, agricultural chemists discovered that plant growth is limited not by the total amount of nutrients available, but by the specific nutrient that is most scarce in relation to need. In most cases, the limiting factor is nitrogen in forms that plants can readily use. There is proportionately less of it in most ecosystems than of other essential nutrients, and the total amount in the biosphere doesn't increase over time. In the oceans and on land, nitrogen is, as Australian ecologist Thomas White wrote, "the most limiting chemical."

As a nutrient, nitrogen is required in quantities second only to carbon. It is a key constituent of all living cells. Without nitrogen proteins cannot be built. Proteins are the basic physico-chemical structures of all living things, and are made from amino acids. Nitrogen is the key component of these amino acids which all organisms must have. No organism—plant, animal, or protist—can survive, let alone grow, without an adequate supply of nitrogen for the synthesis of proteins. The productivity of all life on Earth, in both terrestrial and aquatic environments, is limited by biologically available nitrogen.[11]

Globally and in most ecosystems, the availability of reactive nitrogen has limited the amount of living matter on Earth, and natural selection has favored organisms that use it efficiently. Scientists from Germany's Max Planck Institute explain that the "microbial nitrogen-cycling network" maintained a consistent level of reactive nitrogen in the global biosphere for billions of years:

> There is an astonishing diversity of microorganisms that transform nitrogen, and each of these microorganisms has discrete physiological requirements for optimal growth. . . . Very little bioavailable nitrogen escapes to the atmosphere, and the small amount lost as dinitrogen gas is balanced by nitrogen fixation.[12]

In the past century, that balance has been disrupted by the production of unprecedented amounts of reactive nitrogen. Biogeochemist James Galloway warns: "We are accumulating reactive nitrogen in the environment at alarming rates, and this may prove to be as serious as putting carbon dioxide in the atmosphere."[13]

Guano Imperialism and Fossil Nitrogen

By the time Justus von Liebig showed that crops required specific

Nitrogen: From Shortage to Glut

minerals to grow, much of England's soil was already low in nitrogen, phosphorus, and potassium, and crop yields were stagnant or falling. The repeal of tariffs on foreign grain in 1846 exposed English farmers to competition from North America, where nutrient-rich soils produced cheap and abundant wheat and oats. Imported grain soon dominated the market, and many farmers switched to livestock. Those who could afford to do so recharged their land with manufactured fertilizers, especially nitrogen-rich mixtures based on seabird excrement imported from a unique ecosystem off the coast of Peru.

The Humboldt Current, flowing north along the west coast of South America, brings huge quantities of small fish up from deep, cold waters. For millennia, those fish have attracted millions of seabirds that nest on the rocky Chincha Islands off Peru's coast. Their *guano*—from the Quechua word for seabird shit—is rich in nitrogen, phosphorus, and potassium, the most important elements for plant growth. That area receives almost no rain, so for millennia, guano dried and accumulated rather than being washed away. In some places, the deposits were sixty meters thick.

Peasants in the area had long used guano to enrich sandy soil near the shore and rocky soil in the Andes. Local laws and customs limited the amount taken each year, protecting the seabirds that ensured the resource remained plentiful.

In the 1840s, English landowners "discovered" this powerful fertilizer and seized on it as the solution to their soil fertility crisis. Vaclav Smil describes what followed as "guano mania," a mad rush to acquire every possible scrap of guano, as quickly as possible.[14] The damage done to the environment and the livelihoods of Peruvian farmers played no part in the calculations of merchants who stripped the islands bare. Nor were they concerned about the lives of indentured laborers from China who were literally worked to death digging guano.

In 1856, the U.S. Congress, concerned that British merchants had an effective monopoly on Peruvian guano, passed the Guano Islands Act, authorizing U.S. citizens to take "peaceable possession" of any uninhabited island with guano deposits. Nearly one hundred small islands were eventually seized by U.S. companies under the act, but none of them had the quantity and quality of guano found off the coast of Peru.

Over three decades, some twelve million tons of guano a year were shipped north, mainly to England and Germany. The fertilizer-quality guano was removed far more quickly than seabirds could replace it, so the deposits were soon exhausted. By the 1880s, the guano trade had all but collapsed.[15]

Northern investors turned their sights inland, where the extremely dry climate had preserved another source of nitrogen. Millions of years ago, in the Atacama Desert, salts carried by ocean spray dried and accumulated to form caliche, an ore rich in sodium nitrate. Caliche was harder to extract and refine than guano, but there was a lot more of it. After a five-year war in which Chile seized the nitrate-rich area from Bolivia and Peru, leaving the latter country landlocked, exports reached 1.3 million tons in 1900, and 2.5 million tons in 1913.[16] Sodium nitrate from Chile, laid down in the Miocene epoch, became a major source of reactive nitrogen in the Holocene.

Coal was a source of even older fossil nitrogen. To make coke for steel production, and gas for municipal lighting, coal was heated in the absence of oxygen to drive out impurities, which included small amounts of nitrogen left by ancient plants that had not been entirely reduced to carbon. The manufacturing process converted the nitrogen to ammonia, which, until the 1880s, was simply released into the air. However, when technology was developed to capture the ammonia, it was widely adopted in Britain and Western Europe.

By 1900, mining and manufacturing processes were producing more than enough phosphorus and potassium to replace the amounts removed from the soil by agriculture, but fossil nitrogen didn't even come close. Vaclav Smil calculates that the total production of Chilean nitrates and ammonia from coke ovens that year was about 340,000 tons of reactive nitrogen—"on the order of 2% of all nitrogen removed by that year's crops and their residues."[17]

Restoring the world's soil with fertilizer would require a qualitative leap in nitrogen production. That could only be done by extracting it from the air—and that would require support from powerful forces that would use nitrogen to kill people, not feed them.

Military Nitrogen

By the end of the nineteenth century, knowledgeable observers knew that a European war was coming. Britain, once the world's greatest industrial power, had been matched or surpassed by Germany and the United States. As early as December 1887, Frederick Engels accurately predicted that rivalry between the great capitalist powers would lead to "a world war . . . of an extent and violence hitherto unimagined."

> Eight to ten million soldiers will be at each other's throats and in the process they will strip Europe barer than a swarm of locusts. The depredations of the Thirty Years' War compressed into three to four years and extended over the entire continent. . . . That is the prospect for the moment when the systematic development of mutual one-upmanship in armaments reaches its climax and brings forth its inevitable fruits.[18]

The "mutual one-upmanship in armaments" was an arms race that involved heavy investment in high-powered guns, battleships, and submarines, and accumulation of modern warfare's most essential chemical, nitrogen.

Although most accounts of the nineteenth-century nutrient rift emphasize nitrogen's importance for agriculture, much fossil nitrogen was actually used to make gunpowder and high explosives. A 1909 article by noted industrial chemist Charles E. Munroe, published by the U.S. Naval Institute, gave the following figures for sodium nitrate use in the United States in 1905.

INDUSTRY	TONS
Fertilizer	42,213
Dye	261
Glass	11,915
Acids	29,301
Chemicals	38,048
Explosives	133,034
Total	**254,772**

Fertilizer used less than 17 percent of imported nitrates, while explosives used more than half. Munroe didn't have figures for other countries but believed that "a much larger percentage of Chilean nitrate is used in agriculture in Europe." There, too, the fast-growing armaments and explosives industries depended on fossil nitrogen:

> It may, therefore, be safely asserted that but tor the discovery and exploitation of the nitrate fields of Chile the explosives industry, as it is known to-day, would have been impossible, and the developments in mining and transportation which have characterized the last half century could not have been made.[19]

Ten years earlier, in a widely published address, Sir William Crookes, president of the British Association for the Advancement of Science, had warned that Chilean nitrates could soon be depleted as guano had been, and if that happened, "England and all civilized nations stand in deadly peril of not having enough to eat. . . . We are drawing on the earth's capital, and our drafts will not perpetually be honored."

Crookes's views were a mixture of solid science, crude Malthusianism, and outright racism. He claimed that "the great Caucasian race" owed its superiority to eating wheat, which was "the fit and proper food for the development of muscle and brains." If wheat production fell, the world's "white population" would be surpassed by "other races . . . [who] are eaters of Indian corn, rice, mullet and other grains." Bizarre as such ideas were, they were characteristic of a class that believed it had a God-given right to rule the world.

Without a new and reliable source of nitrogen, Crookes said, England would be at a military disadvantage in a war, because any of the other great powers could block its access to Chilean nitrate. Not only was nitrogen needed for white people's food, but it was also an essential component of gunpowder and other explosives, so such a blockade could be disastrous. "The fixation of atmospheric nitrogen, therefore, is one of the great discoveries awaiting the ingenuity of chemist."[20]

Munroe's 1909 article described several projects for extracting nitrogen from the air that he thought would make it possible to "conduct a prolonged war without robbing the soil, on which people depend for food. of its fertility." He argued that the U.S. government should not only support the nitrogen industry but should intervene to ensure that production was "strategically located throughout the country as to be reasonably well protected from attack, so that they may serve the military establishment in case of foreign invasion from any quarter, or of internal uprisings in any locality."[21]

As Mark Sutton of the Task Force on Reactive Nitrogen writes, by the beginning of the 1900s, "the Western world had effectively become a 'fossil nitrogen economy,' as both food and military security depended critically on these nitrogen sources."[22]

The following years featured intense efforts, particularly in Germany, to end military and agricultural dependence on a resource that could easily be blockaded if an inter-imperialist war broke out.

The eventual key to success was not just clever science, but clever science and engineering combined with sufficient capital to build and maintain massive production facilities. As is often the case with "free enterprise" projects, state support and war played critical roles.

Industrial Nitrogen

Until 1900, all of Earth's reactive nitrogen was produced by a few types of microbes that had evolved the ability to make it from the inert nitrogen in the air. All living organisms depended on—and evolved to live with—the limited amount of nitrogen that microbes could produce.

Then, in just over a decade, industrial production overwhelmed a metabolic cycle that has sustained life on Earth for billions of years. Today, more reactive nitrogen is produced in factories than by all natural processes combined. The capitalist "solution" to limited biological nitrogen led directly to a far more serious environmental crisis in our time.

The global shift to industrial nitrogen began early in the twentieth century, shortly after Sir William Crookes appealed to scientists and industrialists to put more effort into research on nitrogen fixation. The most intense efforts were made in Germany, which was the largest importer of Chilean nitrates and correctly saw itself as the most vulnerable to blockade if war broke out. In the years leading up to the First World War, the world's largest chemical company, Badische Anilin & Sodafabrik—always referred to as BASF—played a leading role in funding research and in commercial production.[23]

Extracting reactive nitrogen from the inert dinitrogen molecules in the atmosphere was a daunting chemical and engineering challenge. Breaking the powerful bond that holds nitrogen atoms together required pressures and temperatures far above those achieved in the 1800s, but three very different nitrogen-fixing technologies were developed and in commercial operation by

Nitrogen: From Shortage to Glut

the beginning of the First World War. Each produced a different chemical compound from which reactive nitrogen could be obtained relatively easily.[24]

The *electric arc process* emulated lightning, sending high-energy electrical sparks through dinitrogen gas, producing nitrogen oxide. The *cyanamide process* heated dinitrogen and other chemicals to over 1000°C, producing calcium nitride. The *ammonia synthesis process* mixed dinitrogen and hydrogen under high pressure and heat in the presence of a catalyst, producing ammonia.

All three were in commercial use into the 1930s, but the third required far less energy than the other two, and so was the most profitable.[25] As a result, today virtually all synthetic nitrogen is produced through ammonia synthesis—commonly called the Haber-Bosch process after its inventors, who won Nobel Prizes for their work.

Fritz Haber, a chemist whose research was funded by BASF, invented and demonstrated the ammonia synthesis process in 1909. Carl Bosch, a BASF engineer, developed the technologies that took Haber's process from laboratory demonstration to mass production. By early 1914, a BASF ammonia synthesis plant in Oppau, in western Germany, was producing twenty tons of ammonium sulfate fertilizer a day, and plans had been made to double production in the following year, but those plans were interrupted by war:

> The First World War brought carnage, destruction, and waste without precedent. Industrial society's capacity to satisfy human need through mass production had turned into its opposite: industrialized slaughter. The war was an extreme expression of the competition between national-capitalist blocs. The whole industrial power of the rival blocs was harnessed to building, arming, and maintaining mass armies. . . .
>
> Two factors were decisive: first, the great powers were divided by imperial rivalry as their industries expanded and competed; and second, when the powers clashed, these same industries could mass produce the means of destruction.[26]

BASF was one of the largest corporations that contributed to industrial slaughter. With government financing and guaranteed profits, the Oppau plant was quickly retooled to produce nitric acid for explosives: shipments to munitions makers began in May 1915. When French air raids demonstrated that Oppau was vulnerable to attack, a much larger plant was built in Saxony, beyond airplane range. By the end of the war, the two factories were producing far more fixed nitrogen than German plants using either the cyanamide process or the older process based on coal.

Smil describes this as "one of the origins of a phenomenon that marked so much of Germany's, and the world's, subsequent history: the rise of a military-industrial complex."[27] Military support made BASF the world leader in the production of synthetic nitrogen. When BASF merged with five other chemical companies in the mid-1920s to create I.G. Farben, its nitrogen fixation operations accounted for two-thirds of the combined organization's immense profits.

Germany wasn't the only country in which the military and private corporations collaborated on nitrogen fixation. In the United States, the 1916 National Defense Act allocated $20 million to build factories to produce nitrogen for the munitions industry, promising that they would produce fertilizer when the war in Europe ended. Two factories were built in Alabama, but the war ended before production began, and the promised conversion to fertilizer manufacturing never occurred.

After the war, the U.S. Army's Fixed Nitrogen Research Laboratory built its own ammonia production plant to test improvements to the Haber-Bosch process and shared its research findings with industry. As historian Timothy Johnston writes, "The General Chemical Company ... adapted technologies from this model plant in their own facilities and as a result became the largest producer of ammonia in the United States until World War II."[28]

The most important technical development of the interwar years was a modification of the Haber-Bosch process to use natural gas (methane) as the source of hydrogen, which was less expensive and produced purer gas than previous methods. Germany had no access to natural gas, so I. G. Farben leased the new process to Standard Oil of New Jersey, whose plant in Louisiana began using it in 1931. Ever since, the nitrogen industry has been tightly linked to the petroleum industry, which provides both energy and feedstock. Today, about 3 percent of the world's natural gas production is used to fix nitrogen, and industrial nitrogen production generates about 3 percent of global carbon dioxide emissions.

After a wartime boom, grain prices collapsed in the 1920s, bankrupting many farmers and radically shrinking demand for fertilizer. The Great Depression of the 1930s made things worse. Although ammonia synthesis plants were built in several countries during those years, their output mostly replaced nitrogen from Chile and from older technologies, and global production of synthetic nitrogen fertilizers grew slowly or stagnated. It would take another war, along with a significant increase in government and military spending, to create a nitrogen boom.

Before it entered the war in 1941, the U.S. government launched a crash program to expand nitrogen production for munitions. Ten factories were built in various parts of the country, paid for with public funds but operated by private companies. Total U.S. production capacity in wartime was about 880,000 tons per year, almost all of it used for weapons.

A Glut of Synthetic Fertilizer

At the end of the Second World War, the U.S. government sold its nitrogen factories for a fraction of their value. Most were bought by the companies that had been operating them.[29] The largest, located in Ohio, was acquired by Allied Chemical. This conglomerate included General Chemical, which got its start in nitrogen fixation in the First World War. The privately owned plants began shipping nitrogen fertilizers in 1947. Sales representatives and government agencies encouraged farmers to use as much as they could afford, and seed companies introduced new strains of corn that responded particularly well to high doses of fertilizer.

Synthetic fertilizer soon replaced animal manure and fallow rotations on most farms, and planting was extended to land previously deemed too nutrient-poor. U.S. agriculture had become addicted to synthetic nitrogen, and new dealers rushed to reinforce that addiction. By 1960, in the United States alone, thirty-eight companies were operating fifty-four plants with a combined capacity of 3.6 million tons of synthetic nitrogen per year, nearly five times the wartime peak.[30]

Synthetic fertilizer quickly spread beyond the United States, first to Europe, then to Mexico and India as part of the so-called Green Revolution, and more recently to China, which now uses more nitrogen fertilizer per hectare than any other country. Worldwide nitrogen fertilizer use has increased exponentially since the mid-twentieth century. In fact, more than half of the synthetic fertilizer ever produced has been applied to farmland in the past thirty years. The UN Food and Agriculture Organization estimates that 107.4 million tons of nitrogen were used in fertilizer in 2019.[31]

The purpose of using fertilizer, of course, is to maintain or (preferably) increase crop yields. There is no doubt that synthetic nitrogen has played a major role in the extraordinary growth of agricultural production since the Second World War. More grains, vegetables, and meat are being produced than ever in history.

But capitalism, as Marxist philosopher István Mészáros argues, "cannot separate 'advance' from destruction, nor 'progress' from waste—however catastrophic the results. The more it unlocks the powers of productivity, the more it must unleash the powers of destruction; and the more it extends the volume of production, the more it must bury everything under mountains of suffocating waste."[32]

That is certainly true of synthetic nitrogen fertilizer. A study published in 1999 found that for cereal crops (corn, wheat, oats, rice) worldwide, nitrogen use efficiency was only 33 percent. Crops only absorbed one-third of the nitrogen fertilizer applied.

In 2019, after two decades of research into more effective farming techniques and the development of genetically modified plants that use nitrogen more efficiently, a follow-up study found that nitrogen use efficiency remained virtually unchanged. Two-thirds of the reactive nitrogen used in fertilizer each year "is unaccounted for and can be lost within the soil system through leaching and/or gaseous forms, potentially contributing to a decrease in air and water quality."[33]

By 2000, the amount of nitrogen in many rivers was far above pre-industrial levels: 400 percent higher in the Mississippi, 800 percent higher in rivers in the northeastern United States, and 1,000 percent higher in the European rivers that drain into the North Sea.[34]

Global agriculture uses about 180 million tons of human-made nitrogen a year—a combination of synthetic fertilizer and atmospheric nitrogen fixed by cultivated legumes, mainly soy. After losses in the rest of the food processing industry, only about 11 percent reaches the food that humans eat.[35] At least 89 percent of synthetic nitrogen in fertilizers enters the environment directly from the soil, and much of the remainder enters it soon after in human and animal excrement.

Agricultural experts have calculated the ideal amount of fertilizer to use for different crops, but following their guidelines would not eliminate nitrogen pollution, because environmental damage plays no role in the calculations. Rather, they attempt to balance monetary cost and revenue, proposing a level of fertilizer that will increase yield without costing more than the probable additional income. And because there are many uncertainties in those calculations, farmers often use more than the supposedly ideal amounts of fertilizer, as a form of crop insurance. It is estimated that farmers in the U.S. Midwest, facing uncertain yields and even more uncertain markets, routinely apply 20 to 30 percent more fertilizer than the recommended amounts.[36] In India, China, and other countries where synthetic fertilizers are subsidized, even more is used, and even more nitrogen escapes into the air and water.

This is a textbook example of a social cost created by the drive for private profit. For individual producers, the cost is the price of fertilizer; for society, the cost is disruption of life support systems. "The moral of the tale," Marx wrote, "is that a rational agriculture is incompatible with the capitalist system."[37] Socialist agronomist Fred Magdoff elaborates: "All of the common decisions and practices of conventional farmers and others in the agricultural system make eminent sense (that is, they are rational) only from the very narrow perspective of trying to make profits within a capitalist system."[38]

As a result, the UN Food and Agriculture Organization tells us, "In most high-income countries and many emerging economies, agricultural pollution has . . . overtaken contamination from settlements and industries as the major factor in the degradation of inland and coastal waters."[39] Agriculture also produces 80 percent of human emissions of nitrous oxide (N_2O). This greenhouse gas is 300 percent more potent than carbon dioxide.[40]

Nitrogen Cascades

Climate change deniers often claim that carbon dioxide cannot be harmful because plants need it to grow. The same false argument can be made about nitrogen, and the same response applies: too much of a good thing can be deadly. The amount of reactive nitrogen produced by all terrestrial sources is now two to three times the pre-industrial level. Organisms and ecosystems that evolved in a world where the supply of reactive nitrogen was strictly limited are now being disrupted, in many cases destroyed, by an unprecedented nitrogen glut.

The concentration of carbon dioxide in the atmosphere can be measured directly, but there is no equivalent way to track the accumulation of reactive nitrogen, or to summarize its environmental effects in simple terms, because the chemical compounds formed by reactive nitrogen transform easily into one another. They have different effects, depending on local conditions:

Many thresholds for human and ecosystem health have been exceeded owing to Nr pollution, including those for drinking water (nitrates), air quality (smog, particulate matter, ground-level ozone), freshwater eutrophication, biodiversity loss, stratospheric ozone depletion, climate change and coastal ecosystems (dead zones). Each of these environmental effects can be magnified by the "nitrogen cascade": a single atom of Nr can trigger a cascade of negative environmental impacts in sequence.[41]

Any given nitrogen cascade may involve a different sequence of chemical transformations and effects. Nitrogen that leaches from agricultural soil into groundwater, for example, will follow a different path than nitrogen produced by gasoline combustion, and each can disrupt multiple biogeochemical processes. *Scientific American* described one possible cascade:

1. The nitrogen produced during fossil-fuel combustion can cause severe air pollution . . .
2. before it combines with water to create nitric acid in rain . . .
3. and joins with nitrogen leaking from fertilized fields, farm animal excrement, human sewage and leguminous plants.
4. When too much nitrogen enters terrestrial ecosystems, it can contribute to biodiversity decline and perhaps to increased risk for several human illnesses.
5. A single nitrogen atom from a factory, vehicle or farm can acidify soil and contaminate drinking water before entering rivers,
6. where it can travel to the oceans and help fuel toxic algal blooms and coastal dead zones.
7. At any point during this chain, bacteria may transform the rogue atom into nitrous oxide, a potent greenhouse gas that also speeds the loss of protective stratospheric ozone. Only bacteria that convert the atom back to innocuous N_2 gas can halt its ill effects.[42]

As they move through the biosphere, the very same nitrogen atoms can increase ozone in the troposphere and decrease it in the stratosphere; increase concentrations of particles in the air; increase acid rain; increase soil acidity; increase or decrease forest productivity; increase surface water acidity; increase hypoxia in coastal waters; and increase greenhouse warming.[43]

Nitrogen cascades are not linear—the atoms may repeatedly cycle through all or part of a sequence, or repeat stages, or begin a different sequence, over time periods ranging from seconds to decades. The overall result can be summed up as more reactive nitrogen in the environment leads to more nitrogen cascades and more disruption of the biosphere. Few ecological problems lack a nitrogen component that is not initiated or made worse by the massive expansion of reactive nitrogen in the soil, air, and water.

Can We End the Glut?

For hundreds of millions of years, there was a rough balance between fixation and denitrification, between the conversion of inert dinitrogen to reactive nitrogen by some species of bacteria, and the reverse process by others. All living things evolved in a biosphere where the overall level of Nr was roughly constant, and different species developed different strategies for survival in a nitrogen-limited world. Constant recycling of reactive nitrogen in multiple forms, "a metabolism prescribed by the natural laws of life itself,"[44] enabled plant and animal life to thrive almost everywhere on the planet.

The irreparable rift in that metabolism is now far more serious—far more deadly—than Marx could have imagined. Rather than closing the rift by restoring the natural nutrient cycle, it was expanded by importing nutrients from elsewhere. First, guano and nitrates from South America, and then industrially produced nitrogen, were added to the now-linear flow of nutrients from soil to air and sea.

Nitrogen: From Shortage to Glut

Before the twentieth century, the natural rate of terrestrial nitrogen fixation was about 60 million tons per year. Reactive nitrogen produced by human activity—mainly by industrial synthesis, but also by intensive legume cultivation, mainly soy, and fossil fuel combustion—has increased from very little to about 187 million tons a year. The amount of reactive nitrogen entering the biosphere each year has risen at least 320 percent.[45]

Planetary boundaries research confirms that the current level of industrial nitrogen "cannot continue without significantly eroding the resilience of major components of Earth-System functioning."[46] About 62 million metric tons of intentionally produced nitrogen—Haber-Bosch plus cultivated legumes—could provide adequate food for all while limiting environmental damage, if known methods of maximizing nitrogen use efficiency were fully implemented. That is less than a third of the amount produced today.

Most proposals for reducing nitrogen pollution have focused on *consumption*, on persuading farmers to use less fertilizer or consumers to eat less meat. The authors of the Planetary Boundaries Framework, by contrast, directed attention to intentional production of reactive nitrogen:

> The simplest and most direct approach is to consider the human fixation of N_2 from the atmosphere as a giant valve that controls a massive flow of new reactive N into the Earth System. The boundary can then be set by using that valve to control the amount of additional reactive N flowing into the Earth System. . . .
>
> This initial boundary would greatly reduce the amount of reactive N pushed into land, ocean, and atmospheric systems. It would eliminate the current flux of N onto the land and could trigger much more efficient and less polluting ways of enhancing food production. It would almost surely also trigger the return of N in human effluent back onto productive landscapes, thus further reducing the leakage of reactive N into ecosystems.[47]

The authors did not discuss how the valve would be controlled or who would control it, but it is hard to imagine that chemical companies will voluntarily cede their "right" to unlimited production and profits. Gaining control of the valve will require directly challenging the power of some of the world's largest corporations and by expropriating their factories.

However it is achieved, social control of nitrogen production must ensure a radical reduction of nitrogen use. That will require balancing the need to prevent ecological damage against the need to produce sufficient food, not just within a country, but globally. It may one day be possible to feed the world without synthetic fertilizer and other chemicals, but undoing the damage that capitalism has caused won't be easy or quick.

CHAPTER 13

Agriculture: The Great Separation

A rational agriculture is incompatible with the capitalist system.
—KARL MARX[1]

Until the mid-twentieth century, almost all of the world's food was grown on small family farms and sold through local dealers or directly to consumers. External inputs were few: on-farm gardens fed the owners and workers; the animals' food was grown on the farm, and their manure fertilized the soil; and part of each year's crop was saved as seeds for next year. One hundred hectares was a large farm: most were well under fifty.

Agricultural yields were modest but stable. Production was safeguarded by growing more than one crop or variety in a field as insurance against pest outbreaks or severe weather. Inputs of nitrogen were gained by rotating major field crops with legumes. Growing many different types of crops over the years in the same field also suppressed insects, weeds, and diseases by effectively breaking the life cycles of these pests. A typical corn-belt farmer grew corn rotated with several crops including soybeans as well as the clovers, alfalfa, and small grains needed to maintain livestock. Most of the labor was done by the family with occasional hired help, and no specialized equipment or services were purchased from off-farm sources. In these types of farming systems the link between agriculture and ecology was quite strong and signs of environmental degradation were seldom evident.[2]

The decades since the Second World War have seen a radical change—a shift from small independent farms to large mass-production operations as the primary source of vegetables, grain, eggs, milk, and meat. The very basis of farming has been transformed:

> The post-World War II capitalization of agriculture was accomplished primarily through the substitution of inputs that were generated from within the farm itself, with inputs that were manufactured outside the farm and needed to be purchased.
> Starting with the early mechanization of agriculture that substituted traction power for animal power, to the substitution of synthetic fertilizer for compost and manure, to the substitution of pesticides for cultural and biological control, the history of agricultural technological development has been a process of capitalization that has resulted in the reduction of the value added within the farm itself.
> In today's farms, the labor comes from Caterpillar or John Deere, the energy from Exxon/Mobil, the fertilizer from DuPont, and the pest management from Dow or Monsanto.[3]

Seeds, which farmers used to save and use for next year's crop, are now patented and must be repurchased year after year. The very essence of organic reproduction has been transformed into commodities controlled by a handful of agribusiness corporations.

The industrialization of agriculture, which began in the United States and has since extended to most of the world, has, as food analyst Michael Pollan writes, "changed the fundamental rules of the game." Food production used to depend entirely on energy from the sun. Now we have "a food chain that draws much of its energy from fossil fuels instead."[4] Without petroleum and natural gas, there would be no tractors or giant combines, no synthetic fertilizer, and no year-round heated enclosures for livestock. The just-in-time transportation networks that distribute crops worldwide in every season would not exist. And agriculture would contribute far less to climate change.

The Great Separation

Industrial agriculture rests on what has been called "the most profound alteration of the animal-human relationship in 10,000 years"[5]—the physical separation of farmed animals from the farms that grow crops.

Low-cost nitrogen fertilizers, heavily promoted by chemical companies and supported by government subsidies, broke the circle. By eliminating the need for animal manure and the nitrogen-fixing crops that had enriched the soil and fed livestock, it paved the way for the divided agricultural system that rapidly became dominant worldwide, in which large farms raise just one or two crops, year after year. The matrix of small fields growing different crops that characterized traditional farming has been replaced by immense monocultures, endless fertilizer- and pesticide-soaked fields growing genetically identical plants. And almost all chickens, pigs, and cattle are raised in enclosed livestock factories that process thousands and even millions of animals annually.

On landscapes that were once dotted with farms that raised a variety of crops and animals, we now see either unbroken expanses of grain or windowless buildings that house tens or even hundreds of thousands of chickens, pigs, or dairy cows.

There are still millions of small farms growing multiple crops, but production and sales are dominated by a small number of very large farms, each raising just one or two species of plants or animals. Worldwide, about 75 percent of plant crop varieties have effectively vanished, leaving a handful of plant species that now comprise a majority of all crops.

Historian Donald Worster describes the transformation of farming as a "radical simplification of the natural ecological order."[6] Complex natural communities of plants, animals, insects, and microorganisms, above and below ground, have been replaced by monocultures, in which large areas devoted to single crops enable pest species to spread and outcompete beneficial organisms.

Livestock Factories

The separation of livestock from the land extended the separation of town and country that caused the metabolic rift Marx described in the nineteenth century. The animal counterparts of ever-growing cities are Confined Animal Feeding Operations (CAFOs) in which huge numbers of chickens, pigs, and cows are fattened on corn and sent to slaughter as quickly as possible. Living conditions for farm animals in CAFOs are appalling, diseases spread rapidly, and excrement is a major environmental problem.

Confined animal production was introduced on a limited scale in England as early as the 1850s. Discussing arrangements that kept beef cattle in stalls most of the time, Marx wrote that animals raised in such a "system of cell prison" were "characterized by precocity, in entirety sickliness, want of bones, a lot of development of fat and flesh etc. All these are artificial products. Disgusting!"[8]

He would have been more repulsed by conditions in CAFOs today:

> Some of the worst farm animal welfare practices in CAFOs include very crowded facilities, routine amputations and inhumane slaughter techniques. Besides the animal discomfort and health issues that can arise under such conditions, they can cause symptoms that have consequences higher up the food chain as well; animals subject to stress and pain are

Agriculture: The Great Separation

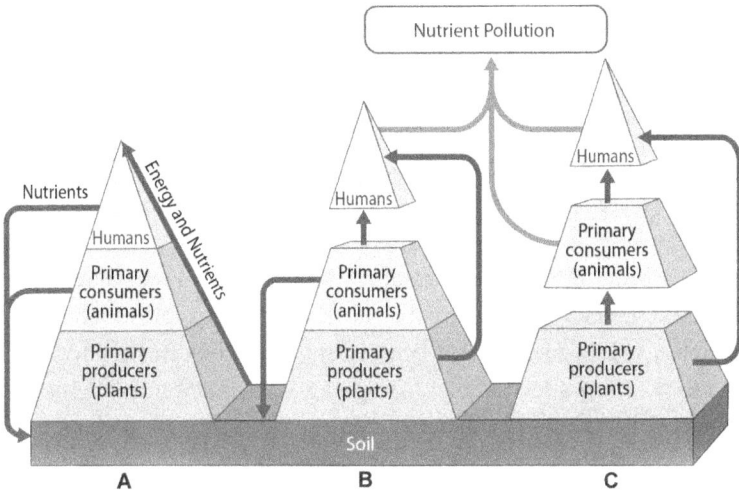

Figure 13.1. The Great Separation: Energy and nutrient flows in (A) Traditional subsistence farming; (B) Mixed commodity agriculture (nineteenth to twentieth century); (C) Industrial agriculture (mid-twentieth to twenty-first century). In traditional farming, nutrients were returned to the soil after the food was consumed by animals and people. When humans and then livestock were separated from the farm, those nutrients became pollution in other environments, and the soil required ever-increasing applications of synthetic fertilizers to maintain crop yields. (Graphic by Ann Sanderson, adapted from Fred Magdoff, Les Lanyon, and Bill Liebhardt, "Nutrient Cycling, Transformation and Flows," *Advances in Agronomy Volume 60*, 1997.)[7]

more prone to disease and produce lower quality meat, milk or eggs.

Animals in confinement are frequently densely crowded or confined to cages without enough space to turn around. Industrially-raised *broiler* chickens (those raised for meat) are raised in large open houses, not cages; but guidelines from the National Chicken Council, an industry group, require less than three-quarters of a square foot per market-weight bird—a space just slightly bigger than a sheet of letter paper. This leads to crowding on barn floors, often with animals standing in feces and other waste. Egg-laying hens, called *layers,* are often raised in *battery cages*, which are too small for the chickens to turn around in or spread their wings. Dairy cows are sometimes tethered in a barn for long periods, unable to take more than a few steps, side to side. Female hogs, known as sows, are confined to farrowing crates shortly before giving birth and while nursing. These are cages only slightly larger than their bodies, not big enough inside for the animals to turn around.[9]

The inhumane conditions in CAFOs have been repeatedly filmed by activists who entered facilities surreptitiously. The industry's response has not been to improve the animals' lot, but to lobby, often successfully, for ag-gag laws that punish whistleblowers. The profits of factory farming are not to be endangered by zealous activists and soft-hearted regulators.

In 1928, a U.S. politician supposedly promised voters "a chicken in every pot." At the time, for most families, chicken was a seldom-served luxury, reserved for special occasions. Most chickens were raised in small flocks for eggs, resulting in a limited meat supply and high prices. Mass production took off during the Second World War, when the U.S. government contracted for large quantities of chickens to feed its armies. The growth of poultry production since then has been spectacular: In 1961, fewer than seven billion chickens worldwide were slaughtered for meat; in 2023, the total passed 76 billion.[10]

Hog farming has been transformed even more rapidly. In the early 1990s, farms with more than 2,000 animals accounted for less than a third of all hogs in the United States. By 2004, the figure had risen to 80 percent. By 2007, it had risen to 95 percent, and the total hog population was growing by 4,600 animals a day.[11]

Worldwide, more than three-quarters of all cows, chickens, pigs, and sheep are confined in industrial production facilities. In the United States, the factory-farmed proportion is higher, including more than 99 percent of chickens and 98 percent of pigs. Farmed animals vastly outnumber wild ones, most of which are in decline. "Farmed poultry today makes up 70% of all birds on the planet, with just 30% being wild. The picture is even more stark for mammals—60% of all mammals on Earth are livestock, mostly cattle and pigs, 36% are human and just 4% are wild animals."[12]

CAFOs in the United States produce more than forty times more solid waste than all publicly owned wastewater treatment plants combined. Almost all of it enters the environment without treatment.[13]

The manure produced by industrial hog operations (IHOs) accumulates in immense cesspools—euphemistically called lagoons—before being sprayed or spread on the land, contaminating soil, sediment, and groundwater. In North Carolina, a state that has more than two thousand giant hog farms and four thousand manure lagoons, researchers found that "people living near IHO liquid waste application sites have elevated rates of infection with methicillin resistant *Staphylococcus aureus*," and that African Americans, Latinos, and Indigenous people are disproportionately affected.[14]

Animals and poultry were once a free source of nutrient-rich manure for multi-crop farms. With poultry, pigs, and cattle housed too far away for their manure to be transported, monocrop farmers must purchase ever-increasing amounts of synthetic fertilizer to maintain production. As we've seen, more than two-thirds of the nitrogen in that fertilizer is lost, becoming a major source of air and water pollution. At the same time, industrial livestock operations in the United States produce and discard about 1.5 billion tons of manure a year, making them a major contributor to the poisoning of air and water and to the spread of deadly algae blooms in rivers and lakes.[15]

As David Montgomery writes in his book on restoring soil health, "We have a systemic problem with nutrient transfers. Instead of closing the loop, we add fertilizer to the fields and manure doesn't go back to where it came from because cows aren't in the fields, and there's no money in hauling crap. It's a great system—if you happen to be selling fertilizer."[16]

The irony runs deeper. On traditional farms, pigs mostly ate waste and chickens ate insects and worms, while cattle, sheep, and horses grazed on grass. CAFOs, in contrast, buy feed that was grown on farms that no longer raise livestock—about 36 percent of all food crops raised worldwide, including most corn and soy, are fed to animals. This is a highly inefficient way to transfer nutrition from the soil to human mouths—on average, it takes about 25 kilos of grain to produce one kilo of beef; 9.4 kilos to produce one kilo of pork; and 4.5 kilos to produce one kilo of chicken meat.[17]

Food expert Frances Moore Lappe describes CAFOs as "reverse protein factories" because they remove food value from the food chain, passing on a fraction of it as meat. Close to a billion people go to bed hungry every night, but it's more profitable to feed livestock than starving children.

Killing the Soil

On the other side of the great separation, mass production of grains and other plant foods is destroying the world's most important ecosystems.

Soils, the UN Food and Agriculture Organization says, "play a pivotal role in regulating the flow and transfer of mass and energy between the atmosphere, biosphere, hydrosphere and lithosphere." They are "the biogeochemical engine at the heart of many of the Earth System cycles and processes on which life depends."[18] Indeed, as ecosystem ecologist Whendee Silver and her associates write, "In the most fundamental sense, soils are the basis for life on the Earth."

> Soils provide the habitat for a vast biodiversity and biomass of soil organisms, and both generate and serve as the repository for most of the carbon and nutrient elements that support life. Soils retain the water that plants and soil organisms use to survive and grow, and slow the rate of water movement and thus limit the rate of erosion and soil loss. Soils also contribute to the composition of the atmosphere, and by association impact climate, and are both a significant source and sink of

Agriculture: The Great Separation

greenhouse gases. At a societal level, one of the most obvious contributions of soil to people is the role that soils play in the provision of food for human populations and feed for livestock.[19]

Even under ideal conditions, it takes nature centuries to make a centimeter of soil, and vastly more time to produce deep topsoil. Which means, as far as human use is concerned, that soil is a non-renewable resource.

Since about 95 percent of our food depends on this fragile, non-renewable resource, one might expect that great care would be taken to preserve it and repair the damage that has been done. In reality, soil worldwide is being lost at a rate up to twenty times faster than new soil can form.[20] "Soil degradation has reduced crop yields on about 20% of all the world's cropland and on 19–27% of the grasslands and rangelands. The majority of agricultural soils are in only fair, poor or very poor condition."[21] If degradation continues at current rates, the health of 95 percent of the earth's land area could be significantly reduced in this century.[22]

Nineteenth-century scientists discovered that plants take essential nutrients from the soil, and that crop yields decline when those nutrients are not returned. Those discoveries, together with the Haber-Bosch technology for extracting nitrogen from the air, laid the basis for the twentieth-century fertilizer industry. What nineteenth-century science didn't know—and fertilizer corporations hope that farmers don't learn—is that chemical depletion is only part of the story, and not the most important part. Loss of organic matter, combined with an agricultural system that treats food as a commodity and soil as a free gift of nature, is the primary cause of soil degradation.[23]

Soils aren't just "dirt," and they don't just provide chemicals and physical support for growing plants. They are complex ecosystems, the most species-rich habitat on Earth. They are home to thousands of insect species, nematodes and earthworms, along with millions of bacterial and fungal species, and even more kinds of microbes. A handful of healthy soil can contain over a hundred million live organisms.

The term "soil health" has been defined as "the continued capacity of soil to function as a living ecosystem that sustains plants, animals, and humans"—and that capacity doesn't exist without soil organic matter. "Indeed, soil life and organic matter are foundational for soil health and soil carbon sequestration, nutrient cycling that provides crops with micronutrients and phytochemicals, limiting options for pathogens, and sustaining yields with lower nitrogen fertilizer and fossil fuel use."[24]

As Hannah Holleman writes:

> Plant roots break up rock, animals burrow, and worms, as Darwin observed, dig and till the soil, providing space for water and air. All plants and animals also provide nutrients to the soil. And teams of microorganisms—such as bacteria, fungi, protozoa, nematodes, and arthropods—break down waste, help decompose living matter, and take nitrogen from the atmosphere and transform it into forms that plants can utilize.[25]

Below ground, living matter breathes, driving a constant exchange of oxygen and carbon dioxide between the atmosphere and the soil. Undisturbed soil usually absorbs and sequesters more carbon dioxide than it releases, so over time it acts as a carbon sink, reducing the amount of climate-changing gas in the atmosphere:

> Organic material in soil is a prominent reservoir of terrestrial carbon and participates in the global cycling of carbon. . . .
> About three times as much carbon is stored in soils than occurs in the atmosphere as carbon dioxide. A soil that has 1 percent organic matter (or about 0.6 percent carbon) in its surface seven inches would be holding the approximate equivalent of the carbon in the carbon dioxide in the atmosphere above the field.[26]

Agriculture: The Great Separation

Industrial agriculture has broken a major part of the global carbon cycle. As soil scientist Fred Magdoff writes, plowing "causes a huge increase in inorganic matter decomposition, with carbon converted to carbon dioxide and diffusing into the atmosphere above. Generally, this converts soils from being carbon sinks to carbon sources, with the net effect of enriching the atmosphere with carbon dioxide instead of removing it." Magdoff refers to this "massive carbon relocation to the atmosphere" as the soil-carbon rift and warns that it is accelerating:

> As soil organic matter decreases as a result of the rift, soils hold less water, provide lower levels of nutrients to plants, and have lower biological diversity. As the soil structure deteriorates, plants become more susceptible to disease and insects. As less water is able to infiltrate, more runs off, carrying soil particles. A downward spiral occurs, with lower organic matter leading to more erosion of topsoil and more loss of organic matter, severely degrading soil in an accelerating, self-reinforcing feedback loop.[27]

The Intergovernmental Panel on Climate Change estimates that between 2010 and 2019, land use changes and forestry caused between 13 percent and 21 percent of anthropogenic greenhouse gas emissions, second only to burning fossil fuels.[28]

As we've seen, synthetic nitrogen seemed to provide a magic solution to declining crop yields. Applying fertilizer doesn't just increase production. It is cheap and requires far less labor than spreading manure, rotating crops, and the many other tasks that traditional farming required. The massive use of fertilizer, together with mechanization, played a key role in eliminating farm jobs. In 1945, farms employed 16 percent of all U.S. workers; in 2000, less than 2 percent.[29]

But unlike those lost jobs, adding synthetic fertilizer does not maintain soil health. Some of the nitrogen is taken up by the crops, but most of the rest washes through the soil, polluting groundwater and streams, and entering the air as nitrous oxide, a greenhouse gas that is three hundred times more powerful than carbon dioxide. Excess nitrogen harms healthy soil by significantly reducing the amount of organic matter in the soil.[30] England's famous Rothamsted Experimental Station has maintained test fields for many years. A recent analysis found that the fields treated with nitrogen fertilizers now contain 83 percent fewer worms and 50 percent less soil organic matter than those fertilized with farmyard manure. The evidence "clearly proves that, from its earliest days, chemical farming as at Rothamsted has been detrimental to soil life and certainly is responsible for killing the soil."[31]

Healthy soils are the product of soil organic matter being actively used by the multitude of diverse organisms in the soil. Some consume added organ residues directly, while others, higher in the "trophic ladder," eat organisms lower down. But when insufficient crop residues from harvest, cover crops, and manures are used, soil organic matter decreases. Using heavy applications of fertilizer instead of organics deprives soil organisms of food—those that thrive tend to be the ones that attack the actual crop. The decline in soil organism diversity can lessen a crop's ability to resist diseases and insect infestations.

This is the metabolic basis of the fertilizer treadmill, which German socialist Karl Kautsky described more than a century ago: "Fertilisers allow the reduction in soil fertility to be avoided, but the necessity of using them in larger and larger amounts simply adds a further burden to agriculture—not one unavoidably imposed by nature but a direct result of current social organisation."[32]

The technologies and techniques known variously as regenerative agriculture, agroecology, and permaculture include proven methods of maintaining and strengthening soil health over time:

> Shifting to no-till practices minimizes physical disturbance of the soil, and even low-till methods may sustain soil health in settings with high inputs of organic matter (e.g., through additions from compost, manure or cover crops). Minimizing or

eliminating the use of chemical fertilizers and pesticides helps to re-establish diverse communities of soil life that can support crop health and thereby reduce the need for chemical inputs in the first place. Planting cover crops between cash crops so as to always keep a living plant growing in the soil promotes continual production of exudates that support soil life. Diverse crop rotations and cover crop mixes increase the diversity of soil life, resulting in more complex and resilient communities of soil organisms.[33]

More generally, maintaining soil health requires understanding the differing characteristics of soils in different areas and responding accordingly. There is no one-size-fits-all solution, but the overriding goal should be to build healthier habitats by creating and maintaining a high level of biological diversity both above and below ground. Relevant practices include more complex rotations, the routine use of cover crops, combining animal and plant agriculture, and creating habitats for beneficial insects within field boundaries or strips within fields.

In practice, however, most farmers have little flexibility in deciding what inputs to use, what products to produce, or how to produce them. Most farmers raising poultry and pigs are locked into contracts with integrators who provide all the inputs, lay down strict regulations for their use, and set the prices paid for the completed products, for which they are the only purchasers. Even farmers who are not under contract are squeezed on both sides by a handful of giant agribusiness corporations—monopoly sellers and monopsony buyers that control the farming and food business. Companies whose quarterly profits depend on selling chemicals to farmers, or commodity foods to supermarket chains or processors, are typically unwilling to support changes that might reduce their profits. Capitalism's need for short-term gains prevents rational agriculture.

The radical biologists Richard Levins and Richard Lewontin wrote four decades ago that "because farmers are a small, although essential, part of the production of foods, the conditions of their part of production are set by the monopolistic providers and buyers of farm inputs and outputs."[34]

Even for farmers who are willing to work outside the mainstream food system, the cost of switching to regenerative agriculture is often a disincentive. Most farms operate very close to bankruptcy at all times—the owners depend on outside employment or government subsidies just to stay afloat. Even with production costs as low as possible, they sometimes have to sell their crops at a loss.

The *New York Times* recently reported the case of an Iowa farm family which is switching from raising hogs to raising mushrooms. They estimate that the transition will cost them more than $1 million—and there is no certainty the new venture will cover its costs, let alone make a profit.[35] That's an expense and a risk few farmers could afford.

So, while some independent (mostly small) farmers are making valiant efforts to save the soil, most continue to plow their fields and drench them with chemicals or squeeze ever more animals into CAFOs—while the soil is dying beneath their feet.

Rational Agriculture?

Agriculture, no matter how sustainable, always changes the natural environment. Left alone, plants grow wherever their seeds fall, and animals move as they please. Natural environments include multiple species of both—there are no natural monocultures. Agriculture imposes order, concentrating a few species of plants and animals in limited areas, organized for human convenience. Unwanted species—weeds and undomesticated animals—are physically excluded.

To grow food successfully, our ancestors had to learn how to work with nature's nutrient cycles, minimizing disruption as much as possible and mimicking them when disruption couldn't be avoided. For thousands of years, farming communities around the world fed themselves and others by doing just that. Through trial

Agriculture: The Great Separation

and error and careful observation, they learned how to maintain or restore soil health through techniques such as crop rotation, spreading compost and manure, leaving crop residues in the fields, pasturing sheep and cattle in fallow fields, and more.

Of course, traditional agricultural knowledge varied a great deal, and soil destruction did occur, sometimes on a large scale. Nevertheless, effective methods of maintaining soil health have been known and practiced for millennia. In conscious or unconscious emulation of nature, nutrients were cycled from the soil through plants, animals, and humans, and returned to the soil as manure and plant waste, creating mostly closed-loop agroecological systems. Energy lost in the cycle was replenished by photosynthesis.

The loop was broken when production for local consumption was supplanted by production geared primarily to cash crops. As environmental sociologist Hannah Holleman explains, producing for markets radically changed agriculture's dynamics:

> Cash-crop agriculture is very different in its social and ecological consequences from subsistence agriculture, or even farming by locals to supply local markets. It is volatile, subject to global market fluctuations. And there is an insatiable quality to it, as long as there is money to make or, because of the role of finance in agriculture and taxes, debts to pay. As a consequence, fields are planted when they should rest, herds are expanded when they should be reduced, and so on, leading to the rapid degradation of the land.[36]

The second half of the twentieth century saw extraordinary increases in agricultural production. More grains, vegetables, and meat are produced than ever in history. But, as agronomist Steve Gliessman writes, those gains have been achieved through means that exact terrible environmental and social costs:

> The industrial agriculture model that dominates agriculture

today is at the core of a fundamental contradiction: the techniques, innovations, practices, and policies that constitute industrial agriculture, and which have played the largest role in increasing agricultural productivity, have also undermined the basis for that productivity. They have overdrawn and degraded the natural resources upon which agriculture depends. They have created a dependence on nonrenewable, increasingly costly fossil fuels, the use of which exacerbates climate change. And they have helped to forge a system that concentrates ownership of food-system infrastructure in the hands of a few while taking it away from farmers and farmworkers, those who are in the best position to be stewards of agricultural land. In short, the contradictions inherent in our industrial agriculture-dominated system of food production make it unsustainable—it cannot continue to produce enough food for the growing global population over the long term because it deteriorates the conditions that make agriculture possible.[37]

In an important article published in the ecosocialist journal *Monthly Review*, Fred Magdoff builds on Karl Marx's famous statement that "a rational agriculture is incompatible with the capitalist system."[38] He then shows, step-by-step, that the operational decisions made by individual corn and soy farmers in the U.S. Midwest are "formally rational, given the economic system in which the farmer operates." Yet, the result is an irrational and anti-ecological agricultural system:

> The pulls and pushes of the capitalist system, and the way it inherently develops as all sectors strive to maximize profits, produces an agriculture in which: (a) there are hungry people although there is an abundance of food; (b) there is little true cycling of nutrients, increasing the reliance on fertilizers at the same time that excess nutrients accumulate on factory animal farms and in the cities; (c) animals are raised inhumanely; (d)

poor rotations are used; (e) farm labor and animal slaughterhouse labor is commonly treated unfairly (and/or cruelly); and (f) pollution with pesticides and fertilizers is widespread, among other problems. All of the common decisions and practices of conventional farmers and others in the agricultural system make eminent sense (that is, they are rational) only from the very narrow perspective of trying to make profits within a capitalist system.

Rational agriculture, Magdoff argues, "would be carried out by individual farmers or farmer associations (cooperatives) and have as its purpose to supply the entire population with a sufficient quantity, quality, and variety of food while managing farms and fields in ways that are humane to animals and work in harmony with the ecosystem."

Two centuries of practical experience prove that such a system is indeed incompatible with the rule of capital. Working with nature, not against it, is the only way to build a system that feeds everyone without exception. At every step, capitalism's exploitive metabolic order violates that simple rule.

CHAPTER 14

Triple Crises in the Oceans

> For the globe as a whole, the ocean is the great regulator, the great stabilizer of temperatures. . . . Without the oceans, our world would be visited by unthinkably harsh extremes of temperature.
>
> —RACHEL CARSON[1]

The ocean's metabolism is a vital part of the Earth System. As famed oceanographer Sylvia Earle writes, our fate and the oceans are inextricably intertwined:

> Our lives depend on the living ocean—not just the rocks and water, but stable, resilient, diverse living systems that hold the world on a steady course favorable to humankind.[2]
>
> The *living ocean* drives planetary chemistry, governs climate and weather, and otherwise provides the cornerstone of the life-support system for all creatures on our planet, from deep-sea starfish to desert sagebrush. . . . If the sea is sick, we'll feel it. If it dies, we die. Our future and the state of the oceans are one.[3]

The two massive metabolic rifts discussed in previous chapters—the carbon dioxide glut in the air and the nitrogen glut in soil and water—are also sickening the oceans.

Although global warming is usually expressed as increased air temperatures, the ocean is much better at storing heat than the atmosphere—one degree of ocean warming stores more than 1,000 times as much heat energy as one degree of atmosphere warming. Since the 1980s, the sea surface has been consistently warmer than at any time since reliable observations began in 1880.[4]

Scientists measure the ocean's heat content in joules—the amount of energy required to produce one watt of power for one second. In 2020, Lijing Cheng of China's Institute of Atmospheric Physics calculated that the increase in ocean heat since 1995 required the addition of 228 sextillion joules of heat—that's 228 followed by twenty-one zeroes:

> That's a lot of zeros indeed. To make it easier to understand, I did a calculation. The Hiroshima atom-bomb exploded with an energy of about 63,000,000,000,000 joules. The amount of heat we have put in the world's oceans in the past 25 years equals to 3.6 billion Hiroshima atom-bomb explosions.[5]

That's about *five Hiroshima bombs a second*, and the rate is accelerating. The IPCC projects that even if emissions are substantially reduced, by 2100 the ocean will heat two to four times as much as it has since 1970—and if emissions are not cut, it will heat five to seven times as much.[6]

The top few meters of the world's oceans contain as much heat as the planet's entire atmosphere. By absorbing and storing such immense amounts of energy, the ocean delays the impact of Earth's energy imbalance on the global climate system. In oceanographer Grant Bigg's words, the ocean "acts as a giant flywheel to the climate system, moderating change but prolonging it once change commences."[7]

The price paid for that storage and delay is record-setting heat that is disrupting the world's largest ecosystem in a multitude of ways, none of them beneficial to humans. The living ocean has changed before, but never, since an asteroid killed the dinosaurs, as rapidly as today. In the transition from Holocene to Anthropocene, marine ecosystems are entering unknown territory:

> In the coming decades and centuries, the ocean's biogeochemical cycles and ecosystems will become increasingly stressed by at least three independent factors. Rising temperatures, ocean acidification and ocean deoxygenation will cause substantial changes in the physical, chemical and biological environment, which will then affect the ocean's biogeochemical cycles and ecosystems in ways that we are only beginning to fathom. . . .
> Ocean warming, acidification and deoxygenation are virtually irreversible on the human time scale. This is because the primary driver for all three stressors, i.e. the emission of CO_2 into the atmosphere, will cause global changes that will be with us for many hundreds, if not thousands, of years.[8]

Marine ecologists have described ocean warming, acidification, and oxygen loss as a "deadly trio" because when they occurred together in the past, mass extinctions of animal and plant life followed.[9]

Permanent Heat Waves

As we've seen, long-term global average changes in the atmosphere's temperature can conceal destructive short-term extremes. The same is happening in the ocean.

The very idea of marine heatwaves is new. The term itself first appeared in 2011, in scare quotes, in a government report on "a major temperature anomaly" in which "water temperatures off the south-western coast of Western Australia rose to unprecedented levels."[10] As recently as 2015, only five articles in English-language scientific journals had "marine heatwave" in the title. In 2019 there were ninety-two, an increase that reflects what the journal

Nature said was "the appearance an entirely new subdiscipline: the study of marine heatwaves (MHWs), discrete periods of unusually warm temperatures in the ocean."[11]

The sudden growth of scientific interest in marine heatwaves reflects a real shift in the ocean's climate in this century: a radical increase in the frequency, intensity, and duration of periods of much higher-than-normal water temperatures. Organisms that have evolved to live within a limited temperature range must adapt, flee, or die when that range is exceeded.

Marine heatwaves are usually defined as five or more consecutive days in which sea surface temperatures were in the top 10 percent of the thirty-year average range for the region. Using an even stricter definition—temperatures in the top 1 percent—the IPCC says that since 1982, marine heatwaves "have doubled in frequency and have become longer lasting, more intense and more extensive," and "the observed trend towards more frequent, intense and extensive MHWs . . . cannot be explained by natural climate variability."[12]

This century has seen particularly devastating marine heatwaves in the Mediterranean (2003 and 2024), Bay of Bengal (2010), western Australia (2011), northwest Atlantic (2012), northeast Pacific (2013–2016), Tasman Sea (2016), New Zealand (2016), Southern California (2018 and 2019), Arctic Ocean (2020), central North Pacific (2021), and northeast Atlantic (2023).

In 2023 and 2024, the number of marine heatwave days worldwide was 240 percent higher than in any previously documented period.[13]

This is only the beginning. In 2019, the IPCC concluded that it is very likely that "MHWs will increase in frequency, duration, spatial extent and intensity throughout the ocean under future global warming. . . . A one-in-hundred-day event at pre-industrial levels is projected to become a one-in-four-day event by 2031–2050 and a one-in-two-day event by 2081–2100."[14]

The largest, longest, and deadliest marine heatwave to date, from 2013 to 2016 in the northeast Pacific, was nicknamed "the

Blob" after the 1958 science-fiction movie. Like its space monster namesake, it grew rapidly and destroyed much of the life it enveloped. After forming in the Gulf of Alaska in the autumn of 2015, it expanded south to Mexico in less than a year, ultimately covering about ten million square kilometers and penetrating up to 200 meters down.

Food webs that had sustained life for millennia collapsed from unprecedented heat. Populations of phytoplankton, copepods, krill, and other small creatures plummeted, and animals that normally feed on these creatures, including more than 100 million cod and millions of seabirds, starved to death. So did thousands of sea lions when their prey disappeared. Hundreds of kilometers of kelp forests wilted and died. Heat killed 95 percent of Chinook salmon eggs in the Sacramento River. The largest toxic algae bloom ever seen released deadly neurotoxins, forcing the closure of clam and crab fisheries from Vancouver Island to California.

Until the Blob, no one imagined that a marine "temperature anomaly" might encompass an area as large as Canada and last more than two years. Past research on ocean climate change has focused on the effects of long-term changes in average water temperatures, but now, as eighteen leading specialists in the field write, "Discrete extreme events are emerging as pivotal in shaping ecosystems, by driving sudden and dramatic shifts in ecological structure and functioning." They warn that marine heatwaves "will probably intensify with anthropogenic climate change [and] are rapidly emerging as forceful agents of disturbance with the capacity to restructure entire ecosystems and disrupt the provision of ecological goods and services in coming decades."[15]

The size and frequency of marine heatwaves are projected to increase so much that many parts of the ocean will reach "a near-permanent MHW state" by late this century.[16] Even if greenhouse gas emissions start to fall by midcentury, by 2100 about half of the global ocean will experience year-round heatwaves. If emissions don't decline, by 2100 there will be permanent heatwaves in 90 percent of the ocean, and more than two-thirds of those will be

Category IV, the most extreme level. (For comparison: the Blob was only Category III.)

In 2023, MHWs were so intense and frequent that some scientists adopted the term "super-MHW" for the most extreme. Super-MHWs occurred in all parts of the ocean, including in the Arctic region.[17]

By 2080, if emissions remain high, the Earth System will be in a "time when the MHW climate has changed completely from the range that species have previously experienced and represents a qualitatively different climate."[18] Since 1982, the average duration of ocean heatwaves has doubled, from twenty to forty days, and "in 2023, 22% of the global ocean surface experienced at least one severe to extreme marine heatwave event."[19]

Corrosive Seas

Ocean acidification has been called the equally evil twin of global warming. Sylvia Earle describes it as "a slow but accelerating impact that will overshadow all the oil spills that have ever occurred put together."[20]

Gas molecules constantly cross the air-sea interface between atmosphere and ocean. CO_2 from the air dissolves in the water; CO_2 from the water bubbles into the air. Until recently, the two flows were roughly balanced: The amount of carbon dioxide on either side didn't change much for millions of years. Now the flow is out of balance. More CO_2 is entering the sea than leaving it, and that is changing the ocean's chemistry, making seawater more acidic.

Scientists measure water's acidity using the pH scale: a lower pH number indicates higher acidity. Over the past century, the ocean's pH level has fallen from 8.2 to 8.1. That doesn't sound like much, but the scale is logarithmic, so that drop means that the oceans are now about 30 percent more acidic than they used to be.[21] That's an average—the top 250 meters are generally more acidic than deeper water, and acidification is more severe in high latitudes, because CO_2 dissolves more easily in colder water.

The present rate of acidification is a hundred times faster than any natural change in at least 55 million years. If it continues, ocean acidity will reach three times the pre-industrial level by the end of this century. A growing body of research suggests that acidification will decimate some commercially important species in this century, causing the collapse of major fisheries.[22]

Although scientific concern about CO_2 emissions began in the 1950s, little attention was paid to ocean acidification until recently. It was first named and described in a brief article in *Nature* in September 2003, and first discussed in detail in a 2005 Royal Society report that concluded acidification would soon go "beyond the range of current natural variability and probably to a level not experienced for at least hundreds of thousands of years and possibly much longer."[23] There is now no doubt that ocean acidification is a major threat to the stability of the Earth System, one that is contributing to the sixth mass extinction of life on our planet.

Though formally correct, the word *acidification* is misleading, since the oceans are actually slightly alkaline, and the shift now underway only makes them less so. Just as raising the atmospheric concentration of carbon dioxide to 0.041 percent is causing global climate change, a small increase in the amount of CO_2 in seawater poses major threats to the organisms that live in that water. Reduced pH has already significantly changed the habitats that marine plants and animals depend on. Any further reduction could be deadly for many of them.

Lower pH levels have weakened coral reefs, and the problem will get much worse if CO_2 emissions aren't reduced soon:

> The skeletons of corals on Australia's Great Barrier Reef have weakened measurably in the last twenty-five years and now contain 14 percent less carbonate by volume than they did before.... Ocean acidification has been dubbed "osteoporosis for reefs" because of this skeletal weakening....
> If carbon dioxide in the atmosphere doubles from its

current level, all of the world's coral reefs will shift from a state of construction to erosion. They will literally begin to crumble and dissolve, as erosion and dissolution of carbonates outpaces deposition. What is most worrying is that this level of carbon dioxide will be reached by 2100 under a *low*-emission scenario of the Intergovernmental Panel on Climate Change.[24]

Approximately 25 percent of all fish depend on coral reefs for food and shelter from predators, so a collapse would be disastrous for marine biodiversity.

Other animals weakened by ocean acidification include oysters, mussels, crabs, and starfish. Of particular concern are foraminifera and pteropods, tiny, shelled animals near the bottom of the food chain: if their numbers decline, many bigger animals will starve.

Acidification also affects animals whose metabolisms function best when the pH level of their internal fluids stays within a narrow range. This is particularly problematic for marine animals, including fish, whose blood pH tends to match the surrounding water. For some species, even a slight reduction in blood pH can cause severe health and reproductive problems, and even death.[25]

In 2008, 155 scientists from twenty-six countries signed a declaration "based on irrefutable scientific findings" about "recent, rapid changes in ocean chemistry and their potential, within decades, to severely affect marine organisms, food webs, biodiversity, and fisheries."

> To avoid severe and widespread damages, all of which are ultimately driven by increasing concentrations of atmospheric carbon dioxide (CO_2), we call for policymakers to act quickly to incorporate these concerns into plans to stabilize atmospheric CO_2 at a safe level to avoid not only dangerous climate change but also dangerous ocean acidification. . . .
>
> Policymakers need to realize that ocean acidification is not a peripheral issue. It is *the other CO_2 problem* that must be grappled with alongside climate change. Reining in this double

threat, caused by our dependence on fossil fuels, is the challenge of the century.[26]

The IPCC's *Special Report on the Ocean and Cryosphere*, published in 2019, concludes that "the ocean is continuing to acidify in response to ongoing ocean carbon uptake," that "it is very likely that over 95% of the near surface open ocean has already been affected," and that "the survival of some keystone ecosystems (e.g., coral reefs) are at risk."[27]

The 2024 update on Planetary Boundaries warned that "the indicator for Ocean Acidification . . . is close to crossing the safe boundary. Several new studies suggest that even these current conditions may be problematic for multiple marine organisms, indicating a need to re-evaluate the safe boundary."[28]

A few months later, an international team of marine ecologists showed that "by 2020, the average global ocean conditions had already crossed into the uncertainty range of the ocean acidification boundary." Their evidence showed that the damage caused by acidification had been underestimated, and the acceptable level of acidification should be reduced to more adequately prevent risk. This "revised and more accurate, ecologically sound definition" means that "the boundary was first crossed during the 1980s, with the entire surface ocean having passed this boundary by the 2000s."[29]

Despite overwhelming scientific evidence that acidification is a major threat to the world's largest ecosystem, the governments of the world's richest countries remain silent. The word *oceans* only appeared once in the Paris Agreement, and "acidification" wasn't mentioned at all. The official program of the 2025 UN Ocean Conference didn't mention "acidification" at all: the word appeared three times in passing in the meeting's final declaration, but not in the section headed "Accelerating Action."[30]

Running Low on Oxygen

The ocean is losing its breath. The decline in ocean oxygen, which ranks among the most "serious effects of human activities on the earth's environment,"[31] has been proposed for addition to the Planetary Boundaries Framework because it "poses widespread and potentially irreversible threats to planetary integrity" and "without it, the PBF will risk overlooking serious Earth System degradation."[32]

In previous chapters we examined two ecological gluts created by capitalism's inherent drive to expand at all costs. Together, nitrogen and carbon dioxide are disrupting the Earth System's metabolism—and making it harder for marine life to breathe.

In the summer of 1972, an environmental assessment study off the coast of Louisiana found something unexpected—an area below the surface where the water contained little or no oxygen. In waters that had long supported a large and profitable fishing industry, there were areas where fish couldn't breathe.

Over the following decade, other low-oxygen areas were found along the continental shelf, but no comprehensive study was conducted until 1985, when a research ship carefully measured what has become known as the "dead zone." That expedition found that hypoxic (low oxygen) or anoxic (zero oxygen) conditions then covered about 10,000 square kilometers on the northern edge of the Gulf of Mexico, from the mouth of the Mississippi west to Texas. It extended up to 130 kilometers offshore, and from about five meters below the surface to the seafloor, sixty meters down.

Subsequent annual surveys found that the dead zone forms off the Louisiana coast every spring and continues through the summer. On average, it covers about 11,000 square kilometers; in 2024, it was 17,366 square kilometers.[33]

Paradoxically, the dead zone is caused by too much life, resulting from excessive plant and bacterial growth that leads to oxygen depletion in bottom waters. Each year, the Mississippi and Atchafalaya rivers carry about 1.6 million tons of dissolved nitrogen into the Gulf of Mexico. When the flow peaks in the spring and early summer, that influx overwhelms the region's natural food webs, causing massive growth of marine organisms that sink to the bottom and are decomposed by microbes, a process that consumes oxygen. (See Figure 14.1.)

Oxygen from the surface normally replenishes deeper water, but the river water floats on top of denser salty seawater, creating a distinct layer that limits or blocks oxygen circulation. The combination of decomposed organic matter and water stratification creates regions where there is too little oxygen to sustain most animal life. "Fish can swim out of the hypoxic waters, or dead zone, to areas with life-sustaining oxygen levels, but other marine animals, such as mollusks, anemones, and worms cannot and die. Hypoxic waters kill high levels of aquatic species, disrupting the food chain and habitat."[34]

The Gulf of Mexico dead zone typically lasts until cooler weather or storms break the stratification and promote downward mixing of oxygen-rich surface waters. It returns the following year when melting snow and spring rains again increase the flow of nutrients.

The discovery of a dead zone in the Gulf of Mexico—and many more at about the same time—raised an obvious question: Was this a previously undetected natural phenomenon? Cores drilled from the seafloor, containing decades of sediment, answer yes and no. Yes, there were low-oxygen episodes in that part of the coast and elsewhere before scientists noticed them in the 1970s. No, coastal hypoxia has never been so frequent, widespread, and long-lasting.

Fertile soil naturally contains nutrients, and the Mississippi has been carrying soil to the ocean for a very long time, so it is not surprising that oxygen was occasionally depleted in coastal waters in the past. However, sediment studies prove that "the low-oxygen events of the last few decades were more extreme than any that occurred in the previous 150 years."[35]

Research on low-oxygen areas in other parts of the United States and Europe leads to the same conclusion: "The modern aggravation of coastal hypoxia is unprecedented and ... must have been forced by excess human-induced nutrient loading."[36]

In 1960, there were a few dozen relatively small coastal dead

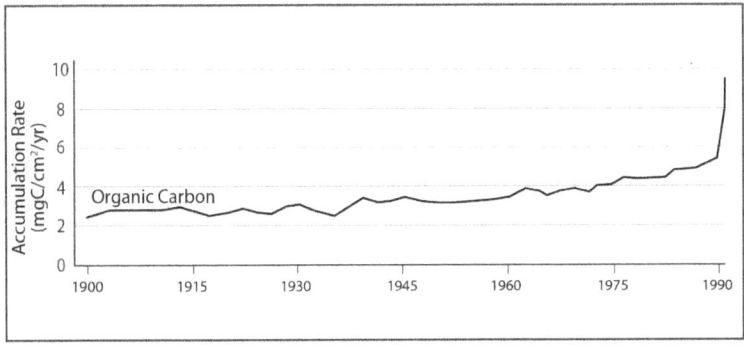

Figure 14.1. Organic matter preserved in Gulf of Mexico near-shore sediment shows increased algal growth in the late twentieth century. (Graphic by Ann Sanderson, adapted from Integrated Assessment of Hypoxia in the Northern Gulf of Mexico, National Science and Technology Council, May 2000.)

zones worldwide. A 2008 study found more than four hundred, with a total area of 245,000 square kilometers; the authors calculated that the number of dead zones had "approximately doubled each decade since the 1960s."[37] In 2019, researchers identified more than 900 coastal areas that experienced eutrophication—more than 700 of those were hypoxic.[38]

Those figures include only scientifically confirmed dead zones, so they omit parts of the world where reporting of coastal water quality is limited or nonexistent. There are probably now more than one thousand dead zones worldwide, and the number continues to rise.

In the Gulf of Mexico and many other coastal areas, marine ecologist Donald Boesch writes, the nitrogen glut has caused "explosive and synchronous intensification of eutrophication," and "dramatic alteration of coastal ecosystems."

> Primary production increased, water clarity decreased, food chains were altered, oxygen depletion of bottom waters developed or expanded, seagrass beds were lost, and harmful algal blooms occurred with increased frequency. Within two decades (roughly 1960 to 1980), large coastal ecosystems were

substantially changed, as areas of hypoxia developed or greatly intensified, phytoplankton production or biomass doubled, and benthic macrophyte meadows contracted.[39]

The 1.6 million tons of nitrogen that pour into the Gulf of Mexico each year is 23 percent of the amount applied to crops in farms in the Mississippi River basin.[40] It is clear that the only way to shrink the dead zone in the Gulf of Mexico is to reduce the amount of fertilizer applied in the thirty-one states in the Mississippi River basin.

In 2008, the U.S. Environmental Protection Agency adopted an "Action Plan" developed by the Mississippi River/Gulf of Mexico Task Force. Its goal was to reduce the average size of the hypoxic zone to less than 5,000 square kilometers by 2015, "through implementation of specific, practical, and cost-effective voluntary actions."[41]

Inclusion of the word *voluntary* was a victory for agribusiness interests that preferred to have no reduction at all. In the following years, the giant corporations that sell agricultural chemicals and profit from the overproduction of corn and soy actively resisted every attempt by state and local agencies to require changes that would protect waterways from fertilizer and other agricultural chemicals. As a result, when 2015 arrived, the dead zone was more than three times larger than the plan promised, so the Task Force extended the timetable by twenty years. The goal now is to reduce the dead zone to 5,000 square kilometers by 2035. If current trends continue, the timetable will have to be extended again. (That, of course, depends on whether the Task Force survives Trump's budget and staff cuts.)

This failure is not unique to the United States. The dead zone in the Baltic Sea is larger and, in many ways, more destructive than the one in the Gulf of Mexico. In 2007, Finland, Sweden, and the other nations that surround the sea adopted an Action Plan "to achieve a Baltic Sea in good environmental status by 2021," including the elimination of eutrophication. They agreed, "by 2010 to halt the degradation of threatened and/or declining marine biotopes/ habitats in the Baltic Sea, and by 2021 to ensure that threatened and/or declining marine biotopes/habitats in the Baltic Sea have largely recovered."[42]

In 2025, a summary report concluded that "the results show little or no improvement in the state of the Baltic Sea environment in 2016–2021 . . . Eutrophication status has shown no signs of recovery."[43] New objectives were adopted, supposedly to be met by 2030.

The Baltic Sea experience reveals an unwillingness to challenge an agricultural system that, as sociologist Philip McMichael puts it, "is ultimately about combining commodified inputs (seeds, fertilizer, antibiotics, privately-owned genetic materials, pesticides and so on) with land or water or factory farms to produce outputs as ingredients of processed commodities to fuel labor or machinery, without regard for social or ecological consequence."[44]

Oxygen is also declining in areas far from the coasts, where the gas is being driven out by warming water. Since 1960, low-oxygen areas in the open ocean have expanded by 4.5 million square kilometers, an area the size of the European Union. Some regions have lost 40 percent of their oxygen, and the volume of water containing zero oxygen has more than quadrupled. The ocean is losing about one billion metric tons of oxygen annually. At present rates, the decline will triple by 2100. Add that to the rapidly growing number of coastal dead zones, and we have a life-support emergency.

An Ocean Anoxic Event (OAE) occurs when the level of dissolved oxygen in a large part of the ocean plunges to (or nears) zero. That has happened previously in Earth's history, most recently about 94 million years ago, when loss of oxygen wiped out a large proportion of marine life. As scientists associated with the Woods Hole Oceanographic Institution point out, ocean conditions today are similar to those that prevailed before that crisis and are rapidly getting worse:

> More widespread perturbation seems realistic under currently projected carbon emissions. Without positive human intervention, ancient OAE studies are destined to become uncomfortably applicable in the not-so-distant future.[45]

Even at present levels of deoxygenation, the damage is extensive. In fact, *any* reduction in available oxygen, not just hypoxia, is problematic for most ocean life. Although some marine animals, such as jellyfish, are little affected by oxygen reduction, others decline when the level falls even slightly.[46] As a result, the population balance in areas where oxygen levels are falling quickly tilts toward hypoxia-tolerant species, while others flee or die.

In addition to directly threatening the lives and habitats of marine organisms, oxygen depletion is disrupting the global nitrogen cycle. For hundreds of millions of years, naturally occurring Oxygen Minimum Zones have played a key role in the nitrogen cycle because the bacteria that convert the reactive nitrogen into inert atmospheric nitrogen can only do so in the absence of oxygen. The expansion of OMZs means that growing numbers of microbes are removing reactive nitrogen from the ocean, unbalancing the cycle and reducing the availability of essential nutrients for marine life.

Furthermore, when bacteria convert reactive nitrogen to inert nitrogen, they also produce nitrous oxide, a greenhouse gas that is approximately three hundred times more potent than carbon dioxide and also depletes the ozone layer. Multiple studies have found large amounts of nitrous oxide rising from the ocean surface above OMZs. This is a classic example of positive feedback—global warming accelerates the production of nitrous oxide, which in turn accelerates global warming.

Finally, it is essential to consider that oxygen depletion does not occur in isolation. For instance, organisms that consume more oxygen also increase acidification by exhaling more carbon dioxide, and fish attempting to escape oxygen-starved water often find that alternative locations are too acidic.

Misery on a Global Scale

The deadly trio of ocean warming, acidification, and oxygen loss is a consequence of the disrupted carbon cycle. Burning massive

Triple Crises in the Oceans

amounts of long-buried carbon has changed the ocean's chemistry, depleted oxygen, and heated the water—metabolic rifts that reinforce each other, making oceans increasingly inhospitable, often deadly, for living things from microbes to whales.

We're seeing rising numbers of compound events, when all three crises occur together. At times in 2020, up to 20 percent of the global ocean volume was simultaneously overheated, acidified, and dangerously low in oxygen.[47]

Worse, the deadly trio isn't acting alone. Overfishing has wiped out many species, and it's predicted that most wild fish populations will be 90 percent depleted by 2050. Pollutants, including tons of plastics that essentially last forever, are poisoning marine life from coastlines to the deepest trenches. Offshore oil wells are leaking deadly hydrocarbons, and mining companies are preparing to dredge rare minerals from the deep-sea floor, destroying some of the few remaining undamaged parts of Earth's surface.

As Jan Zalasiewicz and Mark Williams write, "A wholesale refashioning of the marine ecosystem" is now underway. If business as usual continues, "pervasive changes in the physical, chemical and biological boundary conditions of the sea ... [will] transform, irreversibly, and for the worse, the Earth and its oceans."[48]

The effect of that transformation was summed up by Agence France-Presse, in its account of the IPCC's 2019 report on the oceans: "The same oceans that nourished human evolution are poised to unleash misery on a global scale unless the carbon pollution destabilizing Earth's marine environment is brought to heel."[49]

PART 4

A Fight for Survival

CHAPTER 15

Can We Avoid the Hothouse?

If I had to modify Rosa Luxemburg's dramatic words, in relation to the dangers we now face, I would add to "socialism or barbarism" this qualification: "barbarism if we are lucky."
— ISTVÁN MÉSZÁROS[1]

An important paper on global change published in August 2018, under the unexciting title "Trajectories of the Earth System in the Anthropocene," raised a frightening possibility:

> Even if the Paris Accord target of a 1.5°C to 2.0°C rise in temperature is met, we cannot exclude the risk that a cascade of feedbacks could push the Earth System irreversibly onto a "Hothouse Earth" pathway.[2]

If that happens, humanity will face "conditions that resemble planetary states that were last seen several millions of years ago, conditions that would be inhospitable to current human societies and to many other contemporary species."

Of course, the internet overflows with warnings of imminent

global catastrophes that mainstream scientists have somehow overlooked or are covering up. This article differed from such pseudo-science in two important ways. First, it was published in a major mainstream scientific journal, the *Proceedings of the National Academy of Sciences*. Second, it was written by sixteen of the world's top Earth System scientists, including, to name only three, Will Steffen, founding executive director of the International Geosphere-Biosphere Program, Katherine Richardson, chair of the Danish Committee for Climate Change policy, and Johan Rockström, Executive Director of the Stockholm Environment Institute.

It's possible to disagree with them, but their work cannot be lightly dismissed as fear-mongering. It is an important contribution to our understanding of the planetary emergency, and a call for urgent action.

It's even more important because the authors reject the incremental reformism of liberal greens and most environmental NGOs, and argue that stopping climate change requires systemic change.

Tipping Cascades

The authors of "Trajectories of the Earth System in the Anthropocene," write:

> The Anthropocene represents the beginning of a very rapid human-driven trajectory of the Earth System away from the glacial–interglacial limit cycle toward new, hotter climatic conditions and a profoundly different biosphere.... The Earth System may already have passed one "fork in the road" of potential pathways, a bifurcation taking the Earth System out of the next glaciation cycle.[3]

Discussions of climate change and the models used to forecast future temperatures generally focus on the impact of increased CO_2 in the atmosphere, implicitly treating other aspects of the biosphere as stable background. In contrast, this paper examines large ecosystems that regulate the Earth System in various ways and shows that their nature and roles could change in the near future, multiplying the impact of greenhouse gases. "Feedback processes within the Earth System coupled with direct human degradation of the biosphere may play a more important role than normally assumed."[4]

The long-term evolution of the Earth System is influenced by a multitude of cycles and feedbacks that control the movement of matter and energy in the oceans, soil, and atmosphere. Many large ecosystems are already undergoing changes and could "tip" into new and more dangerous states in this century, possibly in the coming decades. For example:

- Loss of Arctic Sea ice reduces reflection of sunlight (albedo) and raises ocean temperatures.
- Melting of the Greenland ice sheet adds freshwater to the North Atlantic, changing heat circulation patterns and raising sea levels.
- Melting of Antarctic ice sheets reduces reflection of sunlight (albedo) and raises sea levels.
- Melting of the permafrost in Siberia releases frozen methane, a powerful greenhouse gas.
- Dieback of the Amazon rainforest and northern boreal forests, through forest fires, logging, and the expansion of industrial agriculture, releases large amounts of CO_2 and reduces a major carbon sink.[5]

If one such system passes a tipping point, it may trigger a "tipping cascade," permanently accelerating others. "For example, tipping (loss) of the Greenland Ice Sheet could trigger a critical transition in the Atlantic Meridional Ocean Circulation, which could, by causing sea-level rise and Southern Ocean heat accumulation, accelerate ice loss from the East Antarctic Ice Sheet." Such a cascade could alter the Earth System sufficiently to create a planetary threshold beyond which a Hothouse Earth is inevitable and irreversible, regardless of human actions.

The complexity of the Earth System makes cascades impossible to predict. However, the evidence of past changes suggests that such an occurrence could happen in this century if business as usual continues, perhaps before 2040.

> Current rates of human-driven changes far exceed the rates of change driven by geophysical or biosphere forces that have altered the Earth System trajectory in the past; even abrupt geophysical events do not approach current rates of human-driven change.... In terms of their influence on the carbon cycle and climate, the human-driven changes of the Anthropocene are beginning to match or exceed the rates of change that drove past, relatively sudden mass extinction events, and are essentially irreversible.[6]

Crossing the threshold to an irreversible Hothouse Earth pathway would not necessarily lead to immediate runaway heating: more likely, based on past climate changes, would be a transition, over some years, into a permanently hotter state. The transition is likely to be chaotic and dangerous: "It poses severe risks for health, economies, political stability (especially for the most climate vulnerable), and ultimately, the habitability of the planet for humans."[7]

This challenges the "overshoot" climate strategy, which proposes to allow temperatures to rise above 1.5° or 2.0°, expecting to lower the heat later by removing CO_2 from the air. If the planetary threshold is passed before billions of tons of CO_2 can be removed, then Hothouse Earth will be unavoidable.

The Alternative

The authors argue that Hothouse Earth can be prevented if radical changes are made soon in society's relationship with the rest of the Earth System. The "Stabilized Earth" outcome would be hotter and less stable than the Holocene has been, and the oceans would certainly swamp many coastal cities, but the worst impacts of Hothouse Earth would be avoided.

Reaching and maintaining Stabilized Earth would require human society to adopt a permanent active planetary stewardship role toward the planet, consciously becoming "an integral adaptive part of Earth System dynamics, creating feedbacks that keep the system on a Stabilized Earth pathway."[8]

Stabilized Earth, the authors stress, "is not an intrinsic state of the Earth System but rather, one in which humanity commits to a pathway of ongoing management of its relationship with the rest of the Earth System."[9] They don't use these words, but what they propose is a global planned economy with maintenance of a sustainable planet as its prime directive.

Necessary actions to create and maintain what the authors call a super-Holocene state fall into three categories:

(i) reducing greenhouse gas emissions, (ii) enhancing or creating carbon sinks (e.g., protecting and enhancing biosphere carbon sinks and creating new types of sinks), and (iii) modifying Earth's energy balance (for example, via solar radiation management, although that particular feedback entails very large risks of destabilization or degradation of several key processes in the Earth System).

While reducing emissions is a priority, much more could be done to reduce direct human pressures on critical biomes that contribute to the regulation of the state of the Earth System through carbon sinks and moisture feedbacks, such as the Amazon and boreal forests, and to build much more effective stewardship of the marine and terrestrial biospheres in general.[10]

In an interview following publication of the paper, lead author Will Steffen stressed that they used the term "stewardship" to emphasize that what is needed is not new technical methods

Can We Avoid the Hothouse?

of controlling the earth but radical changes in the ways human society interacts with the earth.[11] There is an obvious similarity here, whether the authors realize it or not, to Marx's assertion that humans must "govern the human metabolism with nature in a rational way."[12]

Like a growing number of their peers and other environmentalists, they have concluded that the necessary changes cannot be made within the present social order or by using existing methods. They write that "the present dominant socioeconomic system . . . is based on high-carbon economic growth and exploitative resource use," and that attempts to reform it have been unsuccessful:

> Incremental linear changes to the present socioeconomic system are not enough to stabilize the Earth System. Widespread, rapid, and fundamental transformations will likely be required to reduce the risk of crossing the threshold and locking in the Hothouse Earth pathway: these include changes in behavior, technology and innovation, governance, and values. . . .
>
> The contemporary way of guiding development founded on theories, tools, and beliefs of gradual or incremental change, with a focus on economy efficiency, will likely not be adequate to cope with this trajectory.[13]

"Trajectories of the Earth System in the Anthropocene" makes the case that apparently separate environmental problems are interlocked elements of a global crisis that requires radical global solutions.

Unfortunately, the authors stop short of analyzing the underlying social causes of that crisis. They are frustratingly vague about the "widespread, rapid, and fundamental transformations" that could make Stabilized Earth and planetary stewardship possible, let alone actually implemented, over the certain opposition of the world's richest corporations and their political allies.

Early in the paper, the authors say that this type of analysis "requires a deep integration of knowledge from biogeophysical Earth System science with that from the social sciences and humanities on the development and functioning of human societies."[14] The absence of a concrete program for change suggests that the integration with social sciences and humanities remains more wish than reality, and their list of references indicates that integration hasn't gone beyond consulting a few academic papers. Ecosocialists have clearly not yet succeeded in expanding the horizons of Earth System scientists.

That should not prevent socialists from recognizing this paper as an important contribution to our common concerns. If an irrevocable trajectory to Hothouse Earth is even possible—and this paper shows that it is—then decisive countermeasures must be at the top of the agenda for everyone concerned about humanity's future.

CHAPTER 16

We Only Want the Earth

> The inherent tendencies of capitalist development, at a certain point of their maturity, necessitate the transition to a planful mode of production consciously organized by the entire working force of society—in order that all of society and human civilization might not perish.
>
> —ROSA LUXEMBURG[1]

Speaking at the UNICEF Climate Action Conference in 2019, sixteen-year-old Greta Thunberg berated the assembled dignitaries:

> You say you hear us and that you understand the urgency. But no matter how sad and angry I am, I do not want to believe that. Because if you really understood the situation and still kept on failing to act, then you would be evil. And that I refuse to believe.[2]

I don't know if Greta has changed her mind on this, but it is increasingly hard to resist the conclusion that the people in charge are evil. The causes and consequences of the global environmental crisis are well known and widely publicized. Nothing I've written in this book is a secret: it's impossible to believe that the people with the power to change things don't know all of it. Their response isn't just passive: they are actively and deliberately making things worse every day.

There has certainly been a lot of talk about doing the right thing. Since the Rio Conference in 1992, when the United Nations Framework Convention on Climate Change was adopted, there have been thirty Conferences of the Parties (COPs) and innumerable smaller meetings at which experts and politicians from more than 190 countries have debated how to achieve "stabilization of greenhouse gas concentrations in the atmosphere at a level that would prevent dangerous anthropogenic interference with the climate system."[3] Their deliberations have supposedly been based on the best available science, on thousands of scientific studies and reports, including the massive summaries and synthesis documents compiled by the dedicated volunteer scientists of the Intergovernmental Panel on Climate Change (IPCC).

In 2015, after twenty-three years of talk, they adopted the Paris Agreement, promising to keep the global average temperature rise in this century as close as possible to 1.5° Celsius above pre-industrial levels. But, as philosopher Mark Alizart writes, that was "the vague commitment of public actors to put pressure on indeterminate private actors to limit their carbon emissions in an indeterminate future," so it has had zero effect.[4]

When climate scientist James Hansen called the Paris deal "a fraud ... worthless words," he wasn't exaggerating.[5]

Even Pope Francis agreed that the game is rigged:

> It is remarkable how weak international political responses have been. The failure of global summits on the environment make it plain that our politics are subject to technology and finance. There are too many special interests, and economic interests easily end up trumping the common good and manipulating information so that their own plans will not be

affected. . . . Consequently the most one can expect is superficial rhetoric, sporadic acts of philanthropy and perfunctory expressions of concern for the environment, whereas any genuine attempt by groups within society to introduce change is viewed as a nuisance based on romantic illusions or an obstacle to be circumvented.[6]

After the Paris Agreement, and after the IPCC report on 1.5° said emissions would have to drop 50 percent by 2030, and after the International Energy Agency said there must be "no new oil and gas fields approved for development; no new coal mines or mine extensions"—the industry embarked on a massive expansion program that Andreas Malm and Wim Carton call a "fossil fuel frenzy."

> Not one more pipeline could be built if the world were to avert warming by more than 1.5°C. But in 2022, there were 119 oil pipelines under development—planned, under construction, nearing completion—with a total length of some 350,000 km, enough to encircle the globe at the equator more than eight times. Not one more gas pipeline could be added, but in 2022, there were 477 in progress, with a combined length girding this planet twenty-four times. Over 300 liquified gas terminals were in the works. Not one more coal mine or plant could burden the earth, but underway were 432 new mines and 485 new plants.[7]

Figures published in the *Guardian* in 2022 showed that despite promising to cut emissions, fossil fuel companies worldwide were preparing for massive expansion. "These plans include 195 carbon bombs, gigantic oil and gas projects that would each result in at least a billion tonnes of CO_2 emissions over their lifetimes, in total equivalent to about 18 years of current global CO_2 emissions. About 60% of these have already started pumping."[8]

The Emperor Nero, who allegedly played the fiddle while

Rome burned, had nothing on these global arsonists. As Adam Hanieh writes, "This reality highlights a crucial truth of the climate emergency: left to their own devices there is no chance that the world's largest energy firms ... will willingly walk away from the enormous wealth to be made from continued oil and gas production."[9]

Not one of the governments that voted for the Paris Agreement has acted to stop the deadly expansion of fossil fuel infrastructure in the 2020s. Some are going in the opposite direction, eagerly selling new licenses for exploration and extraction. In North America in 2025, the liberal Canadian government cancelled carbon taxes and planned new pipelines, while to their south, the Trump regime withdrew from the Paris Agreement and radically reduced environmental regulations:

> The warmer the globe became, the more fossil fuels were poured on the fire. The higher the temperatures, the larger the emissions. The closer the earth came to being engulfed in flames—literally and figuratively—the harder companies worked to get oil and gas and coal out of the ground and ferry them off to combustion. . . .
>
> Investing in new fossil fuel infrastructure in the third decade of the Millennium represented not merely moral madness: it was madness without qualifier; madness in the original, clinical sense of the term. . . . Precisely because of the way the economy was constituted, some immoral, clinical madness held the future of the planet in its hands.[10]

In 1845, Frederick Engels wrote that he had never seen a class "so incurably debased by selfishness" as the English capitalists. "In the presence of this avarice and lust of gain it is not possible for a single human sentiment or opinion to remain untainted."

> I once went into Manchester with such a bourgeois, and spoke to him of the bad, unwholesome method of building,

the frightful condition of the working people's quarters, and asserted that I had never seen so ill-built a city. The man listened quietly to the end, and said at the corner where we parted: "And yet there is a great deal of money made here; good morning, sir."[11]

Like that Manchester bourgeois, the people who run fossil fuel companies, and their enablers in government, are quite aware of the damage they are causing. They know that the oil and gas they pump and the coal they dig are threatening humanity's future. As thousands of leaked documents prove, they've known that for decades.[12] They know that burning fossil fuels is causing the climate crisis; they know that global boiling won't stop unless we rapidly reduce and then eliminate fossil fuel combustion. A fraction of their immense wealth, spent wisely, would put a big dent in the problem.

The same is true of the agribusiness tycoons. They know that they are producing and selling more than twice as much synthetic nitrogen as the planet can safely absorb; that soil health is declining; that their plantations, synthetic fertilizers, and pesticides are killing wildlife; that industrial agriculture harms crops, livestock, and consumers.

But we are ruled by capitalism's anti-ecological logic. Commodities must be sold, profits must be made, capital must accumulate. Short-term corporate gains are more important than long-term social losses. Capitalism, in short, is incompatible with the maintenance of the conditions that have made human civilization possible for more than ten thousand years.

The polluters have immense wealth and power. They have most of the world's politicians on their side. They are supported by media propagandists who constantly tell us that there is no alternative. They have a psychopathic determination to maximize their profits no matter what the cost.

But, if I may slightly paraphrase Shelley, we are many, they are few. The thousands at the top of the wealth pyramid depend on the labor and acquiescence of the billions beneath them, and if we choose to resist, they will not last long. Genuine social and ecological change will only come about when millions of working people demand it, fight for it in the streets, and build this world anew by their own power.

As John Bellamy Foster says:

> The only thing that could alter this dire situation, all over the world, is the rise of *another power* in society. We need not millions but hundreds of millions of people, necessarily predominantly working class, in the street day in and day out. There has to be a shift in tactics toward active noncooperation. Mere mass demonstrations, as important as they are, will no longer do the job in this situation....
>
> What is needed is an independent, revolutionary groundswell aimed at the reconstitution of production and consumption in the society, at least to the degree necessary to prevent society from reaching the point of no return with respect to climate change—though the ultimate aims would need to go beyond that. It will have to be internationalist, which means anti-imperialist in character, since global unity of the oppressed, encompassing the many forms of oppression is the *sine qua non* of the movement.[13]

Some components of such a movement can be seen today. Some trade unions are moving away from years of bureaucratic inaction and actually organizing in workplaces. Environmental protests around the world have drawn millions into the streets. La Via Campesina has mobilized hundreds of thousands of peasants and farm workers for land reform.

Indigenous peoples are playing leading roles. As Nick Estes of the Lower Brule Sioux writes:

> Indigenous peoples must lead the way. Our history and long traditions of Indigenous resistance provide possibilities for

futures premised on justice. After all, Indigenous resistance is animated by our ancestors' refusal to be forgotten, and it is our resolute refusal to forget our ancestors and our history that animates our vision for liberation. . . . Whereas past revolutionary struggles have strived for the emancipation of labor from capital, we are challenged not just to imagine, but to demand the emancipation of the earth from capital. For the earth to live, capitalism must die.[14]

Most of our battles are, and will continue to be, for local and partial gains. That's inevitable. If we can't stop a pipeline or the bulldozing of a forest, why would we think we can change the world? More important, why would millions join a movement that doesn't offer real possibilities of concrete gains? Some objectives might include:

- Expand the commons by decommodifying the essentials of life. Food, shelter, health care, education—all should be free, as human rights.
- Close down the fossil fuel industry. Replace private automobiles with free, electric public transportation systems.
- Pay the South-North ecological debt in full. Provide unconditional financial and material support to the people of the world who suffer most from climate change.
- Return farming to working farmers who grow food for local and nearby communities using ecologically sound practices. Raise crops and animals together.
- Expropriate agribusiness. Put control of seeds, fertilizers, and other farm inputs under the democratic control of farmers. Promote efficient and safe nutrient recycling and reduce nitrogen and phosphorus production to within safe planetary boundaries.
- Ban single-use plastics and all other chemical products that nature cannot absorb and recycle.
- Close all military operations at home and elsewhere. Transform

armies into voluntary teams charged with restoring ecosystems and assisting the victims of environmental disasters.
- Restructure existing extraction, production, and distribution systems to eliminate waste, planned obsolescence, pollution, and commercial advertising. Provide full retraining and job opportunities to all affected workers and communities.

That's far from a complete list, and not all would apply everywhere or be implemented in the same ways. What we need now is not a universal ecosocialist checklist, but rather concrete actions that lead toward what scientists refer to as "deliberate management of humanity's relationship with the rest of the Earth System,"[15] and that Karl Marx described as

> the associated producers, govern[ing] the human metabolism with nature in a rational way, bringing it under their collective control instead of being dominated by it as a blind power; accomplishing it with the least expenditure of energy and in conditions most worthy and appropriate for their human nature.[16]

What's needed is not reorganized capitalism, but what Fred Magdoff has called "a truly ecological civilization—one that exists in harmony with natural systems . . . the opposite of capitalism in essentially all respects." It is impossible to know exactly how the future civilization will develop, but to be ecologically sound, it must do the following:

> (1) provide a decent human existence for everyone: food, clean water, sanitation, health care, housing, clothing, education, and cultural and recreational possibilities; (2) eliminate the domination or control of humans by others; (3) develop worker and community control of factories, farms, and other workplaces; (4) promote easy recall of elected personnel; and (5) re-create the unity between humans and natural systems in

all aspects of life, including agriculture, industry, transportation, and living conditions.[17]

We should not underestimate just how great a challenge this is, how big the change will have to be, how difficult it will be, or how long it will take.

More than fifty years ago, Barry Commoner thought the necessary changes needed in the United States alone would require "most of the nation's resources for capital investment . . . for at least a generation."[18] Given the rapid growth and spread of destructive industries and technologies since then, and the even greater destruction that capitalism has caused in the Global South, we should expect the cost and time to be many times greater.

The necessary changes will take decades, in circumstances we can't predict. We need to focus on getting to the starting point. In 1893, William Morris, a pioneer of revolutionary socialism and environmentalism, described the starting point this way:

> The first real victory of the Social Revolution will be the establishment not indeed of a complete system of communism in a day, which is absurd, but of a revolutionary administration whose *definite and conscious aim* will be to prepare and further, in all available ways, human life for such a system.[19]

We could combine that with Fred Magdoff's terminology to summarize the central goal of ecosocialist movements today: "A revolutionary administration whose definite and conscious aim will be to prepare and further, in all available ways, human life for an ecological civilization."

That kind of governance won't come about just because it is the right thing to do. Good ideas are not enough. Moral authority isn't enough. The only way to overcome the forces that now rule, the forces of global destruction, is to organize a countervailing force that can stop them and remove them from power.

In every country, we need governments that break with the

existing order, that are answerable only to working people, farmers, the poor, indigenous communities, and immigrants—in a word, to the victims of ecocidal capitalism, not its beneficiaries and representatives.

What's needed, in short, is an *ecosocialist revolution*.

Marx and Engels posed an alternative: the class struggle would lead either to "a revolutionary reconstitution of society at large" or to "the common ruin of the contending classes."[20]

In this century of environmental crisis, the balance has tilted toward the common ruin of all. The destruction of civilization is a very real possibility that can only be prevented by a mass movement that bridges the gap between the spontaneous anger of millions of people and the revolutionary changes that are so desperately needed.

The late Del Weston powerfully posed the choice we face in the final paragraphs of her brilliant book, *The Political Economy of Global Warming*:

> We can choose to fiddle while the globe burns, to be afraid to be called alarmists, to be secure in the knowledge that we in the West will not be so immediately and devastatingly affected by global warming. That however would leave us morally bankrupt and living in a sea of chaos on a stricken planet.
>
> The task is monumental and complex. The lives of billions of current and future generations of people who share a finite planet, enveloped and interconnected through a thin layer of fragile biosphere—our global commons—are at stake. Any addressing of this task demands that we heal the deep structural chasm that has developed in the metabolic relations between humans and between humans and nature as a result of the social relations of production inherent in the capitalist system.
>
> We can do this by building new political, economic and cultural systems and societies that are metabolically restorative, equitable, resilient, just, diverse and democratic. It is a

challenge that could bring the different peoples of the world together, to build something better together and make history for the benefit of all people. We cannot afford not to try, nor to fail.[21]

I could not agree more.

APPENDIX 1

Metabolism: Lost in Translation?

If metabolism was an important ecological concept for Marx and Engels, why did twentieth-century Marxists take so long to realize it?

There are two answers to that question.

The first was offered in a different context by Rosa Luxemburg in 1903. Marx's work was so wide-ranging and ahead of its time, she wrote, that aspects of it are not recognized as important until the actual class struggle catches up with him. Often, "our needs are not yet adequate for the utilization of Marx's ideas." When new circumstances arise, then, for "the solution of new practical problems . . . we dip into the treasury of Marx's thought, in order to extract therefrom and to utilize new fragments of his doctrine."[1]

The relevance of that insight to Marx's ecology is clear. For most of the twentieth century, socialists didn't find Marx's environmental views because they didn't look for them. It wasn't until the last decades of the twentieth century that global environmental crises and the rise of new environmental movements prompted interest in Marx's views on nature.

The second answer, particularly important for socialists who don't read German or aren't familiar with the natural sciences, is bad translation.

The German word for metabolism is *Stoffwechsel*. Like many German nouns, it combines two root words—*stoff* means substance or material, *wechsel* means exchange—but the combination means something greater than the sum of its parts, as the definition in an 1844 medical encyclopedia shows:

> By *Stoffwechsel* is meant the conversion of body substance into other forms and the rapid production of new and precisely similar body structures by means of the constant supplying of nourishing materials.[2]

The word was used by German scientists as early as 1815, but there was no English equivalent. The word *metabolism*, from the Greek *metabolismos*, meaning change or overthrow, wasn't adopted by English scientists until the late 1870s, and even then, only specialists knew or used it.

So instead of "metabolism," translators rendered the parts of *Stoffweschel* literally, as some variant of exchange of material, or circulation of matter.

The problem is evident in the English translation of Justus von Liebig's influential 1840 book, *Organic Chemistry in Its Applications to Agriculture and Physiology*. A passage in that book refers to "metabolism in blood, the changes in the substance of the existing organs," and to "every organic action being attended by metabolism." But in the 1840 English edition, the same words were translated as "the different changes in the blood," and "a change in the material of the body."[3] Literally correct, but far from clear!

Capital's first translators—Samuel Moore and Edward Aveling for Volume 1, Ernest Untermann for Volume 3—either didn't know the word *metabolism* or didn't know that was what *Stoffwechsel* meant. As a result, their literal translations distorted the meaning of Marx's words. It wasn't until the 1970s that new translations by Ben Fowkes and David Fernbach brought Marx's actual meaning to the fore.

These comparisons illustrate the improvement:

Capital, Volume 1

1888 translation: "Capitalist production . . . disturbs the circulation of matter between man and the soil . . . while upsetting the naturally grown conditions for the maintenance of that circulation of matter, it imperiously calls for its restoration as a regulating law of social production, and under a form appropriate to the full development of the human race."[4]

1976 translation: "Capitalist production . . . disturbs the metabolic interaction between man and the earth . . . by destroying the circumstances surrounding that metabolism, which originated in a merely natural and spontaneous fashion, it compels its systematic restoration as a regulative law of social production, and in a form adequate to the full development of the human race."[5]

Capital, Volume 3

1909 translation: "In this way it creates conditions, which cause an incurable break in the interconnections of the social circulation of matter prescribed by the natural laws of life."[6]
1981 translation: "Large landed property . . . produces conditions that provoke an irreparable rift in the interdependent process of social metabolism, a metabolism prescribed by the natural laws of life itself."[7]

Metabolism involves complex cyclical processes and organic transformations that "circulation" and "interchange" entirely miss. Readers who only had access to the early translations can be forgiven for not recognizing the ecological implications of those passages.

A new translation of *Capital, Volume 1*, published in 2024, changes "the metabolic interaction between man and the earth" to "the metabolizing that goes on between human beings and the earth." In my view, that loses some clarity, but it is still better than the 1888 text.[8]

Literal translation has also affected Marxist works written in Russian, and this has subsequently influenced English works. Russian scientists simply translated the German root words into a phrase, *obmen veshhestv* (обмен веществ), which literally means exchange of substances.

They usually enclosed the words in quotation marks to signal that the literal meaning wasn't intended, but it seems that many Russian-English translators don't know that *obmen veshhestv* is the scientific term for "metabolism." As a result, English translations of

Lenin, Plekhanov, Bukharin, Ilyenkov, and other Russian Marxists feature "exchange of substances" rather than the more accurate and comprehensible "metabolism."

In recent decades, most Russian scientific publications have used метаболизм instead of *obmen veshhestv*—that should reduce confusion, at least for translators.

APPENDIX 2
Has the Anthropocene Been Cancelled?

An overwhelming volume of evidence indicates that a new stage in Earth System history has begun, one characterized by major changes to many aspects of the natural world, heading toward conditions that humans may not survive. Scientists have demonstrated that many of the changes are irreversible on any human time scale. They have dated the beginning of this radical transformation to the mid-twentieth century. They have also shown that physical records of the change can be seen in geological strata.

One might reasonably question whether Anthropocene is the best name for it. But to any reasonable observer, the case that a new epoch has begun is irrefutable.

And yet some prominent scientists deny that a qualitative change has occurred, and one of the world's largest scientific organizations has voted against formal recognition of the new epoch. The research and debates that led to this perverse result help to illuminate the challenges facing scientists and ecosocialists in our time.

The end of the Holocene was first declared and recognized by Earth System scientists, not geologists, but Holocene is a *geological* term: It names the last 11,700 years, the most recent stage in the planet's geological history. It is an epoch in the Geological Time Scale, which was created to ensure that all geologists have a common understanding of the stages of Earth's physical history and use the same terms to describe it. Any change to the Geological Time Scale must be formally approved by the International Commission on Stratigraphy (ICS) and the International Union of Geological Sciences (IUGS), both of which are notoriously conservative and resistant to change.

Not until 2009 did the ICS ask palaeobiologist Jan Zalasiewicz of the UK's University of Leicester to chair a working group to investigate and report on whether geologists should formally recognize the Anthropocene as a new epoch.

The Anthropocene Working Group had to start from scratch: past working groups could base their deliberations on decades of existing research, but no one had yet looked for geological evidence of a break between the Holocene and a possible new epoch. In the years following the formation of the AWG, geologists worldwide conducted dozens of research projects on the subject, with results published in peer-reviewed journals and in books edited by AWG members.

There was an immense amount of data and analysis to assimilate, especially since the group was small and its members were unpaid volunteers. However, by 2015 they had accumulated and evaluated a mass of geological evidence—strong physical indicators that a radical change was underway. An article summarizing that evidence was published in the journal *Science* in January 2016:

> The appearance of manufactured materials in sediments, including aluminum, plastics, and concrete, coincides with global spikes in fallout radionuclides and particulates from fossil fuel combustion. Carbon, nitrogen, and phosphorus cycles have been substantially modified over the past century. Rates of sea-level rise and the extent of human perturbation of the climate system exceed Late Holocene changes. Biotic changes include species invasions worldwide and accelerating rates of extinction. These combined signals render the Anthropocene stratigraphically distinct from the Holocene and earlier epochs. . . .
>
> The stratigraphic signatures described above are either entirely novel with respect to those found in the Holocene and preexisting epochs or quantitatively outside the range of variation of the proposed Holocene subdivisions. Furthermore, most proximate forcings of these signatures are currently accelerating. These distinctive attributes of the recent geological record support the formalization of the Anthropocene as a stratigraphic entity equivalent to other formally defined geological epochs. The boundary should therefore be placed

following the procedures of the International Commission on Stratigraphy.[1]

The AWG concluded, by an overwhelming majority, that a new geological epoch began in about 1950, and that the best stratigraphic signal for the beginning of the new epoch was the presence of plutonium isotopes, created and spread by the atmospheric Hydrogen bomb tests that the United States and the Soviet Union conducted between 1952 and 1963.

Twelve locations on five continents were studied in detail for suitability as reference sites. The onset of the Anthropocene could be clearly identified in all twelve, but the researchers selected Crawford Lake in southwestern Ontario as the best location for a "golden spike." For centuries, unique conditions there have preserved annual layers of sediment, including undisturbed layers containing plutonium. Three other locations, in Japan, China, and Poland, were selected as auxiliary sites.

Opposition

The most common argument against declaring the new epoch was that human beings have always changed the environment, so the Anthropocene is nothing new. Late in the geological debate, this argument took the form of a proposal that the Anthropocene should be considered an informal "event" spanning thousands of years. In that framework, the Great Acceleration was at most an intensification of long-term continuing changes, not a qualitative shift.[2]

AWG members replied, "The Anthropocene is de facto a new epoch, not an encapsulation of all anthropogenic impacts in Earth history." Indeed, that idea "runs counter to the Anthropocene's central meaning," by extending it to all human-induced changes over thousands of years and ignoring "the abrupt human-driven shift to a new Earth System state that has exceeded the natural variability of the Holocene."[3]

In short, the "event" proposal preserved the word but erased its fundamental meaning and radical content.

Other arguments against formalizing the Anthropocene ranged from trivial (the name isn't appropriate; the idea comes from outside geology; other epochs are longer) to insulting (this whole thing is just about getting publicity). In 2017, members of the AWG assembled the published arguments against the Anthropocene and prepared responses to each. The resulting article was polite and collegial but nonetheless devastating. It left the critics with no scientific basis for continued opposition.[4]

And yet, as Jan Zalasiewicz later wrote: "Neither this strengthened evidence base, nor further evidence subsequently gathered, did anything to diminish the outright opposition to the Anthropocene from a minority of AWG members and their colleagues."

> This suggested that this opposition and that of others in the ICS—the strong opposition of the highly influential ICS Chair, Stanley Finney, was a significant factor—even when responded to and countered was not based on the amount and quality of stratigraphic evidence. Rather, it seemed to reflect more deep-seated aspects of the chronostratigraphically proposed Anthropocene. . . .
>
> Evidence-based refutations did nothing to prevent further reiterations of the "event" suggestion, again suggesting that the body of stratigraphic evidence assembled by the AWG was of little relevance to the central question of whether an Anthropocene epoch should exist at all. The Anthropocene clearly touches nerves that more ancient strata do not reach.[5]

In November 2023, when the AWG submitted its formal proposal to recognize the new epoch, it also submitted a complaint to the Geoethics Commission, charging that the executives of the International Commission on Stratigraphy and the International Union of Geological Sciences had deliberately hindered and undermined their work. The Commission reportedly supported the complaint and recommended that no vote be held. The IUGS appears to have ignored the recommendation.

If normal procedures had been followed, the AWG submission should have initiated a period of open discussion. Instead, in March 2024, the AWG's proposal was abruptly voted down after a brief discussion in a closed-door setting. The IUGS did not reply to the AWG submission; it simply announced its rejection.

We can only speculate about the motives that led to this preposterous decision. However, as archeologists Todd Braje and Jon Erlandson have pointed out, this debate "has the potential to influence public opinions and policies related to critical issues such as climate change, extinctions, modern human–environmental interactions, population growth, and sustainability."[6] In that respect, it is surely relevant that geology—a science deeply implicated in the discovery and exploitation of fossil fuels—has been, shall we say, conservative on the question of climate change.

In 2016, the chair of the International Commission on Stratigraphy charged that "the drive to officially recognize the Anthropocene may, in fact, be political rather than scientific."[7] The opposite seems more likely, that opposition to the Anthropocene is political, not scientific. Certainly, he and his colleagues have ensured that no one can use the prestige of the ICS and IUGS in support of decisive action to prevent climate chaos. The price paid for that political victory is a defeat for geology's credibility—the Geological Time Scale no longer accurately reflects Earth history.

The Anthropocene Working Group has not gone away. It continues to operate as an independent group and has published several important papers since the ICS and IUGS rulings.[8] Like Charles Darwin in another time, they are challenging a scientific establishment that is bent on protecting an unscientific worldview—a difficult but essential contribution to the advancement of science.

Eight years before the top bureaucrats in organized geology made their decision, I closed a summary of Anthropocene debates with these words:

It is still possible that the usually conservative international Commission on stratigraphy will either reject, or decide to defer, any decision on adding the Anthropocene to the geological time scale, but as the AWG majority writes, "The Anthropocene already has a robust geological basis, is in widespread use, and indeed is becoming a central, integrating concept in the consideration of global change."

In other words, failure to win a formal vote will not make the Anthropocene go away.[9]

Since I wrote that, the volume and persuasiveness of the evidence have only grown. The highest temperatures in human history, species extinctions on an unprecedented scale, a global glut of plastics and synthetic chemicals that nature can't absorb, multiple pandemics of previously unknown diseases—these and many more crises confirm that massive disruption of Earth's life support systems is underway, in a new and deadlier stage of planetary history.

The Anthropocene may not be official, but it is real.

APPENDIX 3

Can CO_2 Removal Cool the Planet?

> Belief in the omnipotence of technology is the specific form of bourgeois ideology in late capitalism.
>
> —ERNEST MANDEL[1]

In October 2018, responding to a request from the UN climate conference that adopted the Paris Agreement, the Intergovernmental Panel on Climate Change (IPCC) published a *Special Report on Global Warming of 1.5°C*. The report concluded that emissions to that date were not enough to cause a 1.5°C increase, but "lack of global cooperation, lack of governance of the required energy and land transformation, and increases in resource-intensive consumption" mean that emissions will continue, inexorably driving up the temperature.[2]

Accepting that immediate or very rapid reductions will not occur, the authors developed a series of alternative scenarios, all of which would require extensive deployment of carbon dioxide removal technology to make up for the failure. To completely prevent overshoot, the report's *Summary for Policy Makers* says, Carbon Dioxide Removal technology would have to remove between one hundred and one thousand billion tons of CO_2 by 2100. Looking at the report itself, it appears that the actual requirement would likely be close to the high end of that range.

This dependence on large-scale CDR calls the entire scenario exercise into question. As the report admits:

> No proposed technology is close to deployment at scale, and regulatory frameworks are not established. This limits how they can be realistically implemented. . . . There is substantial uncertainty about the adverse effects of large-scale CDR deployment on the environment and societal sustainable development goals.[3]

Nevertheless, policymakers in every country have accepted the fossil fuel industry's argument that it is not practical to reduce emissions rapidly, and assume that some means of pulling CO_2 back out of the air faster than it is emitted will be invented in time.

The Economist, authoritative voice of free market capitalism, tells us that passing 1.5 °C "does not doom the planet . . . but it is a death sentence for some people, ways of life, ecosystems, even countries." And for that reason, "Technologies to suck carbon dioxide out of the atmosphere, now in their infancy, need a lot of attention."[4]

The editors of *The CDR Primer* argue that while priority should be given to cutting emissions, CDR must be deployed at the same time, because some industries will be unable to get to zero, "even with a massive global effort to cut climate pollution."

> The scale of such emissions requires a massive investment in CDR, likely on the order of gigatons of CO_2 removed per year by mid-century. Even larger amounts would have to be removed to draw down atmospheric concentrations from their peak after we reach net-zero global emissions.[5]

That may be what we need, but what is actually possible?

If anthropogenic greenhouse gas emissions continue, temperatures will rise unless concentration increases are matched by removals, which would require removing billions of tons of gas every year. Setting aside the obvious barriers of politics and cost, what physical requirements would have to be met for CDR to stop or (better) reverse global boiling?

Atmospheric Carbon Dioxide Removal: A Physical Science Perspective, a peer-reviewed scientific study published in January by the American Physical Society (APS), provides an authoritative response to that question, and it isn't encouraging.[6] Quite apart from the problem of permanently and safely storing captured CO_2, which the study doesn't address, the scale of the problem is forbidding.

Carbon dioxide capture at oil refineries, where the gas is highly concentrated, has existed on a limited scale for decades. The CO_2 is most often used for "enhanced oil recovery," forcing still more carbon-emitting oil out of the ground.

Technologies for removing carbon dioxide from the open air, on the other hand, are new and untested. There are only a few dozen operating systems, and all are tiny, compared to the task at hand. The authors of the APS report examine a dozen proposed technologies, focusing in particular on scaling—how big can they get? While none is adequate today, three appear to have promise: direct air capture, biological carbon capture, and enhanced rock weathering.

Direct Air Capture (DAC)

DAC gets the most press. You've likely seen pictures of demonstration plants, with giant fans that blow air through chemical filters that absorb carbon dioxide. When the filters are saturated, the CO_2 is extracted, and the chemical is reused.

The best-publicized DAC installation is the Climeworks project in Iceland, whose founder predicted that it would capture 1 percent of the world's annual CO_2 emissions by 2025. It has sold thousands of $250 per month "carbon removal credits" each supposedly representing a quarter of a ton (250 kilograms) of captured CO_2.[7] In fact, as an investigative report in the Icelandic newspaper *Heimildin* showed in May 2025, it has captured only 2,400 tons *in total* since 2021. Its own emissions are much higher than that.[8]

To be fair, the technical challenge facing DAC is enormous. Today's level of CO_2 is enough to significantly change the world's climate but in absolute terms it is a tiny fraction of the atmosphere—carbon dioxide comprises only 0.062 percent of the air's weight, only 0.04 percent of its volume. To remove one ton of CO_2, a perfectly efficient Direct Air Capture system would have to process two thousand tons of air.[9]

As the APS report notes, if we outfitted every air conditioning unit in the world with devices enabling the complete capture of all CO_2 in the air flowing through them, they would remove less than a billion tons a year.[10] Just stabilizing the global temperature would require over 15 times as much equipment; turning the heat down would require much more.

We're told that the technology will improve over time—just look at the exponential improvements in semiconductors, for example—but DAC faces a limitation that computers don't: the second law of thermodynamics. First formulated by German physicist Rudolf Clausius in 1850, the law states that all systems become more disordered over time. Entropy (disorder) increases, and the only way to reverse it is by adding energy from outside. That's not speculation—it is as solid a physical law as any ever discovered. There are no exceptions.

CO_2 molecules in the air are highly disordered, scattered randomly among vastly more molecules of nitrogen, oxygen, and other gases. The second law of thermodynamics allows physicists to calculate, with great accuracy, how much energy would be needed to capture all the CO_2 molecules in a given amount of air and consolidate them in one place.

The calculation applies no matter what technology is used, because we're only measuring how much more energy there is in the consolidated output than in disordered atmospheric CO_2. That's the *minimum* amount of outside energy needed in a perfectly efficient process—real-world processes will require more, usually much more.

Fortunately for the equation-averse, the APS authors have done the calculation for us. Removing one ton of CO_2 from the atmosphere, in a perfect system, requires 120 kilowatt hours of energy. Someone once said that the Second Law doesn't tell you what you can do, it tells you what can't be done. In this case, it isn't saying that you can capture a ton of CO_2 with 120 kilowatts—it is saying that you can't do it with less, regardless of the technology you use.

Scaling up, that means that removing one billion tons a year would require a minimum of 14 billion watts of electricity, twenty-four hours a day, all year, which today would mostly come from CO_2-emitting power plants. Realistically, less-than-perfect CDR would require three to ten times that much energy to remove one billion tons—enough to power New York City several times over, while adding tons of CO_2 to the atmosphere.

Removing the hundreds of billions of tons needed to get Earth's temperature back to Holocene levels would require a very large fraction of the world's energy supply, to the point where it would limit our ability to carry out other energy-hungry programs, including feeding children and combating pandemic diseases.

For Direct Air Capture's contribution to reducing atmospheric CO_2 levels to be more than marginal, there would have to be massive improvements in DAC technology itself, and qualitative leaps in the capacity and efficiency of solar energy systems, so that every DAC installation can have its own high-output zero-carbon solar power plant. Neither is likely to occur in time to prevent dangerous global warming.

Bioenergy with Carbon Capture and Storage (BECCS)

Can we get around the Second Law limit by using natural energy over a longer time? For example, there is enthusiasm in some circles about Bioenergy with Carbon Capture and Storage, which would involve growing crops or trees, then burning them to produce electricity while capturing and burying the released CO_2. Trees naturally remove atmospheric CO_2 using energy from the sun (essentially a free and unlimited source), and the CO_2 at the point of burning would be easier to capture because it would be highly concentrated.

The world's largest BECCS operation, the Drax Power Station in the UK, says it will capture eight million tons of CO_2 a year by 2030, about 3 percent of the UK's annual emissions, but that is misleading. Drax doesn't burn trees that were purpose-grown in Britain—it imports and burns wood pellets manufactured overseas, including hundreds of thousands of tons a year made from old-growth forests in central British Columbia.[11] In other words, Drax is "capturing" CO_2 that was already stored in some of the world's most magnificent forests.

What's more, the Drax plant itself is the largest CO_2 emitter in Britain, pumping twelve million tons into the atmosphere every year. International carbon accounting rules give it a free pass on the specious grounds that the forests will regrow. Hence, their wood is a renewable fuel.

Leaving such scams aside, the physicists' report points out that for a BECCS system that grows new trees, "the low efficiency of photosynthesis in converting energy to biomass . . . means that a lot of land would be required. . . . This land use would compete with existing agriculture and biodiversity efforts."[12]

In IPCC scenarios for keeping the global temperature increase below 1.5°C that include BECCS, energy crops would occupy at least 20 percent of all the world's arable land by 2050, and much more if BECSS is the primary method used. Environmentalists have pointed out that such a massive change in land use would risk "compromising planetary health in areas besides climate change."[13] At each step—planting, fertilizing, harvesting, transporting, burning, and burying—BECCS emits its own greenhouse gases. The Natural Resources Defense Council calculates that if current plans go ahead, by 2040, "emissions from BECCS alone are projected to surpass the U.K.'s total emissions from all other sources."[14]

In short, BECCS will do more environmental harm than good. The European Academies' Science Advisory Council recently told the European Union:

> The role of bioenergy with carbon capture and storage (BECCS) remains associated with substantial risks and uncertainties, both over its environmental impact and ability to achieve net removal of CO_2 from the atmosphere. The large negative emissions capability given to BECCS in climate scenarios limiting warming to 1.5°C or 2°C is not supported by recent analyses. . . .
>
> Deployment of BECCS at the scale in IPCC models could

potentially help mitigate climate change, but at the expense of further exceeding the planetary boundaries related to biosphere integrity, land use and biogeochemical flows, while bringing freshwater use closer to its boundary. . . . BECCS remains associated with substantial risks and uncertainties, both over its environmental impact and ability to achieve net removal of CO_2 from the atmosphere.[15]

Enhanced Rock Weathering (ERW)

In the slow carbon cycle, a key part of the Earth System's metabolism for hundreds of millions of years, exposed rocks combine with atmospheric carbon dioxide to form stable minerals that don't affect the climate. That weathering process naturally removes about a billion tons of CO_2 a year—it is one of the factors that has kept global warming lower than total emissions could otherwise cause.

Proposals have been made to accelerate the process by grinding tons of rock into tiny particles, about one-fifth the width of an average human hair, and spreading them over large areas of land. That would greatly increase the exposed rock surfaces and—some scientists hope—greatly increase the amount of CO_2 removed. Since the United States and other countries already mine and transport very large quantities of ground rock for other purposes, no new technology would be needed, and the energy cost would be much lower than for DAC or BECCS.

It would require a lot of land—an estimated one million square kilometers to remove a billion tons of CO_2 a year—but unlike BECSS, it isn't exclusive use. Ground rock can have fertilizing effects, so it could be spread on existing farmland, depending on local soil characteristics.

It's important to note that the ground rock can only be used once. To keep the removal process working, billions of tons of additional rock will have to be extracted, ground, transported, and spread every year. Nothing even close to that scale has ever been done, and even if it were attempted, no one knows how long removal might take, or how to measure the results.

Ocean Alkalinity Enhancement

Several methods have been proposed for increasing the amount of CO_2 that dissolves in the oceans. The most likely option involves spreading gigatons of ground alkaline minerals on the surface: In theory, they will combine with dissolved CO_2 to create a carbonate that sinks into the deeps, thus freeing the surface water to absorb more CO_2 from the air. The APS Report points out that "many aspects of the ocean chemistry and biological impacts of this approach are poorly understood."

For fossil fuel corporations, keeping CDR on the agenda as a credible climate change solution is a "Get Out of Jail Free" card. Instead of stopping emissions, they promise to capture and bury them. Not now, but someday. As the CEO of Occidental Petroleum told a conference of her peers in 2023, "We believe that our direct capture technology is going to be the technology that helps to preserve our industry over time. This gives our industry a license to continue to operate for the 60, 70, 80 years that I think it's going to be very much needed."[16]

Carbon Dioxide Removal schemes have justly been described as "technologies of prevarication." As Duncan McLaren and Nils Markusson of the Lancaster Environment Centre write, they are the latest in a series of "imagined technologies" that have been promoted "in an ongoing cycle that repeatedly avoids transformative social and economic change."

> Each technological promise has enabled a continued politics of prevarication and inadequate action by raising expectations of more effective policy options becoming available in the future. . . .
>
> Each promise has, to some degree, fed systemic "moral corruption" in which current elites are enabled to pursue

self-serving pathways while passing off risk to vulnerable people in the future and in the Global South. . . .

That for the most part these policies promised future action, rather than immediate sacrifice, clearly made them more palatable to both industry and politicians.[17]

In 2025, the United Nations Environment Program warned that global emissions must be cut by 42 percent by 2030 and 57 percent by 2035 to keep warming under 1.5 degrees.[18] Achieving that, or anything close to it, would require an emergency action program to stop all new extraction of fossil fuels and rapidly phase out major sources of emissions. That's where our focus must be now, not on speculative technologies that might work one day, but now only give polluters a license to continue polluting.

Notes

Internet addresses change frequently, so I have only included them in cases where it might be particularly difficult to find a source with a search engine. Google Scholar may be the best tool for finding articles in academic journals.

The fifty-volume *Marx Engels Collected Works*, published between 1975 and 2004 by Progress Publishers (Moscow) and International Publishers (New York), is abbreviated as *MECW*.

For the three volumes of Marx's *Capital*, I have in most cases used the better-translated Penguin editions rather than *MECW*.

Introduction
1. Marx to Ferdinand Lassalle, January 16, 1861, *MECW*, vol. 41, 246–47.
2. Marx to Engels, February 13, 1866. *MECW*, vol. 42, 227.
3. *MECW*, vol. 3, 276.
4. Andreas Malm, *The Progress of This Storm: Nature and Society in a Warming World* (Verso, 2018), 177.
5. Ian Angus, *A Redder Shade of Green* (Monthly Review Press, 2017), 8.

1. We Are Not the Owners of the Earth
1. V. I. Lenin, Our Programme (1899), *Collected Works*, vol. 4, 211.
2. Lucretius, *On the Nature of Things*, prose translation of *De Rerum Natura* by John Selby Watson (Henry Bohn, 1851), 15.
3. Quoted in D. G. Irving, *The Protein Myth* (John Hunt, 2011), 188.
4. Theodore Schwann, quoted in Stephen F. Mason, *A History of the Sciences* (Colliers, 1962), 389.

5. Franklin C. Bing, "The Origin of the Word 'Metabolism,'" *Journal of the History of Medicine*, April 1971: 158–80.
6. Daniels's influence on Marx's thought is discussed in Kohei Saito, *Karl Marx's Ecosocialism* (Monthly Review Press, 2017), 72–74.
7. Karl Marx, *Capital*, vol.1 (Penguin, 1976 [1867]), 637; Marx, *Capital*, vol. 3 (Penguin, 1981 [1895]), 949.
8. Karl Marx, *Grundrisse: Foundations of the Critique of Political Economy (Rough Draft)*, trans. Martin Nicolaus (Penguin, 1973), 489. Emphasis in original.
9. Marx to Engels, February 13, 1866. *MECW*, vol. 42, 227.
10. Karl Marx, *Capital*, vol. 1, 637.
11. Karl Marx, *Capital*, vol. 3, 195.
12. Frederick Engels, "The Housing Question, Part Three," *MECW*, 384, 337.
13. Hal Draper, *Karl Marx's Theory of Revolution*, vol. I: *State and Bureaucracy*, 24
14. Frederick Engels, *Anti-Dühring* (Bejing: Foreign Languages Publishing House, 1976), 103. This translation is much better than the one in *MECW*.
15. Frederick Engels, *Dialectics of Nature*, 196.
16. Ibid., 291–92.
17. Karl Marx, *Capital*, vol. 3, 959.
18. John Bellamy Foster, "A Failed System," *Monthly Review*, March 2009.
19. Karl Marx, *MECW*, vol. 37, 763. This translation is better than the Penguin edition, which uses *beneficiaries* instead of *usufructuaries*. The latter term, though obscure, correctly identifies the Roman legal concept Marx was referencing. A usufructuary has a legal right to enjoy the benefits of someone else's property without owning it.

2. Ecosocialist Tradition: Bebel, Kautsky, Bukharin

1. V. I. Lenin, *Collected Works*, vol. 4 (Progress Publishers, 1964), 94.
2. V. I. Lenin, "August Bebel" (August 8, 1913), https://www.marxists.org/archive/lenin/works/1913/aug/08.htm.
3. Eleanor Marx and Edward Aveling, "The Woman Question," *Westminster Review*, 1886. https://www.marxists.org/archive/eleanor-marx/works/womanq.htm.
4. The title is *Women and Socialism*, but the most widely circulated English editions, including the one I have used, title it "Women Under Socialism."
5. Jane McDermid and Anna Hillyar, *Midwives of the Revolution* (UCL Press, 1999), 37–38.

6. August Bebel, *Woman Under Socialism*, trans Daniel de Leon (Schocken Books, 1971), 284.
7. Ibid., 69.
8. Ibid., 313.
9. Ibid., 315.
10. Karl Kautsky, *The Agrarian Question*, trans. Pete Burgess (Zwan Publications, 1988), 12.
11. Ibid., 109.
12. Ibid., 59, emphasis in original.
13. Ibid., 52.
14. Ibid., 214.
15. Ibid., 52.
16. Ibid., 54.
17. Ibid., 215.
18. Ibid., 201.
19. Marx, *Capital*, vol. 1 (Penguin, 1976), 860n.
20. Kautsky, *Agrarian Question*, 209.
21. Ibid., 243, emphasis in original.
22. Ibid., 245.
23. Ibid., 245–46.
24. Ibid., 247–48.
25. Ibid., 249.
26. Ibid., 250.
27. Ibid., 251, 252.
28. Ibid., 145.
29. Ibid., 252.
30. Ibid., 335–36.
31. Ibid., 336.
32. Ibid., 217.
33. Ibid., 216.
34. Ibid., 401.
35. Ibid., 215.
36. Ibid., 217.
37. V. I. Lenin, *Collected Works*, vol. 5 (Progress Publishers, 1960), 155.
38. V. I. Lenin, *Collected Works*, vol. 6 (Progress Publishers, 1960), 345.
39. Loren R. Graham, *The Soviet Academy of Sciences and the Communist Party, 1927–1932* (Princeton University Press, 1967) 32–33.
40. Andy Byford, "Revolution and Science under the Bolsheviks," *Culture Matters*, Nov, 3, 2017. https://www.culturematters.org.uk/.
41. Douglas R. Weiner, *Models of Nature: Ecology, Conservation, and*

Cultural Revolution in Soviet Russia (University of Pittsburgh Press, 2000), viii.
42. Salvatore Engel-Di Mauro, *Socialist States and the Environment: Lessons for Ecosocialist Futures* (Pluto Press, 2021), 113.
43. "The Testament of Lenin," https://www.marxists.org/history/etol/newspape/ni/vol02/no01/lenin.htm.
44. Nikolai Bukharin, *Historical Materialism: A System of Sociology* (University of Michigan Press, 1969 [1921]), 65.
45. *Science At the Crossroads* (Moscow: Kniga Ltd., 1931), 7, 12.
46. Nikolai Bukharin, *Socialism and Its Culture*, trans. George Shriver (Seagull Books, 2006); *Philosophical Arabesques*, trans. Renfrey Clarke (Monthly Review Press, 2005).
47. Frederick Engels, *Anti-Dühring* (Progress Publishers, 1947), 147.
48. Helena Sheehan, "Introduction: A Voice From the Dead," in Bukharin, *Arabesques*, 17.
49. Bukharin, *Arabesques*, 100.
50. Ibid.,101.
51. Ibid.,114. Translation adjusted, per Appendix 1.
52. Ibid., 257.
53. Ibid., 264.
54. Ibid.
55. Ibid., 350.

3. Continuity Lost and Restored

1. Raymond Williams, "Socialism and Ecology" (1983), in *Resources of Hope* (Verso, 1989), 214–15
2. Anna Bramwell, *Ecology in the 20th Century: A History* (Yale University Press, 1992), 33–34.
3. E. F. Schumacher, *Small Is Beautiful: A Study of Economics as If People Mattered* (Blond & Briggs, 1973), 15
4. Barbara Harriss-White and Marco Boffo, "Ecology and the Environment," in *The Elgar Companion to Marxist Economics*, ed. Ben Fine and Alfredo Saad-Filho (Edward Elgar, 2013), 102.
5. Perry Anderson, *In the Tracks of Historical Materialism* (Verso, 1983), 83
6. In his history of Maoism in the United States, Max Elbaum says that groups in that current viewed environmentalism as "a backward distraction from the class struggle," and "were unable . . . to appreciate the significance of one of the most crucial issues and vital movements of the 1970s and beyond." Max Elbaum, *Revolution in the Air* (Verso, 2002), 139.
7. Barry Sheppard's detailed history of the Socialist Workers Party, the

largest U.S. Trotskyist group, mentions ecology only regarding articles in a party newspaper and doesn't mention participating in the environmental movement. Barry Sheppard, *The Party: the Socialist Workers Party, 1960–1988*. vol. 1 (Resistance Books, 2005), 251.
8. István Mészáros, *The Necessity of Social Control* (Monthly Review Press, 2015), 27, 49–50.
9. The *Oxford English Dictionary* did not include "ecosocialism" until 2008. Its first citation is the London *Times* in 1985. The word was then at least five years old.
10. Derek Wall, *Babylon and Beyond* (Pluto Press, 2005), 51.
11. Joel Kovel, *The Enemy of Nature* (Zed Books, 2002), 206, 211.
12. Joel Kovel, "A Materialism Worthy of Nature," *Capitalism Nature Socialism*, March 2001, 76.
13. James O'Connor, "The Second Contradiction of Capitalism," *Natural Causes: Essays in Ecological Marxism* (Guilford Press, 1998), 158–77.
14. Samir Amin, *Modern Imperialism, Monopoly Finance Capital, and Marx's Law of Value* (Monthly Review Press, 2018), 9.
15. Paul Burkett, *Marx and Nature: A Red and Green Perspective* (St. Martin's Press, 1999), 6,7.
16. Ibid.
17. Ibid., 196
18. John Bellamy Foster, *Marx's Ecology*, 20.
19. Foster, *Marx's Ecology*, 153.
20. Paul Burkett, *Marx and Nature*, 2nd ed. (Haymarket Books, 2014), xix–xx.
21. Kovel, *The Enemy of Nature* (Fernwood Publishing, 2002), 211.
22. Foster, "Foreword," to Burkett, *Marx and Nature*, 2nd ed., x–xi.
23. Saito, *Karl Marx's Ecosocialism*, 260.
24. Ibid.
25. Andreas Malm, *The Progress of This Storm*, 177.
26. Leigh Phillips, *Austerity Ecology & the Collapse-Porn Addicts* (Zero Books, 2015) 286n.
27. Jason W. Moore, *Capitalism in the Web of Life* (Verso, 2015), 75, 76; "Toward a Singular Metabolism," *New Geographies* 06 (2014), 13.
28. Paul Hampton, *Workers and Trade Unions for Climate Solidarity* (Routledge, 2015), 6.
29. Mackenzie Wark, "The Capitalocene," *Public Seminar*, October 15, 2015. http://www.publicseminar.org/2015/10/the-capitalocene/.
30. McKenzie Wark, *Molecular Red: Theory for the Anthropocene* (Verso, 2015), xiv.

31. Howard Waitzkin, *Second Sickness: Contradictions of Capitalist Health Care*, rev. ed. (Rowman & Littlefield, 2000), 7.
32. Andreas Malm, *The Progress of This Storm*, 177.

4. Six Revolutions that Made the Biosphere

1. Nikolai Bukharin, *Philosophical Arabesques* (Monthly Review Press, 2005), 242
2. Rachel Carson, *Silent Spring & Other Writings on the Environment* (Library of America, 2018), 476.
3. Lynn Margulis and Dorion Sagan, *What Is Life?* (University of California Press, 2000), 23–24.
4. National Research Council, *The Role of Theory in Advancing 21st-Century Biology: Catalyzing Transformative Research* (National Academies Press, 2008) 76, 74.
5. Vaclav Smil, *Cycles of Life: Civilization and the Biosphere* (Scientific American Library, 1997), ix.
6. Michael Jacobson, Robert Charlson, Henning Rodhe, Gordon Orians, *Earth System Science: From Biogeochemical Cycles to Global Change* (Elsevier Academic Press, 2000), 3–4.
7. All land-based and most ocean-based life. Single-celled organisms that live deep in the ocean and in Earth's crust draw chemical energy from the planet's internal heat.
8. Charles Darwin to Joseph D. Hooker, February 1, 1871.
9. Stephen Jay Gould, "Life on Mars? So What?," *New York Times*, August 11, 1996.
10. Tyler Volk, *Quarks to Culture: How We Came to Be* (Columbia University Press, 2017), 73.
11. Ibid., 73, 75.
12. Ibid., 79–80.
13. Nick Lane, *The Vital Question: Why is Life the Way It Is?* (Profile Books, 2015), 29.
14. Ibid.
15. Donald Canfield, *Oxygen: A Four Billion Year History* (Princeton University Press, 2014), 42.
16. Robert M. Hazen, *The Story of Earth: The First 4.5 Billion Years, from Stardust to Living Planet* (Penguin, 2013) 168, 151.
17. R. E. Kopp et al., "The Paleoproterozoic Snowball Earth: A climate disaster triggered by the evolution of oxygenic photosynthesis," *Proceedings of the National Academy of Sciences*, August 2005.

18. Lenton, *Earth System Science: A Very Short Introduction* (Oxford University Press, 2016), 69.
19. Nick Lane, *Oxygen: The Molecule that Made the World* (Oxford University Press, 2016), 150.
20. Lynn Margulis and Dorion Sagan, *Microcosmos: Four Billion Years of Microbial Evolution* (University of California Press, 1997), 117.
21. Nick Lane, *Power, Sex, Suicide: Mitochondria and the Meaning of Life* (Oxford University Press, 2005), 27.
22. Stephen Jay Gould, *Wonderful Life: The Burgess Shale and the Nature of History* (W. W. Norton, 1989), 58.
23. Charles Darwin, *The Origin of Species*, 6th ed. (Modern Library, 2009 [1872]), 438–39.
24. J. William Schopf, "Solution to Darwin's Dilemma: Discovery of the missing Precambrian record of life," *Proceedings of the National Academy of Science*, June 20, 2000.
25. Douglas H. Erwin and James W. Valentine, *The Cambrian Explosion: The Construction of Animal Biodiversity* (Roberts & Company, 2013), 5.
26. Paul Hoffmann et al., "A Neoproterozoic Snowball Earth," *Science*, August 28, 1998, 1342–46.
27. Rachel A. Wood and Franz Anthony, "The Rise of the First Animals," *Scientific American*, June 2019, 24–31.
28. Nicholas J. Butterfield, "Animals and the Invention of the Phanerozoic Earth System," *Trends in Ecology and Evolution* (February 2011), 81, 83, 85.
29. Peter Ward and Joe Kirschvink, *A New History of Life* (Bloomsbury, 2016), 166–67.
30. David Beerling, *The Emerald Planet: How Plants Changed Earths History* (Oxford University Press, 2007), 18.
31. David Beerling, *Making Eden: How Plants Transformed a Barren Planet* (Oxford University Press, 2019), 11.
32. Sandy Hetherington, "How Soils Changed Life on Earth," *The Conversation*, April 17, 2023.
33. Butterfield, "Animals," 86.
34. Carson, *Silent Spring & Other Writings*, 214.

5. Justus von Liebig and the Nutrient Cycle

1. Marx to Engels, February 13, 1866, *MECW*, vol. 42, 227.
2. Born Justus Liebig, he became Justus von Liebig when he was awarded the title of Freiherr (Baron) by Ludwig II of Bavaria in 1845.

3. Quoted in Rosen, "The conservation of energy and the study of metabolism," in *Historical Development of Physiological Thought*, ed. Brooks Chandler and Paul Cranefield, 258.
4. Humphrey Davy, *Elements of Agricultural Chemistry in a Course of Lectures for the Board of Agriculture*, 2nd ed. (Longman, 1814), 272–73.
5. Twentieth-century research found that in addition to nitrogen, phosphorus, and potassium, plants also require small amounts of eleven other elements.
6. Liebig, *Letters on Modern Agriculture* (John Wiley, 1959), 144.
7. Liebig, *The Natural Laws of Husbandry* (London: Walton & Maberly,1863), 274. In the long run, "almost unimpaired" is an important qualification: it isn't possible to recycle endlessly without some external source of energy, usually the sun.
8. Frederick Engels, *Dialectics of Nature* (International Publishers, 1940), 192–93.
9. Twentieth-century research showed that some ocean-dwelling bacteria also fix nitrogen.
10. The nitrogen cycle is actually much more complex than this. More in chapter 12.
11. Liebig, *Organic Chemistry in Its Applications to Agriculture and Physiology* (Taylor and Walton, 1840), 91–92. Carbonic acid is carbon dioxide. Ammonia is a nitrogen compound.
12. Justus von Liebig, *Die Chemie in ihrer Anwendung auf Agricultur und Physiologie*, 7th ed., vol. 1 (Biewig & Son, Braunschweig, 1862), 87. My translation.
13. Quoted in Vaclav Smil, *Cycles of Life* (Scientific American Library, 1997), 6.
14. Matt Huber and Leigh Phillips, "Kohei Saito's 'Start From Scratch' Degrowth Communism," *Jacobin*, March 2024.
15. Leigh Phillips, *Austerity Ecology & the Collapse-Porn Addicts* (Zero Books, 2015), 217.
16. Liebig to Hope, April 1865, in W. Hope, *The Sewage of the Metropolis* (Edward Stanford,1865), 24.

6. Vladimir Vernadsky and the Biosphere

1. Quoted in Alexander Yanshin, "Introduction," to Vladimir I. Vernadsky, *Geochemistry and the Biosphere*, ed. Frank B. Salisbury (Synergetic Press, 2007).
2. Kendall E. Bailes, *Science and Russian Culture in an Age of Revolutions:*

V. I. *Vernadsky and His Scientific School, 1863–1945* (Indiana University Press, 1990), 167.
3. Quoted in ibid., 167.
4. Vladimir I. Vernadsky, *The Biosphere*, trans. David Langmuir and Mark McMenamin (Springer, 1998 [1926]), 91. As Vernadsky pointed out, the Austrian geologist Edward Suess introduced the word *biosphere* in his popular 1885 textbook, *The Face of the Earth*.
5. Vernadsky, *The Biosphere*, 56, 57–58
6. Ibid., 59, 44.
7. Ibid., 72.
8. Jason Ross, ed., *150 Years of Vernadsky*, vol. 1: *The Biosphere* (21st Century Science Associates, 2014), 39, 50.
9. Vernadsky, *Geochemistry and the Biosphere* (Synergetic Press, 2007).
10. Vernadsky, *The Biosphere*, 51. The science of life has made major advances since Vernadsky's time, but non-scientific influences remain.
11. Ibid., 58.
12. Vernadsky to Vernadskaia, May 1913, quoted in Bailes, *Science and Russian Culture*, 127. Later observers compared the landscape around Sudbury to the surface of the moon.
13. Douglas R. Weiner, *Models of Nature: Ecology, Conservation and Cultural Revolution in Soviet Russia* (University of Pittsburgh Press, 1988), 29.
14. Vernadsky, *The Biosphere*, 142. Since Vernadsky's time, it has become clear that living matter exists virtually everywhere on Earth, including in places that humans cannot reach.
15. Ibid., 143.
16. Vernadsky, *Geochemistry and the Biosphere*, 185–86. Despite this observation, he did not connect changes in CO_2 levels with climate.
17. Vladimir Vernadsky, "The Transition from the Biosphere to the Noosphere," trans. William Jones, *21st Century*, Spring–Summer 2012: 27–28.
18. Ibid., 30.
19. Vladimir Vernadsky, "The Biosphere and the Noösphere," *American Scientist*, January 1945, 9.
20. Ibid., 8.
21. Ibid., 10, 9.
22. Vernadsky, *Geochemistry and the Biosphere*, 221.
23. Grinevald, "Introduction," in Vernadsky, *The Biosphere*, 27.

7. Barry Commoner and the Broken Circle

1. Barry Commoner, *Science & Survival* (Viking, 1966), 122.
2. Clifford D. Conner, *The Tragedy of American Science: From Truman to Trump* (Haymarket Books, 2020), 226.
3. Matt Schudel, "Barry Commoner, scientist and influential environmentalist, dies at 95," *Washington Post*, October 2, 2012.
4. Barry Commoner, *Science and Survival*, 122.
5. Ibid., 11.
6. Barry Commoner, *The Closing Circle: Nature, Man & Technology* (Alfred E. Knopf, 1971), 12.
7. Ibid., 39–40.
8. Ibid., 13.
9. Ibid., 33–48. The following discussion of the four laws of ecology includes material, with the author's permission, from Simon Butler, "Barry Commoner: Scientist, Activist, Radical Ecologist," *Green Left*, October 4, 2012.
10. Commoner, *Closing Circle*, 40–41.
11. Ibid., 44–45.
12. Ibid., 45.
13. Ibid., 41.
14. Ibid., 46.
15. Ibid., 140.
16. Ibid., 177.
17. Ibid., 129.
18. Ibid., 258–59.
19. Ibid., 267–68.
20. Ibid., 287.
21. Ibid., 283–84.
22. Ibid, 285.
23. Ibid., 295.
24. Barry Commoner, "Oil, Energy and Capitalism: An unpublished talk by Barry Commoner," *Climate & Capitalism*, July 30, 2013.

8. "We're Not in the Holocene Anymore"

1. Jan Zalasiewicz and Mark Williams, *The Goldilocks Planet* (Oxford University Press, 2012), 237.
2. The Milankovitch cycles did not cause ice age cycles before that because there was too much CO_2 in the atmosphere. It first fell below 350 ppm, a tipping point, about three million years ago.

3. Thomas Slater et al., "Review article: Earth's Ice Imbalance," *The Cryosophere*, January 25, 2021.
4. C. P. Summerhayes et al., "The Future Extent of the Anthropocene Epoch: A Synthesis," *Global and Planetary Change*, November 2024.
5. Will Steffen, Paul J. Crutzen, and John R. McNeill, "The Anthropocene: Are Humans Now Overwhelming the Great Forces of Nature?," *Ambio*, December 2007, 614.
6. Barbara Ward and Rene Dubos, *Only One Earth: The Care and Maintenance of a Small Planet* (W. W. Norton, 1972), 12.
7. For a detailed scientific evaluation, see Toby Tyrrell, *On Gaia: A Critical Investigation of the Relationship Between Life and Earth* (Princeton University Press, 2013).
8. National Research Council, *Earth System Science: Overview: A Program for Global Change* (National Academies Press, 1986), 4.
9. National Research Council, *Global Environmental Change: Research Pathways for the Next Decade* (National Academies Press, 1999), 3.
10. Juan G. Roederer, "ICSU Gives Green Light to IGBP," *Eos*, October 14, 1986.
11. IGBP, "Report No. 12 1990: The Initial Core Projects," 1–3.
12. I have described this process in more detail in chapter 1 of *Facing the Anthropocene* (Monthly Review Press, 2016).
13. Will Steffen et al., "The Emergence and Evolution of Earth System Science," *Nature Reviews Earth & Environment*, January 2020, 59.
14. Martin Head et al., "The Great Acceleration Is Real and Provides a Quantitative Basis for the Proposed Anthropocene Series/Epoch," *Episodes Journal of International Geoscience*, December 1, 2022.
15. Will Steffen et al., *Global Change and the Earth System: A Planet Under Pressure* (Springer, 2004), 93.
16. Will Steffen, Paul J. Crutzen, and John R. McNeill, "The Anthropocene: Are Humans Now Overwhelming the Great Forces of Nature?" *Ambio*, December 2007, 617.
17. A. Ganopolski, S. Rahmstorf, "Rapid Changes of Glacial Climate Simulated in a Couple Climate Model," *Nature*, January 11, 2001, 153–58.
18. William J. Burroughs, *Climate Change in Prehistory: The End of the Reign of Chaos* (Cambridge University Press, 2005), 13, 102.
19. J. R. Petit et al., "Climate and atmospheric history of the past 420,000 years from the Vostok ice core, Antarctica," *Nature*, June 3, 1999.
20. State of the Planet Declaration, https://shorturl.at/8Mf7V.

21. Will Steffen et al., "Planetary Boundaries: Guiding Human Development on a Changing Planet," *Science*, January 15, 2015.
22. Planetary Health Check 2024, https://www.planetaryhealthcheck.org/.
23. L. Caesar, B. Sakschewski et al., *Planetary Health Check Report 2024*, (Potsdam Institute for Climate Impact Research, 2024); Katherine Richardson, "Earth beyond six of nine planetary boundaries," *Science Advances*, September 13, 2023.
24. I discuss this more fully in chapter 5 of *Facing the Anthropocene* (Monthly Review Press, 2016).
25. Helen S. Findlay et al., "Ocean Acidification: Another Planetary Boundary Crossed," *Global Change Biology*, April 2025.
26. John Bellamy Foster, Brett Clark, and Richard York, *The Ecological Rift: Capitalism's War on the Earth* (Monthly Review Press, 2010), 15–19.
27. Ursula Marx et al., eds., *Walter Benjamin's Archive: Images, Texts, Signs* (Verso, 2015).

9. Capital's Anti-Ecological Logic

1. Fred Magdoff and John Bellamy Foster, *What Every Environmentalist Needs to Know About Capitalism* (Monthly Review Press, 2011), 96,
2. Ibid., 38.
3. Karl Marx, *Capital*, vol. 1 (Penguin, 1976), 125.
4. Ernest Mandel, *Marxist Economic Theory*, vol. 1 (Monthly Review Press, 1968), 125–26.
5. Capital One Shopping Research, Number of Products on Amazon, July 14, 2024. https://capitaloneshopping.com/.
6. Frank Ackerman and Lisa Heinzerling, *Priceless: On Knowing the Price of Everything and the Value of Nothing* (New Press, 2005), 17.
7. Michael J. Sandel, "What Isn't for Sale?," *The Atlantic*, April 2012.
8. David Harvey, *Seventeen Contradictions and the End of Capitalism* (Oxford University Press, 2014), 250.
9. Quoted in John Bellamy Foster and Robert W. McChesney, T*he Endless Crisis: How Monopoly-Finance Capital Produces Stagnation and Upheaval from the USA to China* (Monthly Review Press, 2012), 52.
10. Ken Silverstein, "Millions for Viagra, Pennies for Diseases of the Poor," *The Nation*, July 1, 1999.
11. UBS Global Wealth Report 2025, https://www.ubs.com/global/en.html.
12. Omar Ocampo, "Twelve U.S. Billionaires Now Have a Combined $2 Trillion," Inequality.org, December 3, 2024.
13. Marx, *Capital*, vol. 1, 777.
14. James M. MacDonald, Robert A. Hoppe, and Doris Newton, "Three

Decades of Consolidation in U.S. Agriculture," *Economic Information Bulletin* EIB-119 (USDA, March 2018).
15. Istvan Mészáros, *The Challenge and Burden of Historical Time* (Monthly Review Press, 2018), 385.
16. Foster and McChesney, *The Endless Crisis*, 69, 76.
17. Mészáros, *Challenge and Burden*, 386.
18. Oxfam International, "Unpaid and Underpaid Care Work and the Global Inequality Crisis," January 2020.
19. Magdoff and Foster, *What Every Environmentalist Needs to Know about Capitalism*, 43.
20. Marx, Capital, vol. 1, 742, 743.
21. Karl Marx, *Grundrisse: Foundations of the Critique of Political Economy*, trans. Martin Nicolaus (Penguin Books, 1973), 270.
22. Mészáros, *Challenge and Burden*, 384–85.
23. Evgeny Preobrazhenksky, *The New Economics* (1926), trans. Brian Pearce (Clarendon Press, 1965), 49.
24. Andre Gorz, *Ecology as Politics* (Black Rose Books, 1980), 80.
25. Ibid., 82.
26. The phrase was coined by John Bellamy Foster, echoing the title of Ralph W. Estes's book, *The Tyranny of the Bottom Line: Why Corporations Make Good People Do Bad Things* (Berrett-Koeler, 1996).
27. Karl Marx, "The Future Results of British Rule in India" (July 22, 1853), *MECW*, vol. 12, 217.

10. Breaking the Carbon Cycle

1. Robert M. Hazen, *Symphony in C: Carbon and the Evolution of (Almost) Everything* (W.W. Norton, 2019), 238.
2. National Science & Technology Medals Foundation, https://www.nationalmedals.org/laureates/charles-d-keeling.
3. Raymond P. Sorenson, "Eunice Foote's Pioneering Research on CO_2 and Climate Warming," *AAPG Search and Discovery*, January 31, 2011.
4. Tyndall acknowledged several scientists whose work preceded his, so it is unlikely that he deliberately omitted Foote.
5. Henning Rodhe, Robert Charlson, and Elisabeth Crawford, "Svante Arrhenius and the Greenhouse Effect," *Ambio*, February 1997, 2–5.
6. Intergovernmental Panel on Climate Change, *Climate Change 2021: The Physical Science Basis. Summary for Policymakers*.
7. Stephanie Pappas, "Carbon Dioxide Is Warming the Planet (Here's How)," *Live Science*, March 10, 2017.
8. This is a greatly simplified account. For more, see NASA's Earth

Observatory page on "The Slow Carbon Cycle," https://earthobservatory.nasa.gov/.
9. Ibid.
10. Bernadette Bensaude-Vincent and Sacha Laeve, *Carbon: A Biography* (Polity Books: 2024), 117–18.
11. Will Steffen et al., *Global Change and the Earth System: A Planet Under Pressure* (Springer, 2004), 93.
12. Adam Hanieh, *Crude Capitalism: Oil, Corporate Power, and the Making of the World Market* (Verso, 2024), 2.
13. M. Willeit et al., "Mid-Pleistocene transition in glacial cycles explained by declining CO_2 and regolith removal," *Science Advances*, April 3, 2019.
14. *State of the Global Climate 2024*, World Meteorological Organization 2025, https://library.wmo.int/idurl/4/69455.
15. Paris Agreement, https://shorturl.at/w0KbU.
16. Damian Carrington, "World's top climate scientists expect global heating to blast past 1.5C target," *Guardian*, May 8, 2024.
17. Future Earth, The Earth League, WCRP, *10 New Insights in Climate Science 2023/2024* (Stockholm, 2023).
18. United Nations Environment Programme, Emissions Gap Report 2024, (April 2025), xii, xvii.
19. James E. Hansen et al., "Global Warming Has Accelerated: Are the United Nations and the Public Well-Informed?," *Environment: Science and Policy for Sustainable Development*, February 2025.
20. UNEP, Emissions Gap Report 2024 (April 2025), xv.
21. Andreas Malm and Wim Carton, *Overshoot: How the World Surrendered to Climate Breakdown* (Verso, 2024), 69.
22. Will Steffen, Paul J. Crutzen, and John R. McNeill, "The Anthropocene: Are Humans Now Overwhelming the Great Forces of Nature?," *Ambio*, December 2007, 614–21.
23. Global Carbon Project, "2024 Global Carbon Budget."
24. P. Falkowski et al., "The Global Carbon Cycle: A Test of Our Knowledge of Earth as a System," *Science*, October 13, 2000, 295.

11. Rising Seas, Burning Trees, Tipping Points

1. UC San Diego, The Keeling Curve, https://keelingcurve.ucsd.edu/.
2. Global Carbon Project, "2024 Global Carbon Budget."
3. United Nations, "Hottest July ever signals 'era of global boiling has arrived' says UN chief," News Release 27, July 2023.
4. David Archer, *The Long Thaw: How Humans Are Changing the Next 100,000 Years of Earth's Climate* (Princeton University Press, 2016), 1.

5. Simone Fiaschi, Mead A. Allison, and Cathleen E. Jones, "Vertical land motion in Greater New Orleans: Insights into underlying drivers and impact to flood protection infrastructure," *Science Advances*, June 27, 2025.
6. Calum Cunningham, Grant Williamson, and David Bowman, "Increasing frequency and intensity of the most extreme wildfires on Earth," *Nature Ecology & Evolution*, June 2024.
7. Jack D. Cohen and Alan Westhaver, "An examination of the Lytton, British Columbia wildland–urban fire destruction," Summary Report to the British Columbia FireSmart Committee, May 2022.
8. Natural Resources Canada, "Canada's record-breaking wildfires in 2023: A fiery wake-up call."
9. Crystal A. Kolden, John T. Abatzoglou, Matthew W. Jones, and Piyush Jain, "Wildfires in 2024," *Nature Reviews Earth & Environment*, April 11, 2025; *Relatório Anual do Fogo* (MapBiomas, 2025).
10. Matthew W. Jones et al., "Global rise in forest fire emissions linked to climate change in the extratropics," *Science*, October 18, 2024.
11. Brendan Byrne et al., "Carbon emissions from the 2023 Canadian wildfires," *Nature*, August 28, 2024.
12. Alexis Gardiner Jorgensen et al., "The influence of postfire recovery and environmental conditions on boreal vegetation," *Ecosphere*, July 19, 2023.
13. Amazon Frontlines, "The Tipping Point: Is the Amazon Rainforest Approaching a Point of No Return?," September 2024.
14. Timothy M. Lenton et al., *The Global Tipping Points Report 2023* (University of Exeter, 2023), 88.
15. Gernot Wagner and Martin L. Weitzman, *Climate Shock: The Economic Consequences of a Hotter Planet* (Princeton University Press, 2015).
16. Michael E. Mann, "The 'Fat Tail' of Climate Change Risk," *Huffpost*, September 22, 2015.
17. Nico Wunderling et al., "Interacting tipping elements increase risk of climate domino effects under global warming," *Earth System Dynamics*, 12/2, 2021.
18. Lenton, *Tipping Points 2023*, 12.
19. IPCC, Climate Change 2023: Synthesis Report, 77.

12. Nitrogen: From Shortage to Glut

1. UN Environment Programme, Facts about Nitrogen Pollution, https://unep.org/facts-about-nitrogen-pollution.
2. Mark A. Sutton et al., *Our Nutrient World: The Challenge to Produce*

More Food and Energy with Less Pollution (Centre for Ecology and Hydrology, 2013), 1.
3. C. C. Delwiche, "The Nitrogen Cycle," *Scientific American*, September 1970, 137.
4. J. J. Elser, "A World Awash with Nitrogen," *Science*, vol. 334, no. 6062, 2011, 1505.
5. Mark A. Sutton and Hans Van Grinsven, "European Nitrogen Assessment: Summary for Policy Makers," 2011.
6. Johan Rockström, Will Steffen et al., "A safe operating space for humanity," *Nature*, Sept. 23, 2009.
7. Vaclav Smil, *Enriching the Earth: Fritz Haber, Carl Bosch, and the Transformation of World Food Production* (MIT Press, 2001), xiii–xiv.
8. In the ocean, fixation is mostly done by some types of cyanobacteria, which are often misnamed blue-green algae.
9. For a summary of the current state of knowledge (and ignorance) about the roles played by "an astonishing diversity of microorganisms" in the nitrogen cycle, see Marcel M. M. Kuypers, Hannah K. Marchant, and Boran Kartal, "The Microbial Nitrogen–cycling Network," *Nature Reviews Microbiology* 16, no. 5 (2018).
10. Will Steffen et al., *Global Change and the Earth System: A Planet under Pressure* (Springer, 2005), 29.
11. T. C. R. White, *The Inadequate Environment: Nitrogen and the Abundance of Animals* (Springer, 2012), 12.
12. Marcel M. M. Kuypers, Hannah K. Marchant, and Boran Kartal, "The Microbial Nitrogen–cycling Network," *Nature Reviews: Microbiology* 16, no. 5 (2018): 271.
13. Quoted in Fariss Samarrai, "Addressing the 'Nitrogen Cascade,'" *UVA Today*, May 15, 2008.
14. Smil, *Enriching*, 42.
15. Guano is still harvested in the Chincha Islands today, but the quantities are small.
16. Smil, *Enriching the Earth*, 46. The exported ore was about 15 percent nitrogen.
17. Ibid., 57.
18. *MECW*, vol. 26, 451.
19. Charles E. Munroe, "The Nitrogen Question from the Military Standpoint," *Naval Institute Proceedings*, vol. 35 Part 2 (1909), 722–23.
20. William Crookes, "Address of the President Before the British Association for the Advancement of Science, Bristol, 1898," *Science*, October 28, 1898, 562, 571, 573.

21. Munroe, "Nitrogen Question," 727.
22. Mark A. Sutton, "Assessing Our Nitrogen Inheritance," *European Nitrogen Assessment* (European Science Foundation, 2011), 1.
23. BASF was founded in 1865 as a dye-making company. It became part of I.G. Farben in 1926 and reemerged as an independent company in 1952.
24. The best history of the development of nitrogen-fixing technologies is Vaclav Smil's *Enriching the Earth*, to which my brief account is indebted.
25. Kenzi Tamaru, "The History of the Development of Ammonia Synthesis," in *Catalytic Ammonia Synthesis: Fundamentals and Practice*, ed. J. R. Jennings (Springer Science, 1991), 16.
26. Neil Faulkner, *A Radical History of the World* (Pluto Press, 2018), 294, 296.
27. Smil, *Enriching the Earth*, 103.
28. Timothy Johnston, "Nitrogen Nation: The Legacy of World War I and the Politics of Chemical Agriculture in America, 1916–1930," *Agricultural History* 90, no. 2 (Spring 2016): 224.
29. The sale of nitrogen-fixing plants was part of a more general postwar selloff of government-built factories. See Angus, *Facing the Anthropocene*, 138–41.
30. Hugh S. Gorman, *The Story of N* (Rutgers University Press, 2013), 91.
31. World fertilizer trends and outlook to 2022 (Food and Agriculture Organization, 2019), 5.
32. Mészáros, *The Necessity of Social Control* (Monthly Review Press, 2014), 49–50.
33. Omara et al., "World Cereal Nitrogen Use Efficiency Trends: Review and Current Knowledge," *Agrosystems, Geosciences & Environment*, January 2019, 5, 1.
34. Nancy A. Rabelais, R. Eugene Turner, and William J. Wiseman, Jr., "Gulf of Mexico Hypoxia, aka 'The Dead Zone,'" *Annual Review of Ecology and Systematics* 33 (2002), 239.
35. Sutton et al., *Our Nutrient World*, 20.
36. Townsend and Howarth, "Fixing the Global Nitrogen Problem," *Scientific American*, February 2010, 70.
37. Marx, *Capital*, vol. 3, 216.
38. Fred Magdoff, "A Rational Agriculture Is Incompatible with Capitalism," *Monthly Review*, March 2015, 17.
39. Javier Mateo-Sagasta, Sara Marjani Zadeh, and Hugh Turral, "Water Pollution from Agriculture: A Global Review," (Food and Agriculture Organization, 2017), 2.

40. Wozniacka, "The Greenhouse Gas No One's Talking About," *Civil Eats*, September 19, 2019.
41. J. W. Erisman et al., "Consequences of Human Modification of the Global Nitrogen Cycle," *Philosophical Transactions of the Royal Society B: Biological Sciences* 368, no. 1621 (July 2013).
42. Alan R. Townsend and Robert W. Howarth, "Fixing the Global Nitrogen Problem," *Scientific American* 302, no. 2 (February 2010): 65–66.
43. Galloway and Cowling, "Reactive Nitrogen and the World," *Ambio* 31/2, 68.
44. Marx, *Capital*, vol. 3, 949.
45. Peter M. Vitousek et al., "Biological Nitrogen Fixation: Rates, Patterns and Ecological Controls in Terrestrial Ecosystems," *Philosophical Transactions of the Royal Society B*, July 2013. Some studies have made higher estimates of pre-industrial nitrogen fixation, but all agree that current production is at least double the natural rate.
46. Rockström et al., "A safe operating space for humanity," *Nature*, September 23, 2009.
47. Ibid.

13. Agriculture: The Great Separation

1. Karl Marx, *Capital*, vol. 3 (Penguin 1981), 216.
2. Miguel Altieri, "Ecological impacts of industrial agriculture and the possibilities for truly sustainable farming," in *Hungry for Profit: The Agribusiness Threat to Farmers, Food and the Environment*, ed. Fred Magdoff, John Bellamy Foster, and Frederick M. Buttel (Monthly Review Press, 2000), 77.
3. Ivette Perfecto, John Vandermeer, and Angus Wright, *Nature's Matrix: Linking Agriculture, Conservation and Food Sovereignty* (Earthscan, 2009), 50–51.
4. Michael Pollan, *The Omnivore's Dilemma* (Penguin, 2006), 7.
5. Michael Greger, *Bird Flu: A Virus of Our Own Hatching* (Lantern Books, 2006), 109–10.
6. Donald Worster, *The Wealth of Nature: Environmental History and the Ecological Imagination* (Oxford University Press, 1993), 58, 59.
7. The original version of this diagram played an important part in the rediscovery of Metabolic Rift theory. Magdoff and Foster included it in a *Monthly Review* article in July–August 1998, which was then reprinted in *Hungry for Profit* (Monthly Review Press, 2000).
8. Marx's unpublished notebooks, quoted in Kohei Saito, *Karl Marx's*

Ecosocialism: Capitalism, Nature, and the Unfinished Critique of Political Economy (Monthly Review Press, 2017), 209.
9. Foodprint, "Farm Animal Welfare," updated May 17, 2024, https://foodprint.org/issues/.
10. "Yearly number of animals slaughtered for meat, World, 1961 to 2023," Food and Agriculture Organization of the United Nations (2025), processed by Our World in Data.
11. Wenonah Hauter, *Foodopoly: The Battle over the Future of Food and Farming in America* (New Press, 2012), 171.
12. Yinon M. Bar-On, Rob Phillips, and Ron Milo, "The biomass distribution on Earth," *Proceedings of the National Academies of Science*, May 21, 2018.
13. Jay P. Graham and Keeve E. Nachman, "Managing Waste from Confined Animal Feeding Operations in the United States: The Need for Sanitary Reform," *Journal of Water and Health* 8, no. 4 (2010): 649, 653.
14. Steve Wing and Jill Johnston, "Industrial Hog Operations in North Carolina Disproportionately Impact African-Americans, Hispanics and American Indians" (Department of Epidemiology, University of North Carolina at Chapel Hill, August 2014).
15. Paulo Pagliari, Melissa Wilson, and Zhongqi He, "Animal Manure Production and Utilization: Impact of Modern Concentrated Animal Feeding Operations," American Society of Agriculture, January 2020.
16. David R. Montgomery, *Growing a Revolution: Bringing Our Soil Back to Life* (W.W. Norton, 2017), 265.
17. A Well-Fed World, "Feed-to-Meat: Conversion Inefficiency Ratios," https://awellfedworld.org/feed-ratios/.
18. Intergovernmental Technical Panel on Soils, *Status of the World's Soil Resources—Main Report* (FAO 2015), 169.
19. W. L. Silver, T. Perez, A. Mayer, and A. R. Jones, "The role of soil in the contribution of food and feed," *Philosophical Transactions of the Royal Society B*, August 2021.
20. P. R. Shukla et al., *Special Report on Climate Change and Land: Summary for Decision Makers* (IPCC 2019) 5.
21. Fred Magdoff and Harold van Es, *Building Soils for Better Crops: Sustainable Soil Management*, 4th ed. (Sustainable Agriculture Research & Education, 2021), 8.
22. David R. Boyd and Imalka Nilmalgoda, *The Overlooked Environmental and Human Rights Crisis: Desertification, Land Degradation and Drought*, United Nations Special Rapporteur on Human Rights and the Environment (June 2023), 4–5.

23. Socialist agronomist Fred Magdoff has made important contributions to identifying the importance of soil organic matter to agricultural soils. His book *Building Soils for Better Crops* is a practical guide to ecological soil management, and his article "Repairing the Soil Carbon Rift" (*Monthly Review*, April 2021) is an important addition to metabolic rift theory. My discussion draws on those works.
24. David Montgomery, Peter Rabinowitz, Yona Sipos, and Eli Wheat, "Soil Health: A common focus for one health and planetary health interventions," *One Health*, January 2024.
25. Hannah Holleman, *Dust Bowls of Empire: Imperialism, Environmental Politics, and the Injustice of "Green" Capitalism* (Yale University Press, 2018), 19.
26. Fred Magdoff, "Repairing the Soil Carbon Rift: Enhancing Agriculture and Environment," *Monthly Review*, April 2021, 2.
27. Magdoff, "Repairing the Soil Carbon Rift," 6.
28. United Nations Climate Change Secretariat, "Land Use, Land-Use Change and Forestry (LULUCF)."
29. Carolyn Dimitri, Anne Effland, and Neilson Conklin, *The 20th-Century Transformation of U.S. Agriculture and Farm Policy*, United States Department of Agriculture Economic Information Bulletin Number 3, June 2005, 2.
30. S. A. Khan, R. L. Mulvaney, T. R. Ellsworth, and C. W. Boas, "The Myth of Nitrogen Fertilization for Soil Carbon Sequestration," *Journal of Environmental Quality*, February 2007, 1821–32.
31. Robert J. Blakemore, "Critical Decline of Earthworms from Organic Origins under Intensive, Humic SOM–Depleting Agriculture," *Soil Systems*, June 2018.
32. Karl Kautsky, *The Agrarian Question*, trans. Pete Burgess (Zwan Publications, 1988), 215.
33. Montgomery et. al., "Soil Health."
34. Richard Levins and Richard Lewontin, *The Dialectical Biologist* (Harvard University Press, 1985), 285.
35. Cara Buckley, "Meet a Family That's Betting the Farm on a Wild Idea. Literally," *New York Times*, August 14, 2024
36. Hannah Holleman, *Dust Bowls of Empire* (Yale University Press, 2018), 71.
37. Gliessman and Engles, *Agroecology: The Ecology of Sustainable Food Systems*, 3.
38. Fred Magdoff, "A Rational Agriculture Is Incompatible with Capitalism," *Monthly Review*, March 2015; Karl Marx, *Capital*, vol. 3 (Penguin,

1981), 216. The translation of Marx's words in this edition is slightly different.

14. Triple Crisis in the Oceans

1. Rachel Carson, *The Sea Around Us* (Oxford University Press, 1950), 164–65.
2. Sylvia A. Earle, *The World Is Blue: How Our Fate and the Oceans Are One* (National Geographic, 2010), 20.
3. Sylvia A. Earle, *Sea Change: A Message of the Oceans* (Ballantine Books, 1995), xii.
4. United States Environmental Protection Agency, "Climate Change Indicators: Sea Surface Temperature," June 2024.
5. Chinese Academy of Sciences, "Record-setting Ocean Warmth Continued in 2019," News Release, January 14, 2020.
6. IPCC, *Special Report on the Ocean and Cryosphere in a Changing Climate* (IPCC, 2019), 62.
7. Grant R. Bigg, *The Oceans and Climate*, 2nd ed. (Cambridge University Press, 2006), x.
8. Nicolas Gruber, "Warming Up, Turning Sour, Losing Breath: Ocean Biogeochemistry Under Global Change," *Philosophical Transactions of the Royal Society A*, May 2011, 1980, 1992.
9. Jelle D. Bijma et al., "Climate Change and the Oceans—What Does the Future Hold?," *Marine Pollution Bulletin*, September 2013.
10. A. Pearce et al., "The Marine Heat Wave Off Western Australia During the Summer of 2010/11" (Western Australian Fisheries and Marine Research Laboratories, 2011), 1.
11. Mark R. Payne, "Metric for Marine Heatwaves Suggests How These Events Displace Ocean Life," *Nature* 584 (August 8, 2020), 43.
12. IPCC *Special Report on the Ocean and Cryosphere in a Changing Climate*, 2019. 67, 607.
13. Kathryn E. Smith et al., "Ocean extremes as a stress test for marine ecosystems and society," *Nature Climate Change*, February 28, 2025.
14. IPCC, *Report on the Ocean and Cryosphere*, 609.
15. Dan A. Smale et al., "Marine Heatwaves Threaten Global Biodiversity and the Provision of Ecosystem Services," *Nature Climate Change* 9, no. 4 (March 4, 2019).
16. Eric C. J. Oliver et al., "Projected Marine Heatwaves in the 21st Century and the Potential for Ecological Impact," *Frontiers in Marine Science* 6, December 2019.
17. Boyin Huang et al., "Record High Sea Surface Temperatures in 2023,"

Geophysical Research Letters, July 25, 2024.
18. Oliver et al., "Projected Marine Heatwaves."
19. Karina von Schuckmann et al., "The state of the global ocean," *State of the Planet*, September 2024, https://www.state-of-the-planet.net/.
20. Interviewed in John Collins Rudolf, "Q. and A.: For Oceans, Another Big Headache," *New York Times*, May 5, 2010.
21. More precisely, there are 30 percent more hydrogen (H+) ions.
22. See, for example, Martin C. Hänsel et al., "Ocean Warming and Acidification May Drag down the Commercial Arctic Cod Fishery by 2100," *PLOS ONE*, April 22, 2020.
23. Ken Caldeira and Michael E. Wickett, "Anthropogenic Carbon and Ocean pH," *Nature*, Sept. 25, 2003, 365; Royal Society, *Ocean Acidification Due to Increasing Atmospheric Carbon Dioxide* (Royal Society, 2005), 39.
24. Callum Roberts, *The Ocean of Life: The Fate of Man and the Sea* (Penguin, 2013), 108, 110.
25. This is also true of humans. Our normal blood pH is 7.4: a drop of 0.2 can be fatal.
26. "Monaco Declaration," Proceedings of Second International Symposium on the Ocean in a High–CO_2 World (UNESCO, 2008).
27. IPCC, *Special Report on the Ocean and Cryosphere in a Changing Climate* (2019), 59, 66.
28. L. Caesar et al., *Planetary Health Check 2024: A Scientific Assessment of the State of the Planet* (Planetary Boundaries Science, 2024), 55.
29. Helen S Findlay et al., "Ocean Acidification: Another Planetary Boundary Crossed," *Global Change Biology*, April 2025.
30. 2025 UN Ocean Conference, https://sdgs.un.org/conferences/ocean 2025.
31. Quoted in "The Ocean Is Losing Its Breath. Here's the Global Scope," SERC news release, January 4, 2018.
32. Erica M. Ferrer et al., "Why aquatic deoxygenation belongs in the planetary boundary framework," *PLOS Climate*, May 5, 2025.
33. News Release, "Gulf of Mexico 'dead zone' larger than average, scientists find," National Oceanic and Atmospheric Administration, August 1, 2024
34. Amy Gulick, "No Oxygen, No Life: The Gulf of Mexico's 'Dead Zone,'" *Dive Training*, December 2, 2002.
35. USGS, *Gulf of Mexico Dead Zone—the Last 150 Years*, 2006.
36. Sami A. Jokinen et al., "A 1500-Year Multiproxy Record of Coastal Hypoxia from the Northern Baltic Sea Indicates Unprecedented Deoxygenation over the 20th Century," *Biogeosciences*, July 2018, 3975.

37. R. J. Diaz and R. Rosenberg, "Spreading Dead Zones and Consequences for Marine Ecosystems," *Science*, August 15, 2008.
38. Dan Laffoley and J. M. Baxter, eds., *Ocean Deoxygenation: Everyone's Problem: Causes, Impacts, Consequences and Solutions* (International Union for Conservation of Nature, 2019), xi.
39. Donald F. Boesch, "Challenges and Opportunities for Science in Reducing Nutrient Over-Enrichment of Coastal Ecosystems," *Estuaries*, August 2002, 889.
40. K. J. Van Meter et al., "The Nitrogen Legacy: Emerging Evidence of Nitrogen Accumulation in Anthropogenic Landscapes," *Environmental Research Letters*, March 2016.
41. Mississippi River/Gulf of Mexico Watershed Nutrient Task Force, *Gulf Hypoxia Action Plan 2008 for Reducing, Mitigating, and Controlling Hypoxia in the Northern Gulf of Mexico and Improving Water Quality in the Mississippi River Basin* (Environmental Protection Agency, 2008).
42. HELCOM Baltic Sea Action Plan adopted on 15 November 2007 in Krakow, Poland, by the HELCOM Extraordinary Ministerial Meeting. 5, 83.
43. HELCOM, *State of the Baltic Sea, 2023* (Baltic Marine Environment Protection Commission, 2023), 8, 10.
44. Philip McMichael, *Food Regimes and Agrarian Questions* (Fernwood Publishing, 2013), 132.
45. Chadlin M. Ostrander, Jeremy D. Owens, and Sune G. Nielsen, "Constraining the Rate of Oceanic Deoxygenation Leading Up to a Cretaceous Oceanic Anoxic Event (OAE-2: ~94 Ma)," *Science Advances*, August 9, 2017.
46. Guy Claireaux and Denis Chabot, "The Significance of Ocean Deoxygenation for the Physiology of Marine Organisms," in *Ocean Deoxygenation: Everyone's Problem*, ed. D. Laffoley and J. M. Baxter (IUCN, 2019), 461,
47. J. Wong, M. Münnich, and N. Gruber, "Column-compound extremes in the global ocean," *AGU Advances*, 5, 2024.
48. Jan Zalasiewicz and Mark Williams, "The Anthropocene Ocean in Its Deep Time Context," in *The World Ocean in Globalisation*, ed. Davor Vidas and Peter Johan Schei (Brill, 2011), 34.
49. "Oceans Turning from Friend to Foe, Warns Landmark UN Climate Report," Agence France Presse, August 29, 2019.

15. Can We Avoid the Hothouse?
1. István Mészáros, *The Challenge and Burdon of Historical Time: Socialism in the Twenty-First Cen*tury (Monthly Review Press, 2008), 149.

2. Will Steffen, Johan Rockström, Katherine Richardson, Timothy M. Lenton, Carl Folke, Diana Liverman, Colin P. Summerhayes, Anthony D. Barnosky, Sarah E. Cornell, Michel Crucifix, Jonathan F. Donges, Ingo Fetzer, Steven J. Lade, Marten Scheffer, Ricarda Winkelmann, and Hans Joachim Schellnhuber, "Trajectories of the Earth System in the Anthropocene," and "Supporting Information," *PNAS*, July 2018..
3. Ibid.
4. Ibid.
5. Ibid.
6. Ibid.
7. Ibid.
8. Ibid
9. Ibid.
10. Ibid.
11. Radio Ecoshock, September 12, 2018., https://www.ecoshock.org/.
12. Marx, *Capital*, vol. 3, 959.
13. Steffen et al., "Trajectories."
14. Ibid.

16. We Only Want the Earth

1. Rosa Luxemburg, "What Is Economics?," in *Rosa Luxemburg Speaks*, ed. Mary Alice Waters (Pathfinder Press, 1970), 248.
2. NPR Staff, "Transcript: Greta Thunberg's Speech at the U.N. Climate Action Summit," September 23, 2019.
3. United Nations Framework Convention on Climate Change, Article 2.
4. Mark Alizart, *The Climate Coup* (Polity Press, 2021), 51.
5. Oliver Milman, "James Hansen, father of climate change awareness, calls Paris talks 'a fraud,'" *Guardian*, December 12, 2015.
6. *Encyclical Letter Laudato Si' of the Holy Father Francis on Care for Our Common Home* (Vatican Press, 2015), 40.
7. Andreas Malm and Wim Carton, *Overshoot: How the World Surrendered to Climate Breakdown* (Verso, 2024), 93.
8. Damian Carrington and Matthew Taylor, "Revealed: the 'carbon bombs' set to trigger catastrophic climate breakdown," *Guardian*, May 11, 2022.
9. Adam Hanieh, *Crude Capitalism: Oil, Corporate Power, and the Making of the World Market* (Verso, 2024), 277.
10. Malm and Carton, *Overshoot*, 1, 24–25.
11. Friedrich Engels, *The Condition of the Working Class in England* (Penguin, 2009), 275.

12. See, for example, Geoff Dembicki, *The Petroleum Papers: Inside the Far-Right Conspiracy to Cover Up Climate Change* (Greystone Books, 2022).
13. John Bellamy Foster, "There is still time for an ecological revolution to prevent Hothouse Earth," *Climate & Capitalism*, August 25, 2015.
14. Nick Estes, *Our History Is the Future* (Verso, 2019), 256–57.
15. Will Steffen et al., "Trajectories of the Earth System in the Anthropocene," *Proceedings of the National Academy of Sciences*, July 2018.
16. Marx, *Capital*, vol. 3, 959.
17. Fred Magdoff, "Ecological Civilization," *Monthly Review*, January 2011.
18. Barry Commoner, *The Closing Circle* (Knopf, 1971), 285.
19. William Morris and E. Belfort Bax, *Socialism: Its Growth and Outcome* (Swan Sonnenschein, 1893), 285.
20. Karl Marx and Frederick Engels, "Manifesto of the Communist Party," *MECW*, vol. 6, 484.
21. Del Weston, *The Political Economy of Global Warming: The Terminal Crisis* (Routledge, 2014), 197.

Appendix 1, Metabolism: Lost in Translation?

1. Rosa Luxemburg, "Stagnation and Progress of Marxism," in *Rosa Luxemburg Speaks*, ed. Mary Alice Waters (Pathfinder Press: 1970), 111.
2. Franklin C. Bing, "The Origin of the Word 'Metabolism,'" *Journal of the History of Medicine*, April 1971, 158–80.
3. Kohei Saito, *Karl Marx's Ecosocialism* (Monthly Review Press, 2017), 69; Justus von Liebig, *Organic Chemistry in Its Applications to Agriculture and Physiology* (Taylor and Walton, 1840), 369.
4. *MECW*, vol. 35 (International Publishers: 1996), 506–7.
5. Karl Marx, *Capital*, vol.1 (Penguin: 1976), 637–38.
6. Marx, *Capital*, vol. 3 (Charles H. Kerr, 1909), 945.
7. Marx, *Capital*, vol. 3 (Pelican, 1981), 949.
8. Karl Marx, *Capital: Critique of Political Economy*, vol. 1, trans. Paul Reitter (Princeton University Press, 2024), 460.

Appendix 2. Has the Anthropocene Been Cancelled?

1. Colin N. Waters et al., "The Anthropocene is functionally and stratigraphically distinct from the Holocene," *Science*, January 8, 2016.
2. Matthew Edgeworth et al., "The Anthropocene Is More Than a Time Interval," *Earth's Future*, July 18, 2024.
3. Jan Zalasiewicz, Martin Head et al., "Reply to Edgeworth et al., 2024, 'The Anthropocene is a time interval, and more besides," *ESS Open Archive*, December 23, 2024.

4. Jan Zalasiewicz et al., "Making the case for a formal Anthropocene Epoch: An analysis of ongoing critiques," *Newsletters on Stratigraphy*, April 2017.
5. Jan Zalasiewicz, "Foreword" to Martin Bohle, Boris Holzer, Leslie Sklair, Fabienne Will, *The Anthropocene Working Group and the Global Debate Around a New Geological Epoch* (Springer, 2025), ix, xii, xiv.
6. Todd J. Braje and Jon M. Erlandson, "Looking forward, looking back: Humans, anthropogenic change, and the Anthropocene," *Anthropocene*, December, 2013.
7. Stanley C. Finney and Lucy E. Edwards, "The 'Anthropocene' epoch: Scientific decision or political statement?," *GSA Today*, March 2016.
8. Among others: C. P. Summerhayes et al., "The future extent of the Anthropocene Epoch: A synthesis," *Global and Planetary Change*, November 2024; Francine McCarthy et al., "Would Adding the Anthropocene to the Geologic Time Scale Matter?," *AGU Advances*, February 2025; Mark Williams et al., "Palaeontological signatures of the Anthropocene are distinct from those of previous epochs," *Earth-Science Reviews*, June 2024.
9. Ian Angus, *Facing the Anthropocene* (Monthly Review Press, 2016), 58.

Appendix 3. Can CO_2 Removal Cool the Planet?

1. Ernest Mandel, *Late Capitalism* (Verso, 1978), 501.
2. IPCC, *Special Report: Global Warming of 1.5°C* (2018), 95.
3. Ibid., 158.
4. Editorial, "The world is missing its lofty climate targets. Time for some realism," *The Economist*, November 3, 2022.
5. J. Wilcox, B. Kolosz, and J. Freeman, eds., *The CDR Primer*, 2021, https://cdrprimer.org/.
6. Washington Taylor, Robert Rosner, Brad Marston, and Jonathan S. Wurtele, *Atmospheric Carbon Dioxide Removal: A Physical Science Perspective* (American Physical Society, 2025).
7. Climeworks, https://climeworks.com/.
8. Bjartmar Oddur Þeyr Alexandersson and Bjartmar Oddur Þeyr Alexandersson, "Climeworks' capture fails to cover its own emissions," *Heimildin*, May 15, 2025.
9. Calculation by Aatish Bhatia in the excellent *Rate of Change* blog, October 28, 2020.
10. American Physical Society, "APS Releases Report on Atmospheric Carbon Dioxide Removal," News Release, January 27, 2025.

11. Joe Crowley, "Drax: UK power station still burning rare forest wood," BBC, February 28, 2024.
12. Taylor et al., *Atmospheric CDR*, 14.
13. Felix Creutzig et al., "Considering sustainability thresholds for BECCS in IPCC and biodiversity assessments," *GCB Bioenergy*, February 2021.
14. Matt Williams and Elly Pepper, *The BECCS Hoax*, Natural Resources Defense Council, 2024, 4.
15. European Academies' Science Advisory Council, "Forest bioenergy, carbon capture and storage, and carbon dioxide removal: an update," *EASAC Commentary*, February 2019, 2, 6.
16. Quoted in Corbin Hiar, "Oil companies want to remove carbon from the air—using taxpayer dollars," *E&E News*, July 13, 2023.
17. Duncan McLaren and Nils Markusson, "The co-evolution of technological promises, modelling, policies and climate change targets," *Nature Climate Change,* April 2020.
18. United Nations, "'Climate crunch time is here,' new UN report warns," News Release, October 24, 2024.

Index

acidification of oceans, 110, 197–200
Agrarian Question (Kautsky), 31–39
agribusiness, 176, 187, 204, 221
agricultural science (organic chemistry), 75–76
agriculture, 175–76; Bebel on, 30–31; under capitalism, Marx on, 22–23, 175; industrialization of, 176–77; invention of, 13, 107; Kautsky on, 32–37; rational, 188–91; reduced competition in, 119; soils for, 182–88; synthetic fertilizers for, 167–70; Vernadsky on, 89
agroecology, 186–87
algae, 72
Alizart, Mark, 218
Allied Chemical (firm), 167–68
aluminum, 90
Amazon (firm), 115–16
Amazon Frontlines (organization), 148
Amazon River basin: tipping point in, 148; wildfires in, 146
American Physical Society (APS), 239–41
Amin, Samir, 50
ammonia, 160
ammonia synthesis process for nitrogen fixation, 165–67
ammonium, 154
Anderson, Perry, 47
animals, 59; during Ediacaran-Cambrian Period, 71; Kautsky on breeding of, 37–38; on land, 72; livestock, 178–82; in modern Earth System, 73

INDEX

Antarctica, 144, 149
Anthropocene epoch, 140; beginning of, 105–6; in Geological Time Scale, 232–37; noösphere and, 90; scientific support for, 108–9; tipping points in, 211–13; Vernadsky on human activity in, 91; Wark on, 54–55
Anthropocene Working Group (AWG; of International Commission on Stratigraphy), 233–37
Anti-Dühring (Engels), 24, 29
Arrhenius, Svante, 131
atmosphere: carbon dioxide levels in, 133–36, 142–43; carbon released into, by soils, 185; Commoner on threats to, 95; Keeling Curve of CO_2 in, 127–29; nitrogen in, 78, 155; oxygen enters, 66; ozone layer in, 110; reactive nitrogen in, 170; removal of carbon dioxide from, 239–40
atmospheric aerosol loading, 110
Australia, wildfires in, 146
automobile industry, 124–25
autotrophs, 86
Aveling, Edward, 229

bacteria, 64; nitrogen fixing by, 154; nitrous oxide produced by, 206; Pasteur and Liebig on, 79
Baltic Sea, 204–5
banking, 119
BASF (Badische Anilin & Sodafabrik; firm), 164–66
Bebel, August, 29–31, 44
Beerling, David, 72–73
Benjamin, Walter, 112
Bigg, Grant, 193
Bioenergy with Carbon Capture and Storage (BECCS), 242–44
biogeochemistry, 83–84, 86, 111
Biosfera (*The Biosphere*; Vernadsky), 83, 87, 91
biosphere: change in integrity of, 110; Commoner on, 95–96; creation of, 62; as historical phenomenon, 73–74; nitrogen in, 156–58, 172; Vernadsky on, 42, 84–92; Vernadsky on humans in, 82
birds, 37
the Blob (marine heat wave in Pacific Ocean), 196, 197
Boeing (firm), 125
Boesch, Donald, 203–4
Bosch, Carl, 165
Braje, Todd, 236
Bramwell, Anna, 46
Bukharin, Nikolai, 29, 38–45, 58
Burkett, Paul, 50–52
Burroughs, William J., 107
Butterfield, Nicholas, 73
Byford, Andy, 39–40

caliche, 160

Cambrian explosion, 69–71, 73
Canada: fossil fuel growth in, 220; wildfires in, 145–47
Canfield, Donald, 65
Capital (Marx): on ownership of earth, 26–27; varying translations of, 229–30
capital accumulation, 120–23
capitalism, 114–15, 123–26; agriculture under, 39, 190–91; anti-ecological logic of, 221; Bukharin on nature and, 43; commodities in, 115–17; environmental crises caused by, 51; impact on Earth System of, 13–14; Kautsky on agriculture under, 32; Luxemburg on, 217; Marx on agriculture under, 170, 175; Mészáros on, 168; metabolic rift tied to, 22–23; short-term profits in, 119
carbon: recycling of, 132–33; stored in soils, 184; used by early bacteria, 65; in vitalist theory, 21
carbon cycle, 127–29; breaking of, 133–36, 140; climate and, 129–32; industrial agriculture in, 185; ocean threats tied to disruptions of, 206–7
carbon dioxide (CO_2): absorbed by forests, 146–47; absorbed by soil, 184, 185; atmospheric levels of, 142–43, 170; Bioenergy with Carbon Capture and Storage removal from atmosphere of, 242–44; climate and, 129–32; Commoner on, 95; Direct Air Capture of, 240–42; in early Earth's atmosphere, 61, 66; Enhanced Rock Weathering removal from atmosphere of, 244–45; IPCC on removal of, 238–39; Keeling Curve of CO_2 in atmosphere, 127–29; nitrogen in atmosphere and, 155; ocean alkalinity enhancement for removal from atmosphere, 245–46; in oceans, 197–200; *Planetary Boundaries Framework* on, 110; proposed emissions of, 219; removing from atmosphere, 239–40; Vernadsky on, 88
Carbon Working Group (of IGBP), 141
Carson, Rachel, 58, 74; on oceans, 192
Carton, Wim, 139–40, 219
cells: biological evolution of, 63–64; nitrogen in, 158
Cheng, Lijing, 193
chickens, 119, 179–80
child labor, 116
China, synthetic fertilizers used in, 168, 169
Clark, Brett, 111, 112
Clausius, Rudolf, 240
climate: carbon dioxide (CO_2)

Index 277

and, 129–32; heat levels in, 136–40
climate change: arguments for inaction on, 148–49; before Holocene epoch, 107; Planetary Boundaries Framework on, 110; *see also* global warming
Climeworks project (Iceland), 240
coal: atmospheric carbon dioxide resulting from burning of, 143; climate impact of burning, 131, 134; nitrogen in, 160; replaced by petroleum as dominant fossil fuel, 135–36
Commission for the Study of the Natural Productive Forces of Russia, 82
commodities, 115–17
Commoner, Barry, 95–101; on Earth System, 94–95; on metabolic rift, 47; on necessary changes, 225; on pollution, 93
competition, 118–19
Confined Animal Feeding Operations (CAFOs), 178–82
Connor, Cliff, 93
conservation of energy, law of, 21
Constitutional Democratic (Kadet) Party (Russia), 82–83
coral reefs, 198–99

corporatism, 119
cows, 180
Crawford Lake (Ontario, Canada), 234
Crookes, William, 162–64
Crutzen, Paul, 105–6
cyanamide process for nitrogen fixation, 165
cyanobacteria, 65; oxygen produced by, 66

Daniels, Roland, 22
Darwin, Charles, 14, 62, 69, 184
Davy, Humphrey, 76
deforestation, 37, 41, 148
Delwiche, C. C., 152
denitrification, 155, 172
diesel engines, 124–25
dinitrogen, 154
Direct Air Capture (DAC) of carbon dioxide (CO_2), 240–42
Draper, Hal, 24
Drax Power Station (United Kingdom), 242–43
Dubos, René, 104
Dühring, Eugen, 42
Dukes, Jeffrey, 134

Earle, Sylvia, 192, 197
Earth: cycles of life on, 59–60; energy received from sun by, 130; history of life on, 61–62
Earth System: Anthropocene epoch in, 105, 106, 108–9; carbon cycle in, 128; closed

to external matter, 60–61;
Commoner on, 94–95;
creation of, 62, 74; Gaia
hypothesis on, 104; hothouse
conditions for, 210–11;
human-caused changes to,
234; long-term evolution of,
13–14; military spending
on, 94; nitrogen flows in,
152; Planetary Boundaries
Framework on, 109; soils in,
182; Stabilized Earth model
for, 213–14; tipping points
in, 150, 211–13; Vernadsky's
influence on, 91
Earth System Science (ESS),
105
Earth System Sciences
Committee (in NASA), 104
ecological crisis, 112
ecological imperialism, 52
ecological Marxism, 52
ecology: Bukharin on, 42;
coined by Haeckel, 80;
Commoner on laws of,
96–98
economic growth, 122
ecosocialism, 15, 28–29, 225–
26; development of, 48–50;
Marxist, 50–52
Ecosocialist Manifesto (Kovel
and Löwy), 49
Ediacaran-Cambrian Period, 71
Ediacaran Period, 70
Eldredge, Niles, 74
electric arc process for nitrogen
fixation, 165

energy: in Earth System, 61;
law of conservation of,
21; needed for removal of
carbon dioxide from atmosphere, 241–42
Engels, Frederick, 14, 226; *Anti-Dühring* by, 29; on English
capitalists, 220–21; Foster
and Burkett on, 52; Kautsky
and, 31; on Liebig, 79; on
metabolism, 24–26; world
war predicted by, 161
Enhanced Rock Weathering
(ERW), 244–45
entropy, 241
environmental crises: Burkett
on, 52; Commoner on,
98–101; Marx on, 51
environmentalism: Bebel on,
30; Commoner's, 94; ecosocialism and, 48–52; Kautsky
on, 37; Marx on, 228; socialists versus, 47; in Soviet
Union, 40
Erlandson, Jon, 236
Estes, Nick, 222–23
Eukaryotes, 67–69
European Science Foundation,
152
evolution: emergence of, 63–64;
of humans, 107; Vernadsky
on, 89

farms, *see* agriculture
fast carbon cycle, 132
Fernbach, David, 229
fertilizer industry, 183

Index

fertilizers, 33, 52; containing nitrogen, 78, 152; guano as, 159–60; Liebig on, 77, 80, 81; synthetic, 167–70; *see also* synthetic fertilizers
Finney, Stanley, 235
fire weather, 145–47
fixation of nitrogen, 154–56; balance between denitrification and, 172; technologies for, 164–65
Fixed Nitrogen Research Laboratory (U.S. Army), 166
Food and Agriculture Organization (UN), 170, 182
Foote, Eunice, 130–31
forests: Bukharin on deforestation of, 41; Kautsky on deforestation of, 37; wildfires in, 146–47
Fort McMurray (Alberta, Canada), 146
fossil fuels, 219–21
fossil nitrogen, 160–61; used in armaments, 162
Foster, John Bellamy, 15, 114; on capital accumulation, 121; on Marx on metabolic rift, 51–53; on planetary boundaries, 111, 112; on popular working class movement, 222; on socialism and environmentalism, 47
Fourier, Joseph, 130
Francis (pope), 218–19
freedom, Marx and Engels on, 26
freshwater change, 111

fungi, 72, 79
Future Earth (organization), 137–38

Gaia hypothesis, 104
Galloway, James, 158
General Chemical Company, 166, 167
Geological Time Scale, 232, 236
geology, 236
Germany, 165–66
Gilbert, Joseph, 78
Gliessman, Steve, 189–90
global warming: acceleration of, 138–40; fires and, 145; Mann on, 149; *see also* climate change
Gorz, Andre, 123–24
Gould, Stephen Jay, 63, 69, 74
Great Acceleration, 106, 234
Great Barrier Reef (Australia), 198
Greece, wildfires in, 146
greenhouse effect, 130
greenhouse gas emissions, 139; from Bioenergy with Carbon Capture and Storage (BECCS), 243; from coal, 136; Commoner on, 95; in early Earth's atmosphere, 66–67; IPCC on, 185; nitrous oxide in, 152, 170, 171; during Paleocene-Eocene Thermal Maximum, 140–41; Planetary Boundaries Framework on, 110; in Stabilized Earth model, 214

Greenland, 144, 149
green movement, 48–49
Green Revolution, 168
Grineveld, Jacques, 92
growth, economic, 122
guano, 159–60
Guano Islands Act (U.S., 1856), 159–60
Gulf of Mexico, 203–4

Haber, Fritz, 165
Haber-Bosch process (ammonia synthesis process) for nitrogen fixation, 165–67, 173, 183
Haeckel, Ernst, 80
Haldane, J. B. S., 62
Haldane-Oparin hypothesis, 62
Hanieh, Adam, 134–36, 220
Hansen, James, 138–39, 218
Harvey, David, 117
Hazen, Robert, 127
heat levels, 136–40
Hellriegel, Hermann, 79
heterotrophs, 86
historical materialism, Bukharin on, 41
Hoffman, Paul, 70
hogs, 180, 181
Holleman, Hannah, 184, 189
Holocene epoch, 102, 103; break Anthropocene epoch and, 233; climate during, 108; end of, 105, 106, 232; sea levels during, 143
homo sapiens, see humans
"Hothouse Earth," 210–13, 216;

Stabilized Earth alternative, 213–14
Huber, Matt, 80–81
humans: in biosphere, Vernadsky on, 82, 86–87; Bukharin on metabolism between nature and, 41–43; end of Holocene epoch caused by, 103; environment changed by, 234; evolution of, 107; impact on Earth System of, 13–14, 106; making our own history, 106; nature and, Malm on, 53–54; social metabolism of, 22; Vernadsky on economic activity of, 89–91
Humboldt Current, 159
Hutchinson, George Evelyn, 91
hydrogen, 167; used by early bacteria, 65
hydrogen bomb tests, 234

Ibn al-Nafis, 20
Ice Age, 102, 103
ice sheets, 144
I.G. Farben (firm), 166, 167
indigenous peoples, 34, 222–23
Ingenhousz, Jan, 21
Intergovernmental Panel on Climate Change (IPCC), 148; on anthropogenic greenhouse gas emissions, 185; on heating of oceans, 193; on marine heat waves, 195; on ocean acidification, 200; on oceans, 207; on

Index

removal of carbon dioxide, 238–40; on sea levels, 144; temperature goal of, 219; on tipping points, 150
International Commission on Stratigraphy (ICS), 232; Anthropocene Working Group of, 233–37
International Energy Agency, 219
International Geosphere-Biosphere Program (IGBP), 104–6, 134; Carbon Working Group of, 141
International Union of Geological Sciences (IUGS), 232, 235–36
iron, 89–90

Johnston, Timothy, 166

Kapp, K.W., 100
Kautsky, Karl, 44; on agriculture and metabolic rift, 31–38; on fertilizer treadmill, 186; Lenin on, 28, 29, 38–39
Keeling, Charles, 127–28
Keeling, Ralph, 128
Keeling Curve, 127–29
Kenorland (prehistoric supercontinent), 67
Keynes, John Maynard, 117–18
Kollontai, Alexandra, 29
Kovel, Joel, 49, 52

labor theory of value, 46
land system change, 111

Lane, Nick, 64, 68, 69
Lappe, Frances Moore, 182
La Via Campesina (organization), 222
Lavoisier, Antoine, 21
Lawes, John, 78
Lenin, V. I.: areas protected by, 87; on Bukharin, 40; on Kautsky, 28, 29, 38–39; Kautsky and, 31; on Marx's theory, 20; on Vernadsky, 83
Levins, Richard, 187–88
Lewontin, Richard, 187–88
Liebig, Justus von: Bebel on, 31; Marx on, 14, 39; on nutrient cycle, 75–81; on rational agriculture, 24; on soil depletion, 33; translations of, 229
life: biosphere of, 84–86; dependent upon nitrogen, 153–58; Gould on early history of, 63; origins of, 62; symbiotic, 67–69; Vernadsky on origins of, 86
Livermore, Roy, 133
livestock, 178–82
longue durée, 61
Lovelock, James, 104
Löwy, Michael, 49
Lucretius, 20
Luxemburg, Rosa, 210, 217, 228
Lytton (British Columbia, Canada), 145–46

Magdoff, Fred: on capitalism, 114, 121, 170; on carbon

cycle, 185; on ecological civilization, 224–25; on rational agriculture, 190–91
Malm, Andreas, 15, 53–55, 139–40, 219
mammals, 181
Mandel, Ernest, 115, 238
Manhattan Project, 93
Mann, Michael, 149
manure, 30–31; produced by factory farms, 181; replaced by synthetic fertilizer, 168
Margulis, Lynn, 68
marine heatwaves (MHWs), 194–97
Markusson, Nils, 245
Marx, Eleanor, 29
Marx, Karl, 224, 226; on agriculture under capitalism, 170, 175, 190–91; on beef cattle, 178; Benjamin on, 112; Burkett on, 50–52; on capital accumulation, 121–22; on capitalism, 123, 126; on commodities, 115, 116; on Darwin, 14; ecological criticisms of, 46–47, 49–50; on human-nature relationship, 53, 215; on humans making our own history, 106; Lenin on, 20; on Liebig and Schönbein, 75; on metabolism, 22–23, 54, 228–31; on soil depletion, 34
Marxism: ecosocialism and, 49–52; on metabolism, 228–31
mass extinctions, first, 67
Mauro, Salvatore Engel-Di, 40
Mayer, Julius Robert, 21
McLaren, Duncan, 245
McMichael, Philip, 205
meats, 119
Mészáros, István, 120; on economic growth, 47–48; Luxemburg cited by, 210; on transnational corporations, 119; on waste in capitalism, 168
metabolic rift: Commoner on, 47; Foster on, 51–52; Kautsky on, 37; Liebig on, 80–81; Malm on, 55; Marx on, 22–23, 39, 54; in Marx's understanding of nature, 14–15; Vernadsky on, 91
metabolism, 14; of bacteria, 64; Bukharin on, 41–43; of cells within environments, 59; Engels on, 24–26; fire in, 145; history of science of, 21; Ibn al-Nafis on, 20; Liebig on, 75–76; Marx on, 22–23, 228–31; as metaphor, 54–55; recycling in, 85
metazoans, 70
methane, *see* natural gas
microbiology, 24, 79
Milankovitch cycles, 103
military spending, 93–94
mitochondria, 68
money, Keynes on, 117–18
Montgomery, David, 181

Index

Montreal Protocol (1987, on ozone), 110
Moore, Samuel, 229
Morris, William, 225
Munroe, Charles E., 162, 163

Nader, Ralph, 94
narcotics, 116
natural gas (methane): climate impact of burning, 134; in early Earth's atmosphere, 66–67; Haber-Bosch process for, 166–67
Natural Resources Defense Council, 243
natural selection, Kautsky on, 38
nature: Bukharin on metabolism of humans and, 41–43; capitalist view of, 117; humans and, Malm on, 53–54; Marx on humans in, 14; Marx on universal metabolism of, 22
Nero (emperor, Roman Empire), 219–20
New Orleans (Louisiana), 144
nitrification, 154–55
nitrogen: cascades of, 171–72; as crisis, 151–52; current use of, 111; in fertilizers, 80, 81, 177; in guano, 159–60; industrial use of, 164–67; life dependent upon, 153–58; marine levels of, 203–4; military use of, 161–64; Planetary Boundaries Framework on, 173–74; in plant nutrition, 78
nitrogen cascades, 171–72
nitrogen cycle, 79, 152; nitrification and denitrification in, 154–55; Oxygen Minimum Zones in, 206
nitrogen oxide (NO_x), 124–25, 165
nitrous oxide (N_2O): as greenhouse gas, 152, 170, 186; produced by bacteria, 171, 206
noösphere, 88–91
Nordhaus, William, 149–50
novel entities, 111
nuclear weapons, 234
nutrient cycle, 37, 73; Liebig on, 79, 81

ocean alkalinity enhancement, 245–46
Ocean Anoxic Events (OAEs), 205–6
oceans: acidification of, 110, 197–200; carbon dioxide absorbed by, 140, 245–46; heating of, 192–94; hot spots in, 138–39; marine heatwaves in, 194–97; oxygen levels in, 200–206; petroleum and natural gas created under, 134; rising sea levels of, 143–44; threats to, 206–7
oil, *see* petroleum
Oparin, A. I., 62
Oppau (Germany), 165, 166

organic chemistry (agricultural science), 21, 75–76
Organic Chemistry in Its Application to Agriculture and Physiology (Liebig), 76, 80, 229
overfishing, 207
oxygen, 66–67; during Cambrian explosion, 73; discovery of, 21; ocean levels of, 200–206; used by early bacteria, 65
Oxygen Minimum Zones (OMZs), 206
Oxygen Revolution, 66–68
ozone (O_3), 66, 172
ozone layer, 110

Paleocene-Eocene Thermal Maximum (PETM), 140–41
Pappas, Stephanie, 131–32
Paris Agreement (2015), 137, 138, 200; target temperature proposed by, 210, 218; United States withdraws from, 220
Pasteur, Louis, 79
Pavlov, A. P., 90
permaculture, 186–87
petroleum: climate impact of burning, 134; Commoner on, 99; as energy source, 135–36
petroleum industry, nitrogen industry tied to, 167
pharmaceutical industry, 118
Phillips, Leigh, 80–81

Philosophical Arabesques (Bukharin), 42–44
phosphorus, 111, 152, 155
photosynthesis, 64–65; autotrophs live by, 86; nitrogen in, 153; oxygen concentrations increased by, 73; solar energy converted into chemical energy by, 21
pigs, 180
pipelines, 219
Planetary Boundaries Framework, 109–12; on nitrogen pollution, 173–74; on oxygen levels in oceans, 201
Planetary Boundaries Science (organization), 109–10
Planetary Health Check, 109
plants: in carbon cycle, 132–33; carbon dioxide consumed by, 59, 60; on land, 72, 73; Liebig on nutrition of, 76; nutrients taken from soil by, 183; photosynthesis by, 64–65
Pleistocene epoch, 107
plutonium isotopes, 234
political economy, Marx on, 50
Pollan, Michael, 176–77
pollution: agricultural, 170; atmospheric aerosol loading, 110; Commoner on, 93–95, 99; nitrogen as, 151, 173; in oceans, 207; reactive nitrogen as, 171
Potsdam Institute for Climate Impact Research, 107

Index

poultry, 178–80
Preobrazhensky, Evgeni, 123
Priestley, Joseph, 21
production: capitalist, 114–15; *Capital* translations on, 229–30; Commoner on changes to, 98–99; as human priority, 45–46
profits, 117–18; short-term, 119
prokaryotes, 63
proteins: dependent upon nitrogen, 158; Engels on, 25; Rubisco (protein), 65
punctuated equilibrium, 74

radioactive fallout, 94
rational agriculture, 188–91
reactive nitrogen (Nr), 153–54; in atmosphere, 170; in biosphere, 156, 158; in fertilizers, 168; industrial production of, 164; Planetary Boundaries Framework on, 173–74; as pollution, 171
recycling: carbon, 132–33; Commoner on, 100–101; Lucretius on, 20; Vernadsky on, 85
regenerative agriculture, 186–88
Richardson, Katherine, 211
Rockström, Johan, 211
rock weathering, 244–45
Rose, Steven, 58
Rothamsted Experimental Station (United Kingdom), 186

Rubisco (protein), 65
Russia, Vernadsky in, 82–83
Russian Revolution, science and, 39–40

Sagan, Dorion, 68
Sandel, Michael J., 116
Schleiden, Matthias, 21
Schumacher, E. F., 46
Schwann, Theodor, 21
sea levels, 143–44
seeds, 176
Seneca Falls conference on women's rights (1848), 130
Sheehan, Helena, 42
Siberia (Russia), 36
Silver, Whendee, 182–83
Silverstein, Ken, 118
slavery, 116
slow carbon cycle, 133
Smil, Vaclav, 153, 159–61, 166
Smith, Adam, 119
"Snowball Earth" hypothesis, 70–71
Social Democratic Party of Germany (SPD), 29
socialism: Commoner on, 101; defined by Marx and Engels, 26; ecosocialism, 15, 28–29, 48–52; Luxemburg on, 210; on production, 45–46
social metabolism, 22; Mészáros on, 48
sodium nitrate, 162
soil-carbon rift, 185
soil depletion, 77; Kautsky on,

32–37; Marx on metabolic rift and, 39
soils, 182–88
Soviet Union: conservation in, 40; environmentally destructive policies in, 46, 49; hydrogen bomb tests by, 234; under Stalin, 45; Vernadsky in, 83, 91
species, integrity of, 110
Stabilized Earth model, 213–14
Stalin, Joseph: Bukharin purged under, 41, 44, 45; Vernadsky on, 83
Standard Oil of New Jersey (firm), 167
Steffen, Will, 211, 214–15
Stoffwechsel (metabolism), 21, 228–29
Sutton, Mark, 163
symbiosis, 68, 72
symbiotic life, 67–69
synthetic fertilizers, 167–70, 177, 185–86
synthetic nitrogen, 221

technology: for carbon dioxide removal, 239, 245–46; Commoner on, 99–100
Teilhard de Chardin, Pierre, 88
Thunberg, Greta, 140, 217
tipping points, 148–50, 211–13
trees, 72–73, 242–43
Trump, Donald J., 127, 139
Trump administration, 220
Tyndall, John, 131

United Nations Environment Program, 139, 151, 246
United Nations Framework Convention on Climate Change (Rio Conference of 1992), 218
United States: guano trade and, 159–60; hydrogen bomb tests by, 234; nineteenth century agriculture in, 35; nitrogen production in, 166; withdrawn from international climate process, 139; withdrawn from Paris Agreement, 220

Vernadsky, Vladimir I., 80, 82–83; on agriculture, 89; biogeochemistry of, 83–84; on biosphere, 84–88; Bukharin on, 42; current interest in, 91–92; on human activity, 89–91
vitalism, 21
Voit, Carl, 75–76
volcanoes, 133, 141
Volk, Tyler, 63
Volkswagen (firm), 124–25

Waitzkin, Howard, 55
Wall, Derek, 48
Ward, Barbara, 104
Wark, Mackenzie, 54–55
wastes: produced by factory farms, 181; used by early cells, 64
wealth, 118, 121

Weiner, Douglas, 40
Weston, Del, 226–27
White, Thomas, 157–58
wildfires, 145–46
Willfarth, Hermann, 79
Williams, Mark, 102, 207
Williams, Raymond, 45–46
Wöhler, Friedrich, 21
women: Bebel on, 30; Seneca Falls conference of (1848), 130

Women and Socialism (Bebel), 29–31
Wood, Rachel, 71
World War II, 93, 99
Worster, Donald, 178

York, Richard, 111, 112

Zalasiewicz, Jan, 102, 207, 232, 235